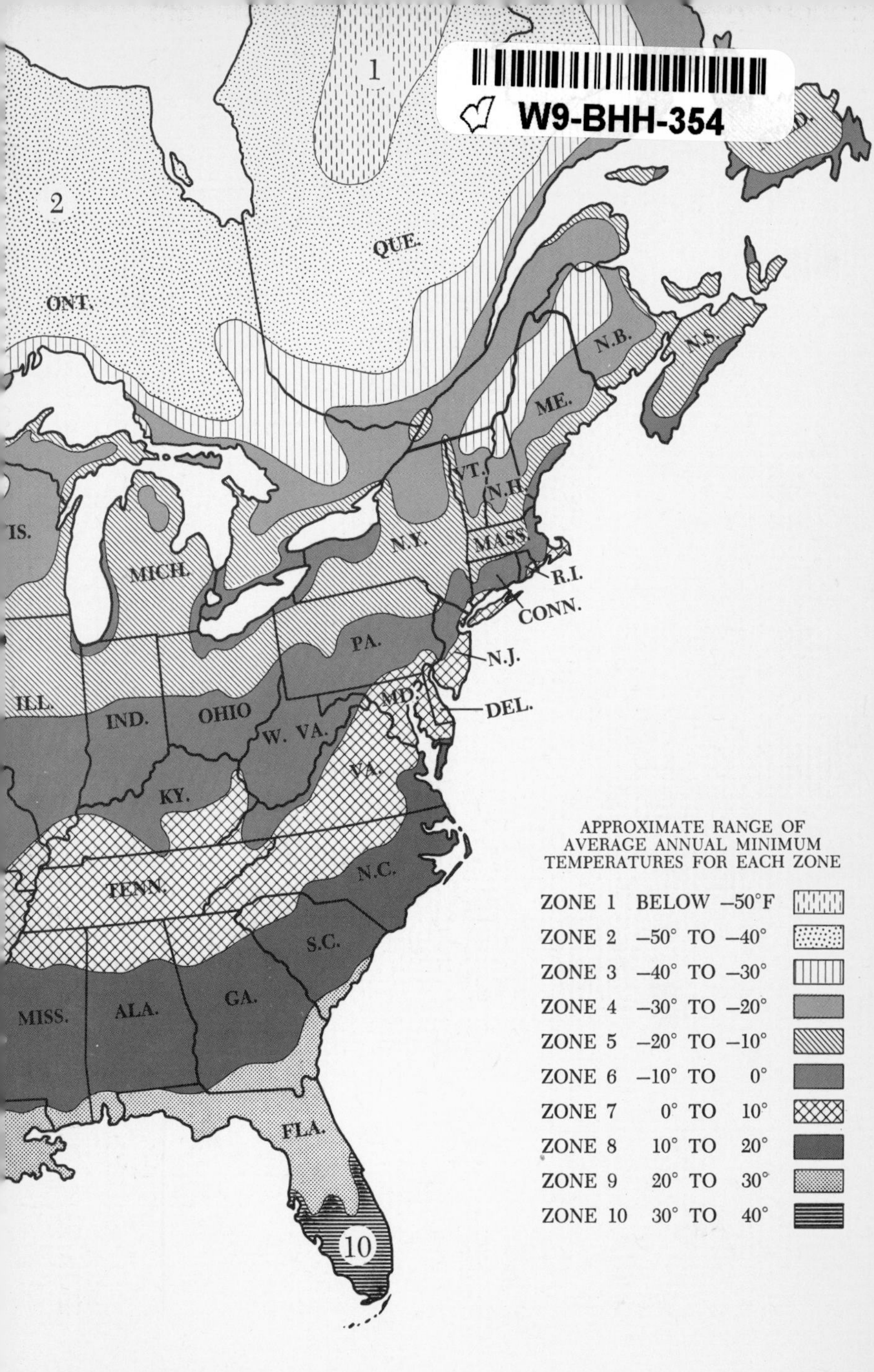
1
2
QUE.
ONT.
N.B.
N.S.
ME.
VT.
N.H.
MASS.
R.I.
CONN.
N.Y.
IS.
MICH.
PA.
N.J.
DEL.
MD.
ILL.
IND.
OHIO
W. VA.
VA.
KY.
TENN.
N.C.
S.C.
GA.
ALA.
MISS.
FLA.
10
APPROXIMATE RANGE OF
AVERAGE ANNUAL MINIMUM
TEMPERATURES FOR EACH ZONE
ZONE 1 BELOW −50°F
ZONE 2 −50° TO −40°
ZONE 3 −40° TO −30°
ZONE 4 −30° TO −20°
ZONE 5 −20° TO −10°
ZONE 6 −10° TO 0°
ZONE 7 0° TO 10°
ZONE 8 10° TO 20°
ZONE 9 20° TO 30°
ZONE 10 30° TO 40°

GARDENING FOR BEGINNERS

GARDENING FOR BEGINNERS

by DANIEL J. FOLEY

ILLUSTRATIONS BY *Katharine Burton,*

Charlotte Edmands Bowen & *Dorothy Waugh*

PHOTOS BY *George Taloumis* AND OTHERS

FUNK & WAGNALLS   NEW YORK

For MITCHELL *May he never lose his sense of wonder*

Acknowledgments

The information contained in these pages is based on nearly half a century engaged in planning and planting home gardens. It all began with a one-cent package of nasturtium seeds purchased in school in 1919. The seed was planted and, as I remember it, every seed germinated. The flowers were bright; the seeds were hot and peppery, but those mean black aphids soon found my nasturtium bed. Thus, my adventure with a garden began.

Over the years, friends and neighbors, too numerous to mention, have shared their plants and their knowledge. As most gardeners know, and beginners soon learn, gardening is a gregarious hobby. It is the sharing of experiences, in success and failure, that makes gardening the pleasantest of hobbies—a pursuit to be enjoyed regardless of age or status. As an aid to longevity, it has few equals.

To my family who have endured my trials and joys, I am ever grateful. For reading the manuscript and for challenging me all the way, I am indebted to: Mrs. Moses Alpers, Robert Bourassa, Gerald Campbell, Rick Eaton, Thomas Gaudette, Priscilla Sawyer Lord, Beatrice Marchand, Gifford P. Scott, David Sinclair, George Taloumis, Robert Thomson, and Wilbert H. Walfield.

For typing the manuscript and for critical comment and assistance, from start to finish, I am greatly indebted to Ann P. Scott.

Katharine Burton and Dorothy Waugh have added immeasurably to the text with their line drawings. George Taloumis has made the chapters more graphic with his photographs.

My thanks to Northrup King Co. and Miss Carol Givens, Pan-American Seed Company and Miss Lulu Brown for photographs. Also to Oxford University Press and Henry Z. Walck for permission to use the drawings in Chapter 1, from Dorothy Waugh's book *Warm Earth*.

To Mr. and Mrs. Moses Alpers, Mr. Donald Dodge, *Down East Magazine*, Mrs. Thomas Hosmer, Miss Viola Kneeland, Mr. and Mrs. Philip H. Lord, Mr. and Mrs. Harvey L. Macaulay, Mr. and Mrs. George S. Moore, Mr. and Mrs. Gordon W. Roaf, Mrs. Harold Ross, Mr. and Mrs. C. Fred Smith, Jr., Mrs. Charles Townsend, Mrs. Foster Whitney, and others for sharing their gardens for photographing.

DANIEL J. FOLEY

Salem, Massachusetts
September 30, 1967

CONTENTS

vii

GARDENING FOR BEGINNERS

INTRODUCTION

"What is a garden for?" is a rhetorical question which stirs the imagination and prompts the beginner to ask many others. Actually, the first question should be, "What is a garden?" According to an ancient and widely accepted definition, a garden is an enclosed outdoor area, devoted to the culture of all types of plants, a kind of living room for relaxation and enjoyment. For centuries, even before the Christian era, plants and flowers were cultivated for adornment, for color, and for fragrance, as well as for culinary and medicinal uses, but, as originally conceived, a garden was more than a plot for the growing of plants; it was an outdoor living room. The idea of a place enclosed suggests privacy, such as one enjoys indoors.

Down through the ages, from the days of the Hanging Gardens of Babylon to the hanging gardens of New York, men and women have planned gardens on level ground, on slopes and terraces, in window boxes, on porches, and finally on the roofs of houses. They have been planned as places in which to relax and enjoy leisure hours, or perhaps to entertain guests in the open air. Gardens also afford men an opportunity to dig in the warm earth. That concept has not changed greatly since the days of the ancient Egyptians, the Greeks, and the Romans. Today, with the advent of the New Leisure, a well-planned garden, more than ever, satisfies all these basic needs, and a modern house is not complete without a garden, however simple. The nurseryman's slogan, "A house is not a home until it's planted," has become part of our way of life.

What is a garden for if it is not an integral part of the place where one lives? Most of us think that a garden is pointless without flower beds and borders, colorful shrubs and ornamental trees, pools, bird baths, pergolas, and window boxes, as well as comfortable chairs in which to relax. These are the raw materials

3

all gardeners use to make a garden, but the end result is only pleasing and satisfying when it is well fitted to the site and so planned as to be enjoyable and easily cared for.

As we strive to make more effective use of our leisure time, the problem of maintenance looms large. A fussy garden that requires too many of our waking hours will soon become a burden. Weeding and watering, spraying and feeding, and all the attendant chores that are essential to good gardening, can become wearisome and tiring; for even if the spirit is willing, all too often the back may be weak.

The idea of planning a garden for easy maintenance is today's great challenge. Most of us want continuous color throughout the season.

Yet, many beginners fail to realize that there is more to gardening than wishing and dreaming. One should be content (at least during the first few years) with gay splashes of seasonal bloom for eye appeal. The notion of continuous bloom is challenging and exciting, but it takes planning and experimenting, constant shifting and rearranging to achieve the desired results. An appreciation of the enduring beauty of a green garden is something one discovers by living with plants and working with them. All in all, making a garden takes both time and patience, but with a little know-how the results can be richly rewarding and completely satisfying.

Some beginners have the space and the urge to grow at least a few of their own vegetables, and there are those who delight in cultivating the various kinds of plants, sometimes making a hobby of one kind.

Some homeowners enjoy cooking out of doors and taking their meals in the open during the summer months. In such cases, provision must be made to accommodate these needs. For an ever-increasing number of homeowners, the evening hours afford the only opportunity during the week to enjoy a home garden. In this instance, outdoor lighting extends this precious time. With the addition of well-placed lights, the pleasant hours of twilight and after dark can be made much more pleasurable.

Even beginners are often eager to specialize in some group of plants, perhaps the free-flowering tuberous begonias or fuchsias. Both are particularly effective for providing color in shady gardens. Then too, the garden may be so limited in space that plants grown in pots and boxes are the answer. Others may be content with an all-green garden. Whatever your desires, strive to realize them. There is no point in modeling your garden after your neighbor's. It should be an expression of your own taste, interest, and enthusiasm.

In these days of increased tension, a place to relax in is more important than ever, and what could be more desirable than an attractive terrace in your own garden, surrounded by green things growing? To look out on your handiwork from such a place is its own reward for the tedious chores involved in maintaining it.

If your home grounds are planned for easy maintenance, they will afford the opportunity for much needed exercise, fresh air, and the personal satisfaction that comes from handiwork well done. A noted amateur gardener who grew roses for more than fifty years once made the statement that he took many a grudge into his garden, but never carried one out! A garden is truly a place for the refreshment of the spirit.

Gardening in one form or another is often the answer for those looking for a hobby as retirement approaches. The growing of plants and flowers can be as exciting and as meaningful as any tyro wants to make it. It is a matter of choosing the things you want to grow, the amount of space you want to cultivate, and the kind of setting you want to create. I am reminded of a noted football coach who found great pleasure in the growing of rock plants in his country place. He took particular interest in raising rare kinds of gentian from seed. At best, these are difficult plants to grow, but by studying their needs he was able to provide the required conditions for flowerings up to killing frosts and early snowfalls. Writing of his gentians, he declared: "They say a last 'au revoir' from the top of the world, and say it so bravely, as winter's snows come swirling down. They have made old age less fearsome and more beautiful to me."

1

SOIL—THE BASIC STUFF
OF PLANT LIFE

❧❧❧ Gardening is fun, great fun, because the pursuit is filled with adventure. There is so much to learn about plants and fertilizers and, particularly, about the soil in which plants grow that the search for information is continual and exhilarating. The adventure begins with the discovery that success in gardening— or the lack of it—usually can be traced directly to the soil. We all tend to take the soil on our property for granted. Yet, its texture, its moisture-holding capacity, its fertility, and general make-up are of prime importance.

It is a common notion that rich, dark color indicates fertility, but this is not necessarily true. Another belief is that soil must be heavy in texture to grow crops successfully, but this fact is easily disproved by the great number of flowering plants which thrive in light sandy soils where water and fertilizer are supplied frequently. It is the ability of soil to retain moisture, to make food available to the roots of plants as they seek it, and to be workable after a heavy rain that determine how well plants grow.

Rarely is the soil on most home grounds ideally suited to all the kinds of plants which are likely to be planted there. However, few soils are so poor that they cannot be improved. At best, a garden is a highly artificial environment in which plants of varying soil requirements are assembled. Consequently, the soundest approach to good gardening begins with soil improvement.

To describe soil is a many-sided task. The breakdown of rocks of varying sizes caused by the physical and chemical weathering by wind, water, heat, cold, plant growth, and animal activity produces the minerals that give soil part of its substance. It is the constant reaction of some of these forces on rock surfaces over centuries of time—plus the penetration of plant roots into the cracks and crevices of disintegrating rock, aided by the various movements of animal life—that causes their breakdown. The particles that result vary in size and are referred to as sand, silt, and clay. These particles are held together by varying amounts of organic matter, water, and soil air.

Yet soil is more than a mixture of minerals and organic matter.

9

*(Left) Particles of gravel in subsoil; (right) topsoil with an un-
usually tiny ant crawling down a crack—all greatly enlarged*

This combination of ingredients teems with microorganisms—
bacteria and fungi which are not visible to the eye. Even a
handful of soil literally teems with life. Certain of these organisms attach themselves to the roots of plants, thus stimulating
growth by making available to them needed plant food. For
example, nitrogen-fixing bacteria are found adhering to the roots
of beans, peas, and clover, and garden flowers such as lupines,
baptisia, and sweet peas. (All are members of the legume family.) The nodules which cling to the roots of these plants develop
as the result of action by soil bacteria which bring free nitrogen

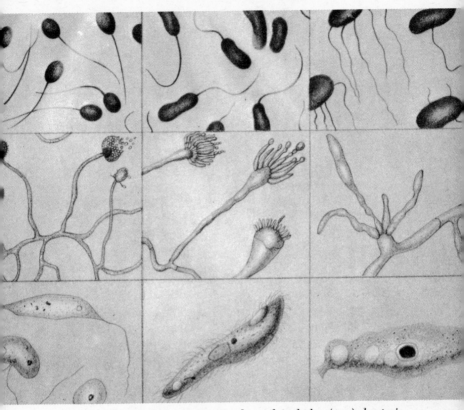

Micro-organisms that function in the soil include: (top) bacteria; (middle) fungi; (bottom) protozoa—all greatly enlarged

absorbed from the air to the tiny root segments. Fungi called mycorrhizae which penetrate the roots of acid-soil plants such as rhododendrons, azaleas, blueberries, and other members of the erica family are believed to predigest needed food for root absorption. Also, these minute organisms not only activate soluble soil nutrients but also conserve and release them, thus increasing the use of the fertilizer which the gardener adds to his soil.

In addition to solids, soil also contains water and air. The water and air present are dispersed in the pore spaces between the solid particles and, consequently, are not continuously in

(Left) Rain water rushing down through the soil; (center) water held back long after a rain where soil grains pinch together; (right) water standing underground—all greatly enlarged

liquid or gaseous form. Both elements are essential for the development of plant roots and the complex life cycles of the various microorganisms which enable plants to grow and thrive. When soil moisture is at its highest level, the ideal condition for growth, the humidity of soil is nearly 100 per cent. Under this condition, the various organisms—bacteria, fungi, and others—become active and chemical reaction is hastened.

Since soil processes are biological in nature, the addition of organic matter to a flower bed and its subsequent breakdown or

Water climbing rapidly through fine pores and falling back to fill coarser pores—all greatly enlarged

decay are essential to the fertility of soil. Actually, the make-up of soil—the basic stuff from which plant life emerges—is far more complex than it appears. Furthermore, the interaction of the various soil components and the part which plant foods play is every bit as fascinating as the growth promoted.

The following soil types are described on the basis of their physical make-up: sand, silt, clay, and loam.

Sandy Soil. The predominant ingredient, varying from two-thirds to three-quarters of its make-up, is sand. The individual particles, or grains, are easily seen with the naked eye. Water and air pass through it quickly, and heat is readily absorbed. Sandy soil is coarse in texture, heavy in weight, and light in substance, because it is deficient in organic matter. Since it dries out quickly, this type of soil requires large amounts of organic matter to absorb and hold water and to retain the plant food one applies to produce healthy plants.

Silty Soil. As grains of sand break down, they form a powdery dust commonly referred to as silt. It is seen on the surface of newly turned fields, along roadsides, in pools of water, and carried in the air by the wind. When silt settles, it is found in the bottom of river beds, lakes, brooks, ponds, and even in puddles. Few garden soils have great amounts of pure silt which is a valued component of loam.

Clayey Soil. Exceptionally fine in texture, the tiniest particles of silt form what is known as clay soil. It forms lumps as it dries, because the surface of each particle is colloidal or sticky, so that little aeration is possible. As a result of its make-up, clay soil holds water too well, since the grains cling to one another when moist. Although referred to as being heavy because of its enduring moisture-holding capacity, it is actually light in weight when thoroughly dry.

Clay soil needs improvement in texture to allow for adequate air circulation, drainage, and the ready absorption of heat. Soil of fine texture is slow to warm up in spring and cannot be worked as early as that of coarser texture. The addition of coarse materials such as sand and fine gravel as well as organic matter, changes its structure. Also, improvement is essential for continuing vigorous growth, since typical clay soil remains cold and wet for extended periods after heavy rain. In summer, the heat of the sun causes it to crack in streaks. Under these conditions, soil organisms do not function normally, and the roots of plants are unable to obtain essential nutrients.

Loamy Soil. The ideal combination of soil structure sought by gardeners is a balanced mixture of sand, silt, and clay. Loamy soil particles are of different sizes and combine to produce a gritty texture known as crumb structure. Because the individual particles vary greatly in size, the pressure of water and organic matter holds them together, making this type of soil retentive of

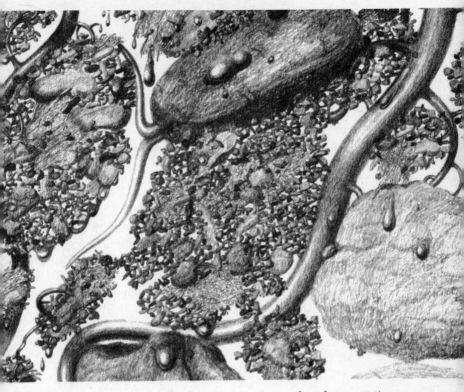

Good soil structure, with three grains of gravel and a sprouting seed—each of pin-head size

both moisture and plant food. Yet, loam crumbles easily, indicating that air can move through it readily. By bulk, nearly half of its make-up is soil water and soil air.

Essentially, the structural make-up of soil is more vital than its richness or fertility, since plant foods are added easily. Generally, loam occurs as a relatively thin layer of soil on the earth's surface, commonly referred to as topsoil. The aim of the home gardener is to increase its depth for the maximum benefit of plant roots. Building and improving soil on the home grounds to obtain good garden loam is a continuing process, accomplished by spading and adding organic matter and plant food.

Improving Sandy Soil

Building up sandy soil is a task of gradual improvement. Because of its loose make-up, this kind of soil must have fertilizers applied to it frequently, since rain and the constant use of sprinklers cause plant food to be leached out. Thus, the problem of feeding is "little and often." There are several ways to approach the problem. Sandy soils may be improved by growing a crop of green manure, or sheet composting as it is sometimes called. Organic materials like peat moss, compost, sawdust, wood chips, chopped bark, partially decayed leaves, or leaf mold may be dug in before the area is planted. If available, rotted cow or horse manure, stable sweepings, and partially rotted hay and straw are other sources of organic matter. Poultry manure should be thoroughly aged before using. Fresh manure is best scattered in late fall and allowed to break down over winter. To be effective, any of these materials should be applied in a layer at least two inches deep. A third method is to thoroughly prepare the individual hole for each tree and shrub set out. Still another approach is to turn under each spring the mulch material used on the surface the previous year.

Green Manure

The planting of such crops as Italian rye grass, buckwheat, and winter rye is a most effective means of improving sandy soils. This procedure, commonly referred to as green manure, requires effort: preparing the soil for seeding, sowing the seed, and turning under the roots and stems. The results, however, in terms of long-range gardening, are well worth the work required. This procedure is an excellent and inexpensive way to improve large areas for lawns, but it should be remembered that a green manure crop requires a growing season before grass seed can be sown or a flower or vegetable garden may be planted.

The soil is prepared in late summer or early fall. A complete fertilizer is scattered at the rate of 50 pounds per 1,000 square feet. Seed of the crop chosen, planted at the rate of one ounce per square yard, is applied with a lawn seeder and raked in. The following spring the area is again sprinkled with a complete fertilizer, and the crop is turned over before it has matured. If sulphate of ammonia is scattered on the surface before turning the crop over, the decay of the vegetable matter will be hastened and the broken-down crop will result in a supply of humus.

Humus

Humus may be defined simply as decomposed vegetable or organic matter. Leaf mold or woods soil found on the forest floor is the prime form of humus. Many gardeners make their own in compost piles, by growing cover crops as previously discussed, or by adding various types of organic matter to the soil. The microorganisms present in the soil aid the breakdown of all of these organic substances. When the breakdown is complete, the resulting humus provides the process energy beneath the soil that is comparable to photosynthetic effect of light on green plants. (Aided by the sun and the green coloring matter which they contain, leaves produce the sugar and starch that are essential for plant growth.) Thus, the importance of humus in building healthy soil is apparent.

How to Make a Compost Pile

Where space is available, a compost pile is a sound and practical means of obtaining organic matter for the home garden, provided that it is properly made and maintained. Some gardeners build a concrete bin or make one of brick and cement or wood. Easier still, simply mark out an area at least 3 by 5 feet in the service area of your grounds or in some screenable part of the garden. Dig out 10 to 12 inches of soil to make a shallow pit.

Making use of disease-free garden refuse, such as leaves, grass clippings, discarded plants, or bits of sod, build the compost pile in layers of 8 to 10 inches. Coffee grounds, tea leaves, vegetable trimmings, bones, or other forms of greaseless garbage may be added. If available, separate each layer with 1 or 2 inches of soil and stable manure. As the pile is built, layer by layer, add a thin

covering of a complete fertilizer. Ground limestone, superphosphate, and wood ashes, scattered thinly, may be added from time
to time.

Compost piles, which usually range from 3 to 4 feet in height,
should always be kept covered with soil. Soak thoroughly and
turn the pile every few months. Bacterial agents (such as Adco)
that hasten the breakdown of plant materials are worth using and
should be applied according to directions. These agents are
especially valuable when animal manure is not available. To
provide for ventilation, make two or more holes in each pile,
using a stick or a tube made of hardware screening. Strips of
burlap may be used for cover. By keeping the compost pile well
covered with soil, turned frequently, and moist, the breakdown
of the various ingredients is hastened.

Treating Raw Organic Materials

When fresh or raw sawdust, wood chips, ground bark, hay, or
straw are added to soil—to improve its organic content—or a
compost pile, it should be remembered that these materials in the
process of breaking down rob the soil of some of its existing
nitrogen. Therefore, it is essential to add nitrogen. For each cubic
yard of raw sawdust, wood chips, or similar material used, add
1½ pounds of ammonium nitrate or ammonium sulphate or 3
pounds of nitrate of soda. The same procedure should be followed when using materials for mulching, if they have not been
thoroughly composted before they are dug in or scattered.

Peat Moss and Compost

To be effective, organic matter such as that mentioned above
needs to be spread and turned under in layers at least two inches
deep. When peat moss or compost are used in this manner, a
similar layering is essential if any marked degree of soil improvement is to be obtained. For most beginners, however, adding an
inch in the spring and another inch in the fall may prove more
convenient. For any type of soil, its improvement necessitates
a gradual and continuing program.

Improving Clay Soils

Lime is of prime value for improving the structure of clay soils, since it aids in forming crumb structure. Lime unites clay's tiny soil particles into larger units, thus allowing air to penetrate and improving drainage. The amount of ground limestone required for a particular clay may vary from 20 to 40 pounds per 1,000 square feet, depending on the soil's stiffness. Often, the amount needed can best be determined by consulting your local county agent. Since spring weather is often uncertain and garden operations must be started early, fall is the ideal time to begin an improvement program on clay soils. Furthermore, if the lime-treated soil is turned over and left in a rough state over winter, the action of weathering will prove of considerable value.

Sand is another means of improving clay soil, but it must be added in sufficient quantity to achieve the hoped-for results. Stiff clay requires a considerable quantity of sand to condition it effectively. A layer 2 inches deep, turned under may not be sufficient to produce the desired texture. It may take an additional inch, or even two, to produce friable soil—the type that crumbles easily when a handful is squeezed into a ball.

Where large areas need improvement, such materials as sifted coal ashes, medium to fine gravel, or cinders from power plants are useful. When cinders are used, they need to be weathered over winter; if unusually coarse, they may need screening. On the other hand, small flower beds may respond to the addition of vermiculite or Perlite—materials commonly used by commercial growers. Light, easy to handle and slow to disintegrate, they are efficient conditioners. Vermiculite is expanded mica and Perlite, a volcanic mineral; both are white or grayish-white in color. The extent to which they are used is determined largely by the cost involved.

Since all of these methods are concerned with the improvement of the physical structure of clay soils, humus in some form is also an essential element of the improvement program. The various methods for its addition are the same as those recommended for sandy soils.

Chemical soil conditioners, produced by reliable firms have merit but are costly and, in the long run, accomplish no better or more permanent results than the practices that have been used by home gardeners for generations. However, in combating heavy clay soils, it is sound practice to attempt to improve only areas large enough to be handled efficiently in a given season.

Acid, Alkaline, and Neutral Soils

Any basic understanding of soils involves reference to the degree of acidity or alkalinity which they contain, since certain popular garden plants have distinct needs and preferences for the kind of soil in which they grow. Soils may vary somewhat in this respect, even within the small area of the average home garden. For example, in a garden where the soil is known to be acid, the degree of acidity may be greater on a flat surface than on a slope where it tends to leach. Most home gardeners think of only two kinds of soil—acid or sour, and alkaline or sweet. (These terms are often employed carelessly and without thought to their true meaning.) Yet, soils, neither decidedly acid nor alkaline, are spoken of as neutral soils.

The degree of acidity or alkalinity in soil is determined by a system known as pH. Soil reactions as revealed by simple chemical tests are expressed by numbers. For example, neutral soil has a reading of pH 7. Soil tests showing indications higher than 7 are on the alkaline or sweet side; those lower than 7, on the acid or sour side. Tests may indicate an extreme situation on either side of the neutral scale, resulting in a toxic condition, but this is not common.

Home gardeners are rapidly learning the value of soil testing. While there are test kits available, which are simple and easy to use, they are not always completely satisfactory. The beginner—and for that matter the gardener with a fair amount of experience —may obtain entirely satisfactory results by having tests made by competent soil analysts at his county or state experiment station. This service is usually free. A telephone query or a letter will result in a set of instructions to be followed in preparing and sending the test soil sample.

Improving Acid Soil

A goodly number of wild flowers—as well as azaleas, rhododendrons, and other broad-leaved evergreens—and such native shrubs as blueberries, hollies, and others require an acid soil. Although most garden soils in which these plants are commonly grown need little preparation to make them suitable, it is sometimes necessary to alter soil acidity for successful culture. Acidity in the soil can be increased by use of acid leaf mold (easily made from oak leaves), hardwood sawdust, sulfur, and such fertilizers as ammonium phosphate, ammonium sulfate, and urea. Commercially prepared acid-soil fertilizers, sometimes referred to as rhododendron and azalea plant food, often solve the problem.

With most plants that require acid soil, a lack of acidity is indicated by pale green to yellow leaf coloring accentuated by veins of darker green. Such plants look unhealthy and often are; to verify these symptoms, however, a soil test should be made. Send a representative soil sample, a specimen of the affected plant, and any pertinent details to your county or state testing station. Lowering of acidity may be due to an alkaline condition in the local water supply, drainage from walls in which plaster has been used, or rubble left in the soil by builders. Certain types of fertilizer are known to produce salts which are toxic to acid-loving plants. Then, too, when plants are grown on sloping ground, the acidity tends to leach out of the soil.

To counteract these conditions, the use of aluminum sulphate is widely recommended, but its prolonged use may cause a toxic condition in some soils. An easy and safe method to increase soil acidity in the home garden is by using ordinary dusting sulfur. Apply it in late spring or early summer by scattering a quarter pound around an average-size rhododendron, azalea, or any other needy broad-leaved evergreen and then water it in. Too much sulfur can be injurious to plants, but if it is scattered in this recommended amount, no harm is likely to result.

On the other hand, some soils are too highly acid to produce satisfactory growth. In such instances, the degree of acidity needs to be learned. Following your local county agent's recommendations usually counteracts such a condition.

Uses of Lime

Lime improves soil in a variety of ways when properly used. It has many valuable properties which—when clearly understood—make its use of prime importance in many types of soil. Yet, some gardeners hold curious notions about its merits. The term *Lime* is used loosely to cover several specific kinds. For instance, hydrated lime is air-slaked (containing at least 70 per cent calcium oxide), light in weight, easy to use, and rapid in its reaction. (Some types of agricultural lime, commonly sold at low prices, are not up to standards.) Composed of larger particles, ground limestone is slower acting and requires one-third more by weight to obtain the results of hydrated lime. Finely ground oyster shells are equal in value to ground limestone.

Improving Clay Soil. Lime acts as a conditioner reducing the sticky quality of clay and improving soil structure by building the crumb structure. Thus, air can penetrate and the improved drainage that results enables the soil to warm up more rapidly.

Improving Sandy Soil. Lime makes these soils more compact and thus more moisture retentive.

Counteracting Acidity. Sour or acid soils in which rhododendrons, azaleas, and other plants of the Heath family (*Ericaceae*) thrive, together with most woodland and bog plants, are not suitable for growing many types of annual flowers, some perennials, and vegetables. To grow specific crops in such soils, lime must be added to alkalize or sweeten them.

Lime for Lawns. When new lawns are made or established, sod is renewed in areas of known acidity: lime is applied to sweeten the soil, improve its texture, aid in the liberation of plant food, and check certain types of in-soil pests.

Lime Liberates Plant Foods. When lime reacts on existing humus or organic matter in soil, it liberates soil chemicals which supply plants with essential food. In soils of heavy texture, lime makes potash available.

Effects on Insects and Diseases. Lime aids in counteracting certain soil diseases and is injurious to slugs, wireworms, and other pests. However, it is not a panacea for controlling insects and diseases.

Lime as Aid to Plant Growth. Many plants require a certain amount of lime to flourish, particularly vegetables, but lime is not a fertilizer. Such plants as clematis, dianthus, chrysanthemums, columbines, and delphiniums are greatly improved by the addition of lime when grown in soils known to be heavily acid. Determining these needs by soil testing is important.

Plants That Dislike Lime. As previously mentioned, certain plants have a strong dislike for lime and are adversely affected by it. Thus, its use must be avoided in soils for rhododendrons, azaleas, blueberries, and other members of the Heath family, which includes many of our native plants. If lime is accidentally applied to these plants, the results are immediately apparent.

How to Use Lime. Generally, hydrated lime is applied at the rate of 3 to 5 pounds per 100 square feet. If ground limestone is used, increase the quantity by one third. Scatter it evenly over the surface of the soil and turn it under lightly. A lawn seeder makes the task of spreading easy. If soil is dug in the fall and left rough, lime can be scattered and left to act by the action of weather. A soil test should be made to determine if larger amounts are required to correct specific conditions.

It is most important to remember that hydrated lime is not added to the soil simultaneously with animal manures or commercial fertilizer, because the nitrogen in these plant foods is likely to be lost. At least two weeks should elapse before lime is applied under these conditions.

Drainage

Drainage is vital to the successful growth of plants, even those that thrive in naturally moist soils. Waterlogged soils prevent air from circulating around the individual soil particles and the roots of plants. When subjected to this condition for any period of time, roots are killed, growth is checked, and plants eventually die. Even plants growing in boggy and swampy areas are usually found on hummocks of soil, which enables air to circulate around their roots at various times during the year. Most cultivated trees and shrubs, perennials, and bulbs are not adaptable to soils that are constantly wet. Flat surfaces on which water tends to stand after a heavy rain during winter sometimes can be drained by excavating the area and putting in a layer of gravel. If the area is lower than its surroundings, raising the grade is the answer. The problem of drainage often presents itself in heavy clay soils. Where it cannot be corrected by improving the texture of the soil, agricultural tile can be utilized to carry off the surplus soil water. Hardpan subsoil beneath the surface may be a cause of poor drainage. When this condition exists, the subsoil can be loosened by excavating the topsoil and using a pick mattock to break the hard surface. Electric drills are sometimes used when large areas are involved.

Mistaken Notions and Common Errors

1. Color is not necessarily a clue to the degree of soil fertility. Questions relating to this problem can and should be answered by your county agent.

2. The presence of various size stones in soil does not impede plant growth, and such soil does not need to be raked free of all stones. Stones help to retain soil moisture and may prove to be a drainage aid. For general garden use, rocky soil does not have to be removed and replaced by screened topsoil. However, when a new lawn is being built, the soil should be thoroughly and carefully raked to remove small stones, which damage lawn mowers.

3. Since lime is not a cure-all for every type of soil problem, it should be used discriminately.

4. Wet soil should be neither cultivated nor dug until it has drained properly.

5. Earthworms, despite popular notions and advertising, are not wonder workers. They are commonly found in garden soils of good fertility, manure, and compost piles, because they require an abundance of organic matter and moisture to survive. When "planted" in poor soil to improve it, they do not survive. In

essence, earthworms contribute comparatively little to the general health, fertility, and conditions of soil.

6. Beware of peddlers offering humus or compost at bargain prices—or at any price—unless the material is known to have been obtained from a reliable source. Oiled sawdust and other spurious mixtures are sometimes peddled from door to door by slick hucksters.

7. Topsoil purchased for lawns and gardens is most safely obtained from reliable sources. Good topsoil is seldom cheap. Beware of bargains and extravagant claims.

8. Use weed killers with caution and precisely as directed on the container; otherwise, these preparations may have a bad effect on your soil.

2

GROWING ANNUALS

FROM SEED

❦❦❦ Annuals, which produce the predominant bloom in summer gardens, are the flowers that lure most beginners to start a garden. An annual is a plant that completes its life cycle—from seed to seed—within a single season. Some annuals tend to self-sow, reappearing as volunteers the following year, since the ripe seed drops to the ground, lies dormant through the winter, and germinates when the ground warms up the following spring. In seed catalogs, annuals are classified according to their ability to endure cold temperatures and are referred to as hardy, half-hardy, or tender annuals. The proper time to plant each group is based on this consideration.

Some annuals have to be started indoors rather than directly in the garden, because they require a longer season to produce bloom than outdoor conditions allow in the colder parts of the country. Others are by nature not true annuals; they may be either biennials or perennials in their native habitat but will produce flowers in a single season if given an early start. Pansies, English daisies, and forget-me-nots are typical biennials which, when started early, bloom the same season. The snapdragon, while actually a perennial, is treated as an annual in cold climates.

Hardy annuals are those that endure cold temperatures and may be sown in the open ground as soon as the soil is workable, even before the frost has left the ground entirely. In fact, these may be sown also in late autumn to obtain early bloom the following season. Typical examples include:

Baby's-Breath	Cornflower	Pinks
Bachelor's-Button	Gaillardia	Poppies
California Poppies	Larkspur	Snow-on-the-Mountain
Calliopsis	Love-in-a-Mist	Sweet Alyssum
Candytuft	Lupines	Sweet Peas

Half-hardy annuals may be planted before the ground has become thoroughly warm, since the young seedlings are not usually harmed by light spring frosts; they include:

Annual Phlox	Lavatera	Petunia
Calendula	Lobelia	Portulaca
Cleome	Marigold	Salvia
Cosmos	Mignonette	Scabiosa
Everlastings	Nemesia	Snapdragon
Godetia	Nicotiana	Verbena

Tender annuals are so sensitive to frost or severe drops in temperature as to be impeded or stunted in growth if planted too early. Beginners are advised to consult with experienced gardeners before setting out any tender plants from the window garden or greenhouse or the following annuals:

Ageratum	Coleus	Salpiglossis
Balsam	Cup-and-saucer-vine	Scarlet runner
Begonia	Datura	Statice
Bells of Ireland	Heliotrope	Strawflower
Blue lace flower	Lobelia	Sunflower
Celosia	Morning Glory	Tassel-Flower
China Aster	Nasturtium	Tithonia
Chrysanthemum	Petunia	Wishbone Flower
Clarkia		Zinnia

To enjoy early bloom, many tender annuals are started indoors, or they may be purchased from local growers in small flats or boxes. Despite their susceptibility to frost, a sizable number self-sow. Petunias, flowering tobacco, balsam, and others often appear as volunteers when the soil warms up; the seed remains dormant in the soil until temperatures for germination are ideal. Of all the kinds mentioned, self-sown petunias are the least desirable because of their magenta color.

Sowing Hardy Annuals in the Open

When forsythia blooms, seed of hardy annuals may be sown in the open ground, but first the soil must be prepared. The area to be planted needs to be spaded or turned over with a digging fork, then raked to remove stones and other debris. If the soil crumbles easily when a handful is squeezed, it is in workable condition. However, if exceptionally moist, it must be allowed to dry out before seed is sown.

Soil Preparation. Areas that have not been cultivated the previous year require preparation to a depth of 8 to 10 inches and the addition of a complete fertilizer such as 5-10-5 (see Chapter 16) at the rate of 3 to 5 pounds per 100 square feet. This is scattered on the surface and turned under as the soil is prepared. Allow the prepared area to settle for a few days before planting.

Light Requirements. For success with annuals, the site must have direct sunlight for at least half the day. Many kinds such as zinnias and marigolds require full sun to produce their best bloom.

Sowing in Open Ground. Since most annuals are easily transplanted, they are sown in rows in a seedbed. However, some that have long taproots do not transplant successfully without special care, and the usual practice is to broadcast the seed where blooms are wanted. When large enough to handle, these plants are thinned to allow ample room for the remaining plants to develop.

Experienced gardeners may take issue with some of the plants in the following list, since with care they can be transplanted, but the effort involved is usually not worth the time required. When the delicate roots are damaged or broken, seedlings of the kinds listed below do not survive in most cases. Professional growers offer many of these in plant bands or small flats that can be transplanted safely. Hence, the usual practice for beginners is to scatter the seed and then thin the seedlings so they are the following distances apart:

African Daisy—12"	Clarkia—8"	Love-in-a-Mist—6"
Annual Chrysanthemum—12"	Four-O'Clock—24"	Lupines—12"
Annual vines—24"	Gilia—12"	Mallow—18"
Baby's-Breath—6"	Godetia—12"	Mignonette—6"
Bachelor's-Button—12"	Larkspur—12"	Nasturtium—24"
Chinese Forget-me-not—12"	Lavatera—18"	Poppies—12"

Sowing in a Seedbed. Tiny seeds are best mixed with sand before planting. If sown in rows, scatter thinly and press into the soil with a block of wood. Larger seed is distributed as evenly as possible in the row and covered with soil to a depth of twice the diameter of the seed. Cover the seedbed with burlap or cloth and water with a fine spray through this material to prevent exposing the seed.

Broadcasting Seed. When seed is scattered over a bed, aim for even distribution (mixing fine seed with sand is practical) and rake it in lightly. Watering should be done carefully enough not to cause soil to wash. Seeded areas must not be allowed to dry out. Keep them moist but not soggy. Following the critical period of germination, the tiny seedlings must be kept moist.

Thinning. As seedlings emerge, the tender shoots produce a pair of seed leaves that provide food for the stem. These are followed by a pair of true leaves. When two or more sets of true leaves have developed on seedlings from broadcast seed, thin them as indicated above. Moisten the soil before thinning and pull out the unwanted seedlings, leaving those showing the greatest vigor.

Transplanting. Seedlings grown in the seedbed are transplanted as soon as they have developed two or more sets of true leaves. Moisten the soil first, then remove them with a putty knife or narrow-bladed trowel, being careful to dig deep enough to get each entire root. To avoid wilting, handle the seedlings in small groups. In replanting them in their permanent positions or to a bed for later transplanting, make the holes deep and wide enough to accommodate the roots without crowding them. Firmly but gently compress the soil around each seedling with the thumb and forefinger of each hand. After transplanting, water and provide shade for several days until the seedlings have become established. (Brush cut from nearby shrubs is useful; or old window screens covered with lightweight cloth supported on stones provide the necessary protection from sun and wind.) Keep seedlings moist, but not soggy. After 3 or 4 days, the cover may be removed.

Using Flats, Plant Bands, Peat Pots. If beds are not ready for seedlings, some gardeners find it practical, at first transplanting, to place seedlings in flats, spacing them 2 to 3 inches apart in rows. Plant bands or peat pots may be used. Although this step necessitates a second transplanting, it aids in developing sturdy plants with well-developed root systems. (This is basically the practice of the professional grower who raises annuals for sale.)

In removing annuals from a flat, first soak its soil thoroughly; then lift out the seedlings with a knife or trowel, removing each with as much soil as possible attached to its roots.

Pinching. After plants have become well established, most kinds need to be pinched back to produce bushy, well-developed specimens for a maximum of bloom. This is done by removing the tip growth with the fingers or shears.

Feeding. If the beds have been prepared and fertilized before transplanting (the usual practice), no plant food will be needed until flower buds begin to form. Then, scatter a complete fertilizer lightly around the plants and water it in. Two additional feedings may be given at 4-week intervals. Some gardeners use foliar feeding (see Chapter 16).

Cultivating. In most gardens, as summer approaches, soil tends to cake or form a crust that prevents water from penetrating easily. Every 2 to 3 weeks, loosen the soil around plants with a hand cultivator. The long-handled kinds eliminate the need to bend or stoop.

Mulching. The use of a convenient mulch eliminates cultivating, a considerable amount of weeding, and conserves moisture (see Chapter 18).

Starting Annuals Indoors

Seed of certain annuals needs to be started earlier than is possible in the open because of the time required to produce flowering plants. With others, the purpose of indoor sowing is an early start to obtain early bloom. Kinds such as petunias, salvia, snapdragon, China asters, and verbenas belong in this category. Local growers usually offer all these kinds in boxes, but the number of available varieties is often limited. Consequently, many gardeners find that the only way to obtain desired varieties is to raise them from seed.

Timing. Schedule seed sowing for 8 weeks prior to time of setting out.

Light Requirements. Unless window space is available that receives sun most of the day, your seedlings are bound to be leggy and thus disappointing. If available, greenhouse conditions are ideal and electrically heated hotbeds are also useful. Cold frames are needed if many kinds of annuals are to be raised in this way.

Some gardeners start seedlings under artificial light. With proper controls this method is successful, but constant care and timing of light are required. For most beginners, it is a specialized and complicated approach but can be a most rewarding adventure.

Where only a few kinds are desired, a sunny window suffices. Satisfactory results can be expected, if seedlings are properly handled from the time of germination until they are large enough to set out.

Equipment

This includes bulb pans, cigar boxes, wooden flats, or plastic trays. Five-inch wooden labels for identifying varieties. For drainage: broken flowerpots, stone chips, or screened gravel. Soil mixture (or vermiculite or sphagnum moss). Glass or plastic for covering or plastic domes. Seed sower.

Bulb pans are wide but shallow flowerpots such as used by florists for tulips, daffodils, azaleas, and other plants. They may be clay or plastic. Clay types are porous, and the soil dries out more rapidly than in nonporous plastic, but they are usually safer for the beginner to use, since soil in plastic pots can easily become waterlogged.

Cigar boxes, or other small wooden ones of similar size, fit conveniently on many windowsills.

Wooden or plastic trays, 2 to 3 inches deep, are frequently used. Holes must be made for drainage. Cookie tins make good "saucers" for them.

Soil Mixture. Equal proportions of sand, peat moss (screened), and good garden soil (screened), leaf mold, or soil from compost pile. Some amateurs start seed in sand, others use vermiculite or chopped sphagnum moss.

Vermiculite. (A finer grade is known as terralite.) This is a lightweight mineral substance valued for its sterile quality. It is weed- and insect-free, but since vermiculite contains no plant food, this must be added in liquid form as soon as seed germinates. Many gardeners find vermiculite useful for starting seeds since there is little or no chance of damping-off.

Sphagnum moss, chopped, treated, and offered in packages, is used by some gardeners for starting seed. It is sterile, weed-free, and holds moisture well, but, as with vermiculite, terralite, and similar media, once germinated, seedlings need feeding with a water-soluble fertilizer every 10 days. However, for starting seeds that are slow to germinate (certain perennials, shrubs, and wild flowers), it has proved most satisfactory. The value of sphagnum moss lies in its moisture-holding capacity and loose, fibrous texture that does not become waterlogged and allows air to circulate. Sphagnum moss, vermiculite, and terralite are preferred by many amateurs who garden under artificial light.

Drainage. Before containers are filled with soil, drainage should be provided in the form of pebbles or pieces of clay pots, broken up small. Use at least a one-half-inch layer. Cover the drainage material with screenings from soil, sphagnum moss, rough compost, or coarse soil. Then fill the pot or flat to within three-fourths of an inch of the top. Tamp soil with a block of wood to remove excess soil air. Once the surface is flat and even, seeds are ready to be planted.

Damping-off is a soil fungus that kills seedlings as they emerge. It occurs in the presence of too much moisture or damp weather. Methods used to combat it are sterilized soil, a sterile medium, or disinfecting the soil or the seeds.

Sterilizing soil need not be a chore if certain methods are used. Heating soil in an oven for an hour at 200° F. is a good one. Another is formaldehyde; sprinkle a teaspoonful into a flat of the soil mixture and stir thoroughly. Sow the seed, place the flat in water to soak the soil, then cover with wet newspaper until the seedlings push through.

Disinfecting Seed

The most convenient method for the beginner is to use a chemical solution for treating seed, such as Anti-damp, Semesan, or Arasan, following the simple instructions on the package.

These materials are valuable for controlling damping-off both indoors and in the garden.

Seed-Sowing Techniques

Sowing seed requires patience, but care exercised at this stage makes transplanting easier and more efficient. Seeds vary in size from some as fine as dust to those the size of a pea or bean. The finer the seed, the greater the chance of planting too deep, which results in faulty germination.

Metal and plastic seed sowers make the task of sowing fine seed easy. Before sowing, treat the seed with one of the disinfectants for control of damping-off. Drop a pinch of the powder into the seed packet and shake it thoroughly to coat the seeds. This simple operation is well worth the effort. Scatter the seed as evenly and thinly as possible on the surface.

Handling Fine Seed. Mix tiny seed with finely screened sand or soil, or scatter it on sphagnum moss or vermiculite. These materials provide even moisture, essential to germination. Water from the bottom by placing the pot in a pan of water until bubbles cease to rise from the water; this method of watering is best until germination occurs. Then water with a fine spray and cover with a piece of glass, a plastic cover or dome. Place pots in a warm location until the seedlings emerge. Then move them to full sun. Seeds do not require light until the tiny sprouts break through the soil.

Light. Once germination has occurred pots must be turned daily, since seedlings always reach for the strongest source of light. Fresh air is also essential when seedlings have developed a set of true leaves. When large enough to handle, they can be transplanted.

Handling Large Seed. Seed large enough to be handled is sown in rows, using flats, plastic trays, or cigar boxes. Space seed carefully for even distribution. Patience is required, but the effort simplifies transplanting. Cover the seed and firm the soil with a block of wood.

Watering. It is essential to keep soil from drying out—moist but not waterlogged.

Transplanting. Use the techniques previously outlined.

Peat Pots and Plant Bands. In lieu of flats, some gardeners prefer to use either peat pots (Jiffy-pots) or plant bands, placing one seedling in each. When peat pots are used, they are set directly in the ground at planting time since they soon disintegrate. Plant bands (rectangular container—made of a thin layer of wood) are removed before planting seedlings in the ground. In either case, the small plants are saved the shock of a second transplanting since the roots are not disturbed.

Buying Annuals Already Started

Many home gardeners find it convenient and practical to buy some or all of their annuals from local growers. Conveniently boxed in wood or plastic, usually 12 to a box, these seedlings are easy to handle. Some growers offer annuals in individual peat pots, plant bands, or plastic or clay pots, but these are always more costly. Whatever the container, the soil in it should be thoroughly watered and allowed to drain before the seedlings are removed for setting out. Well-prepared soil and periodic feeding are essential for better than average results. See Chapter 1, for information about soil preparation and Chapter 16, for fertilizing.

A Selected List of Popular Annuals

In the following pages are the most commonly grown annuals. Seed catalogs list many other worthwhile kinds which are worth trying, once beginners have become acquainted with the easy-to-grow types. The brief descriptions contain only the essential facts, and no attempt has been made to list or evaluate all the strains and hybrids now available.

Annuals flourish in well-drained soil and in full sun throughout the day. Many perform well if they have sun for a bit more than half the day. The few that thrive in varying degrees of shade are discussed in Chapter 13.

Given reasonable care and periodic booster feedings of a complete fertilizer when needed, and if faded blooms are removed, annuals are among the most rewarding of flowers to grow.

Ageratum (Floss Flower) —6-15″

A tender annual, ageratum is widely used for edging and window boxes. Shades of blue are dominant, but there are white and rose-pink varieties. A tall kind for cutting, with 15″ stems, is sometimes grown. Free-blooming, it forms compact mounds of foliage, partially concealed by the flowers. Sow seed 8 weeks prior to setting out, or buy small plants in flats or pots. Certain varieties are grown from cuttings to obtain uniform plants. Shallow-rooted, it needs moist soil and frequent watering in dry weather.

Alyssum—4-6″

The best of the annual edging plants, sweet alyssum is a tough, hardy, fragrant white annual which self-sows with abandon. Pink and purple varieties are also grown. Seed may be sown directly in the open ground and plants set 6 inches apart. It is a good companion for portulaca in hot, dry, rocky sites.

Asters—10-20″

Topnotch as cut-flowers, China asters may be obtained in single or double forms. Blooms may be trim, shaggy, quilled, or with crested centers; colors range from white to deep red. There are early, midseason, and late-flowering varieties. Asters were formerly plagued by wilt and aster yellows, but disease-resistant strains are commonly offered. Seed of these half-hardy annuals may be sown in the open and transplanted to stand 6 to 12 inches apart, according to variety. Most growers offer plants.

Baby's-Breath—15-18″

Primarily grown for cutting, baby's-breath is offered in white, pink, and rose. Sow in rows and thin the plants to stand 6 to 8 inches apart. For a continuous supply, sow seed evey two weeks.

Balsam

Well-suited to shady sites (see Chapter 13). It is equally adapted to sun.

Begonia

Ideal for shady gardens (see Chapter 13). In sunlight, the foliage of some varieties turns red, but there are varieties particularly adapted to full sun.

Bells of Ireland—2′ *Molucella laevis*

This picturesque plant's decorative green bell-shaped flowers (calyces) are much prized for fresh and dried arrangements. Sow seed where plants are to be grown, as early in spring as the ground can be worked, by merely pressing the seeds into the soil. This plant does not transplant easily because of its taproot. Frequently, Bells of Ireland self-sow.

Browallia

Useful in shady gardens (see Chapter 13). It also grows effectively in sun.

Calendula—15″

An old-time favorite, the calendula or pot marigold is easy to grow, showy in the garden, and ideal as a cut flower. Colors are orange, lemon, and apricot; it blooms best in cool weather. Sow seed early in the open, and thin seedlings to stand a foot apart. Remove dead flowers for continuous bloom. The calendula self-sows readily.

California Poppy—15″

In hot, dry places, especially where the soil is rocky and sandy, the California poppy is at home. This American native with its glaucous, fern-like foliage makes a bright splash in the landscape, but the flowers are of little use for cutting. Although yellow is the common color, the Mission Bells strain features blooms in pink, rose, cherry, scarlet, and gold. Sow the seed where the poppies are to flower as early as the soil is workable, since the California poppy does not transplant successfully. Thin the seedlings to stand 8 to 10 inches apart. It usually self-sows.

Calliopsis—1-3′

A rather weedy annual of the easiest culture, it self-sows readily. Dwarf varieties make compact plants about a foot high, while the tall kinds branch freely to 3 feet in height. The daisy-like blooms are bright and showy, including yellow, maroon, and bronze. Sow seed in the open as soon as the ground can be worked.

Candytuft—10-15″

A sweetly scented annual bearing clusters of small flowers on stiff stems, candytuft is easy to grow from seed and often self-sows. A tall kind known as giant hyacinth-flowered is an outstanding white cut flower with good keeping qualities. Sow seed as soon as the ground can be worked and transplant to stand 6 inches apart.

Castor Bean—8-10′

A gigantic tropical annual, it is used to conceal unsightly areas or to amuse children with its Jack-in-the-Beanstalk-like growth. Castor bean produces enormous fan-shaped leaves 1 to 2 feet across in rich red or bright green, according to the variety planted. Sow seed in the open when the soil is thoroughly warm.

Celosia—12″-4′

Those who enjoy exotics and flower arrangers with a flare for dried bouquets are partial to the plumed celosia, the coxcomb, and the Chinese wool-flower. All make a spectacular display in late summer and autumn, lasting until heavy frost. Plumed celosias are broadly pyramidal, branching freely to 3 feet or more. Colors range from yellow through the deepest red, with plume-like flower heads of silky texture. The flower heads of the Chinese wool-flower are round-headed, but otherwise are similar in habit. Coxcombs are stiff and formal with velvety-textured, comb-shape flowers. Red is the favorite color in both the tall (3 foot) and dwarf forms (1 foot), but there are yellow, rose, and salmon varieties with silvery and soft-hued edges. The tiny black seeds of all celosias may need an early start indoors and at least one transplanting before setting them in the open when all danger of frost has passed. For the tall kinds, space plants at least 18 inches apart each way; dwarf forms, 8 to 10 inches each way.

Chrysanthemum—18-24″

The annual kinds are called painted daisies. This name admirably describes some of the single kinds, which may have dark centers and dark circular zones, contrasting with a lighter background. There are doubles, too, and some of solid color, ranging from white to maroon, with an abundance of yellows. Foliage is delicately cut and plants are usually well-branched. Sow seed in the open ground and allow a foot each way between plants.

Cleome—4′

Spider flower is an apt name for this tropical annual with spiny stems, rather coarse palmate leaves, and handsome heads of bloom. White is the common color, but there is an excellent pink variety. Cleome is big scale and rather coarse but highly ornamental and well adapted to sun or shade. It thrives in the poorest of soils, makes an attractive quick-growing hedge or background plant, spreading to 2 feet or more and half again as high. Sow seed in the open ground and space plants 2 feet apart. It self-sows readily.

Coleus

Especially well suited to shade, coleus is described in Chapter 13. It is equally well adapted to moist soil in full sun.

Cosmos—4-5′

As background plants for annual borders, fillers among shrubs, or for a temporary flowering hedge, cosmos meets the need, either in full sun or light shade. The more they are transplanted or moved, the sturdier they become. The foliage is lacier than most ferns, and the large, single, daisy-like flowers are produced freely on long stems. Colors are white, pink, rose, and crimson. The Klondyke strain has much bolder foliage with brilliant orange flowers. Sow seed in the open as soon as the soil can be prepared and set the plants 2 feet apart each way.

Dahlia—2-2½′

Growing dahlias from seed is a rewarding experience, often filled with surprises. There are single and semi-double strains producing flowers which measure about 3 inches across. The single blooms of the Coltness Hybrids have distinctive yellow centers surrounded by velvety-textured petals containing practically every color but blue. Unwin Hybrids produce mostly double flowers and are equally good. For cutting and for show, these dahlias have great merit. Dahlias quickly form tuberous roots, and some gardeners dig and store the roots of favorite colors, enjoying them from year to year. Allow 18 inches between plants each way. Given an early start indoors (or buy seedlings from a local grower), they can be counted on to bloom until frost.

Everlasting—6-30″

Commonly referred to as strawflowers, these papery-petaled flowers of several distinct kinds are popular with devotees of dried arrangements. They are also decorative in the garden and effective as fresh cut flowers. Globe amaranth (*Gomphrena*) produce flowers, shaped like red clover, in purple, rose, and white. It is available in either dwarf form, half a foot high, or a taller strain nearly 2 feet tall. Immortelle (*Xeranthemum*) with its distinctive buds and flat, open-centered flowers on wiry, 18-inch stems is truly delightful. Colors include pink, white, purple, and red. Acroclinium and Rhodanthe are others of similar appeal, offered by seedsmen.

Best known of all is the common strawflower (*Helichrysum*), interesting to look at in all stages of flowering from tight bud to full-blown flower. Plants are sturdy and grow 2 feet or more. The winged everlasting (*Statice*) produces a rosette of foliage from which the flower stems rise. Flowers are small, varying in color from white through purple. They are borne in wavy branching sprays on winged stems 15 to 18 inches tall.

When grown in quantity for winter bouquets, everlastings are best planted in rows and thinned to stand half the distance of their respective heights. To use for bouquets, the flowers are cut with long stems as the buds begin to open. (If allowed to fully develop on the plant, the blooms, in drying, display their open yellow centers instead of the more appealing effect of unfolding petals.) After removing the foliage, the stems are tied in bunches and hung upside down to dry in a dark, well-ventilated place. When completely dry, they can be stored in boxes for later use.

Feverfew

Well suited to shady gardens (see Chapter 13). Easy to grow, feverfew does equally well in full sunlight.

Flowering Tobacco

Because it flowers well in shade, it is described in Chapter 13. Sunny situations suit it equally well.

Forget-me-not   See Chapter 3.

Four O'Clock—3′

These tropical annuals with shrub-like growth bear an abundance of small, tabular, fragrant flowers which open in the late afternoon and close when the sun reaches them in the morning. Useful for hedges and temporary landscape effects, each plant makes a trim small shrub. Seed is sown in the open ground and seedlings set 2 feet apart.

Gaillardia—18″

The 2-inch single blooms of the common type are bright red and yellow, resembling a gay Indian blanket, hence the name blanket flower. There are double forms in shades of yellow, bronze, and rich red. Gaillardias are ideal for hot, dry places. Sow seed in the open and transplant to stand a foot apart.

Gloriosa Daisy—3′

These are giant single and double black-eyed susans, carrying blooms that are yellow, mahogany, or a blend. Although the foliage and growth are coarse, the gloriosa daisy is well suited to hot, dry locations where summer flowers are desired. Blooms are exceptionally long lasting. Actually, it is a perennial which blooms the first year from seed, and self-sows readily. Sow seed in the open and transplant to permanent locations, spacing seedlings 2 feet apart. Many local growers offer seedlings.

Gomphrena   See Everlasting.

Gourds—10′

For the quick cover they provide on unsightly fences as well as for their fascinating fruits, gourds are grown in gardens where there is ample room for their development. The lush, tropical foliage and rapid-growing vines need some sort of support; otherwise they sprawl far and wide. There are many kinds, both large and small fruited. Sow seed in the open, after all danger of frost has passed, placing several seeds together in groups 2 feet apart. Allow the strongest seedling in each to remain and pull out the others. Foliage usually needs spraying because of chewing insects and borers.

Heliotrope—2′

Fragrant lavender, purple, or white flowers are borne in loose spray-like clusters on 2-foot plants. This is a plant of sentimental associations, charming as a cut flower and effective in borders or containers. Most beginners buy small plants, seedlings, or rooted cuttings from local growers. Heliotrope flourishes in moist, well-drained soil and shows the effects of drought quickly.

Impatiens

See Patient Lucy, Chapter 13. Because of its adaptability to limited light, it is discussed as a shade plant, but impatiens flowers as well in full sun.

Larkspur—3-4′

Annual larkspur is not only a showy garden flower but highly desirable for cutting with its fern-like foliage and showy spikes of white, pink, lavender, or purple blooms, mostly double. Several strains are offered by seedsmen. Sow as early as the soil can be worked by broadcasting the seed and raking it in. Thin seedlings to stand a foot apart, because larkspur does not transplant easily. Some gardeners sow seed in autumn; the young plants live over winter to bloom in late May and early June.

Lobelia

See Chapter 13, for use in shade. Equally useful in full sun or as an edging plant, lobelia is also a favorite for window boxes.

Lupine—2½′

Where lupines flourish, there is usually an ample supply of nitrogen, and these plants increase its supply by means of the nitrogen-fixing nodules which develop on their roots. White, blue, purple, and pink varieties are available as well as mixed packets. Annual lupines grow readily from seed, flowering in 8 to 10 weeks, and usually self-sow. Plant seed where the lupines are to flower, since they do not transplant easily. Thin to a foot apart.

Marigold—1-3′

A garden is hardly complete without marigolds; their easy culture, free-flowering habit, long-lasting blooms, and ability to endure heat—even drought—are the noteworthy features of these Mexican natives. The greenest beginner can be assured of success if he plants marigolds. Do not overfeed them or they will foliage at the expense of blooms. In the past two decades, marigolds have been widely hybridized and selected; more than a hundred varieties are offered today by seedmen.

Tall, medium, and dwarf kinds are offered with double or single flowers, according to variety. The large flowered types, referred to as African marigolds, include Chrysanthemum-flowered kinds and those that resemble the carnation in form. Heights vary from 2 to 3 feet or more, and the color range extends from pale yellow to deepest orange, with blooms to 5 inches across. African marigolds used to make their great display in late summer and fall, but now there are early-flowering kinds. Some of these are dwarf, less than a foot tall, some slightly taller, and others about 18 to 24 inches.

French marigolds are those with smaller blooms, many with a conspicuous collar of broad-lipped petals surrounding the central cluster. These plants are usually more compact, two feet and under in height; some are less than a foot, forming mounds. Single and double flowers are characteristic of this group and so, too, is red coloring, combined with yellow or orange. The hybridizers have produced a new race by crossing the Africans with the French, resulting in a rich array of red and gold flowers. Daintiest of all is the Signet marigold. It has tiny, single flowers and lacy foliage.

Marigolds are the easiest annuals to raise from seed in the open. Sow seed when the ground is thoroughly warm and transplant when four true leaves have appeared. If a second transplanting is needed because of too close planting, it will do no harm. Space tall kinds 2 feet apart and dwarfs one foot apart. Marigolds flourish in full sun with no special care. Soil of average fertility is sufficient. Beware of high nitrogen fertilizer which produces heavy foliage and delays flowering.

Mignonette—12″

A curious flower of delicate scent, mignonette recalls the quaint gardens of the 19th century, when fragrant flowers were important. The flower spikes are reddish, buff, or white. Seedsmen offer several improved strains. Sow the seed in the open ground where it is to bloom and thin the seedlings to stand 6 to 8 inches apart. For a succession of bloom, make several sowings. Grow it in sun or part shade and remember that cool weather suits it best.

Morning Glory—10-15′

Popular and ornamental, this is the most widely planted of all annual climbing plants. It makes a good temporary cover for banks and slopes, lends itself to trellises and pergolas, and makes a decorative plant for tubs. Flowers may be white, pink, blue, purple, or red, according to the variety planted. Heavenly Blue is the prime favorite. Morning glories make delightful cascading effects, as well as dense growth on fences.

Seeds have a hard coating and need to be soaked for a day before planting. When started from seed, plant where the vines are to be used, since this annual does not transplant easily. Plants in pots can be purchased from many local growers. Morning glories flower best when grown in poor soil, in a sunny location.

Nasturtium—5-6′

A familiar annual vine for hot, dry places, it prefers poor, sandy soil for abundant bloom and has long been a favorite seashore flower. Fragrant blooms in a variety of colors, soft green foliage, plus a rapid-trailing habit make it a most useful ground cover for banks, the tops of walls, or rocky areas. However, it tends to become something of a pest in warm climates, because of the ease with which it reseeds. Both double and single flowering kinds are popular. Trained on supports, nasturtiums make effective plants for pots and boxes on porches and terraces.

Best-planted where it is to grow, it can be started from seed, or seedlings are sometimes planted in pots for transfer to the open ground. Despite its vigor and ease of culture, it is notably sensitive to cold weather and cannot be planted until all danger of frost has passed.

Nemesia—12″

A tender annual, native to South Africa, nemesia makes a colorful display when planted in solid beds or in irregular "drifts." It is useful for container gardens and a superb cut flower. Start the seed indoors or in the open ground, and set seedlings 6 inches apart. It responds to fertile soil and thrives in cool weather.

Nemophila—10″

A delightful California wild flower, it is known as baby blue-eyes. Essentially a filler or edging plant, nemophila grows best in cool weather. Sow the

seed in the open ground and space the plants 4 inches apart. Make several
sowings for a succession of bloom.

Nicotiana   See Flowering Tobacco, Chapter 13.

Nierembergia—6″

Frequently beginners are either bewildered or amused by the plant names
they encounter. *Nierembergia caerulea* is one of these, but its common name,
blue cup-flower, is easy to remember and apt. (There is a perennial species,
N. rivularis, known as white cup-flower.) The lavender-blue blossoms,
resembling shallow chalices with golden centers, are borne on compact
mounds of finely cut foliage. Blue cup-flower makes an attractive edging and
lends color to the summer rock garden. Seed needs an early start indoors
since it takes nearly four months to produce flowering plants from seed.
Most growers offer small plants.

Pansy—8″

Pansies, English daisies, and forget-me-nots are biennials which if started
early enough under glass bloom the same year they are planted and, as such,
are treated as annuals. (See Chapter 3, Catering to Biennials, for another
common practice used in raising these plants.) Beginners and, in fact, most
experienced home gardeners prefer to buy plants already started from local
growers. This is the most practical and economical approach. There are
several outstanding strains of pansies commonly grown and a number of
named varieties, in separate colors, which are often preferred by those
planning special color schemes. Hybridizers have aimed to develop flowers
of unusually large size and plants of compact habit. Violas or tufted pansies
which bear smaller blooms have been selected for separate colors. These
endure heat more readily and often prove to be short-lived perennials.

Essentially cool weather plants, pansies can be set out as soon as the
ground can be worked in spring. It is far better to obtain small plants, just
beginning to flower, than larger sizes in full bloom since the smaller plants
become established more quickly. Space plants at least 10 inches apart.
Booster feedings every two weeks with a complete fertilizer pays dividends.
Keep blooms picked to prevent seed formation and extend flowering. By
cutting back leggy growth, new shoots are induced from the base, and the
life span of the plants is lengthened. Full sun or light shade suits them, and
the better the soil, the finer the bloom.

Patient Lucy   See Chapter 13.

Periwinkle   See Chapter 13.

Petunia

Where varied or separate color effects and continuous bloom are desired in full sun or semi-shade, petunias are usually the answer. The list of available varieties runs into the hundreds, and blooms range from single, funnel-shaped to full-double forms. There are many variations in petal formation, from simple ruffles to heavy fringing. Colors run the full gamut, including many subtle variations in solid values. Some petunias have contrasting throats and others conspicuous blotching and veining or star-shaped throat and petal markings. There are compact and wide-spreading types and some that trail. For beds and borders, window boxes, hanging pots—every type of container—there is sure to be a suitable type and color. Hybridizers are constantly working on selections and new crosses to obtain improvements in habit, size, color, and general vigor. A visit to a trial garden of new varieties is a rewarding experience indeed.

The term F_1 hybrid is used commonly with petunias, referring to the result of crossing two separate selected plants that has produced a first-generation of seed of outstanding quality. Carefully controlled hybridizing results in evenness in color, flower form, habit, and disease resistance. However, when plants of F_1 hybrids set seed in the garden and germinate the following spring, as frequently happens, the results vary greatly with an abundance of unwanted magenta-colored blooms of inferior size.

Those varieties listed as Multiflora hybrids produce comparatively dwarf flowers from 2 to 3 inches in diameter, a foot or so high, free-branching, and broad spreading in habit. Grandiflora petunias bear flowers considerably larger in size, with ruffling and fringing. Somewhat taller, they spread wider than the Multifloras and include semi-trailing types. Double varieties may be large- or small-flowered with conspicuous fringing of the petals. There are also selections in which ruffling and trailing occur in single and semi-double forms, making these a separate group. Hanging basket or trailing types and miniature or mound petunias are among other available kinds.

Because petunia seed is finer than dust and is comparatively expensive, many beginners prefer to buy plants from local growers. Blooming-size plants are usually desired by early June, and most home gardeners do not have the facilities, time, or space required to produce the quantity they require, so that purchase of seedlings is practical and economical. The technique described for sowing fine seed (earlier in the chapter) is particularly pertinent to petunias. Considerable handling care is required plus time and patience. It requires 10 to 12 weeks for the average home gardener to obtain seedlings large enough to set out. Set seedlings 12 to 15 inches apart each way. Crowding results in matting growth, especially in wet weather. In midsummer, petunias often become somewhat rank and need to be cut back to induce new shoots from the base. Follow this practice with an application of a complete fertilizer to stimulate both growth and bloom. Destroy diseased plants immediately.

Phlox—15"

Annual phlox, a showy annual of both bright and subtle coloring, makes a most desirable cut flower. In beds and borders and in the rock garden, it gives an effective display for 8 to 10 weeks. There is a dwarf type about 8 inches tall, a mixture with fringed and pointed petals, and the Globe strain with individual florets—an inch or more in diameter—borne in sizable clusters. Named varieties in separate colors are available. Sow seed in the open when the soil is thoroughly warm, and thin the young plants to stand 8 to 10 inches apart. If the dead flower heads are cut, flowering is prolonged until frost.

Pinks—12-15"

Most of the pinks commonly grown in gardens are perennials such as the cinnamon pink or biennials like sweet William. Those referred to as annuals may often live over to bloom a second or a third year, but they bloom most satisfactorily the first year from seed. Best known of these are the China pinks used for edging, bedding, or in rock gardens. Usually mixed colors are offered; these bear single, double, or fringed flowers, and there are named varieties as well. Seed may be sown in the open ground as soon as the soil is workable. Allow 8 inches between plants. All pinks like lime which can be scattered lightly around the plants.

Poppy—15-30"

Poppies flaunt their flamboyant beauty in gardens without requiring any special care. They are most effective in broad masses, whether sown in mixture or in separate varieties, and many gardeners grow them in separate beds. Then, it is possible to pull them out after flowering and replant the area with such fall-blooming annuals as marigolds, China asters, and others. The corn poppy of Europe is the source of the delightful Shirley varieties, including both single and double forms. There are also carnation-flowered and peony-flowered varieties in a wide color-range.

Poppy seed may be sown in the fall for early flowering, followed by successive sowings in early spring for midsummer bloom. For even distribution, mix the tiny seed with sand or finely sifted loam and scatter it lightly where the poppies are to bloom. Since seedlings are difficult to transplant, thin them to stand 10 to 12 inches apart. Once established, they return each year.

Portulaca

An easy annual for everybody's garden, portulaca needs only a hot, sunny location, since it grows easily in any kind of soil. Sun-rose, sun-plant, wax-pink, and rose-moss are some of its many common names. An ideal ground-cover for hot, dry areas, it blooms incessantly, and requires no care except weeding. Plant portulaca where grass is difficult to grow. It has been used to advantage in driveways, between and along the sides of paved areas. Single and double-flowering kinds are obtainable in many colors. Broadcast the seed and press it in lightly with a board.

Salpiglossis—2′

An aristrocrat among annuals, the dainty salpiglossis is sometimes called painted-tongue. Poised in loose clusters, the tubular blossoms, similar to petunias in form, stand erect on graceful stems. Colors include maroon, purple, golden yellow, and related shades. A dwarf strain is available also. For an early start, sow seed indoors; in the open, wait until the soil is warm. Set plants 9 inches apart. Pinch the plants to make them branch.

Salvia—1-3′

Scarlet sage or salvia is commonplace in public plantings and in gardens as well because of its showy flowers and the fact that it blooms until hard frost. For those who prefer other colors than red, there are old rose, purple, pink, and white varieties. Hybridizers have developed dwarf forms less than a foot high, intermediate types about 15 inches tall, and the more familiar kind 2 to 2½ feet. In marked contrast, there is the refined blue salvia or mealycup sage as it is sometimes called. This flourishes in sun or shade and is described in Chapter 13. Salvia is rather slow to germinate since it requires considerable heat. Usually it is sown indoors early or in open when the soil is thoroughly warm. Practically every grower of annuals offers plants; most amateurs buy young plants. Depending on the kind grown, space plants 8 to 24 inches apart.

Scabiosa

Sweet scabiosa, pincushion-flower, and mourning bride are the most commonly used names for this attractive annual. Its free-flowering habit, showy blooms on long, slender stems, and extensive color range make scabiosas most desirable. Lavender, several shades of pink, red, blackish-red, yellow, and white kinds, in addition to named varieties, are widely grown. Scabiosas are ideal plants for middle-ground planting in annual or perennial borders. Sow the seeds in the open and set the plants 9 to 12 inches apart. They are at their best in full sun, but grow satisfactorily even in light shade.

Snapdragon—6-36″

Truly magnificent in their color-range, the many improved varieties of snapdragons are highly valued for cutting, bedding, bright massing in many parts of the garden, and edging. The improved types may be grouped according to height: tall, medium, and dwarf. Those of medium height, up to 2 feet, are best suited to the average home garden, since no staking is required. The Rocket strain and Tetra, giant ruffled types, are particularly worthwhile. Among the novelties are the Magic Carpet and Floral Carpet strains, seldom more than 6 inches tall, desirable for edging and rock-garden use. Pure white, many shades of pink, rose, red, orange, and yellow, some of which are pastel tints and others of infinitely brilliant hues, are obtainable among the dozens of named varieties of all types. The comparatively new double-flowering varieties are most desirable.

For early bloom, the seed must be started indoors or in a cold frame at least 8 weeks before they are to be set out. Unless sunny windows and ideal growing conditions are available, it is more practical to buy seedlings from growers. When planning to grow snapdragons in quantity, it is best to buy separate colors. Pinch the centers of the seedlings and set them in rich garden soil. Determine the space between plants by the height of the particular strain; usually the distance between plants is equal to one-half the maximum height. Snapdragons bloom freely as long as seed pods are not allowed to develop.

Snow-on-the-Mountain—2′

This flower combines well with other annuals and perennials, serving as a garden highlight. A showy cut flower, snow-on-the-mountain is often used as a filler for decorative effects with such large blooms as marigolds, zinnias, and the like. Truly a "hard-luck" annual, it is not particular as to soil, grows in partial shade as well as in sunny areas, and self-sows readily. In hot, dry places, it grows compactly and does not require staking. The milky juice in the stems can be irritating to the skin, also to the eyes and to cuts.

Statice   See Everlasting.

Stock—12-18″

Stock is a cool weather annual displaying spikes of double or single flowers on stately stems, superb for cutting. It requires an early start and needs to be kept growing vigorously to produce flowers of acceptable quality; otherwise, it develops a heavy mass of foliage and no bloom. Lavender, purple, pink, white, soft yellow, and dark red are typical colors. Start the seed indoors or in a coldframe and transplant the seedlings as soon as the soil can be worked. Those who prefer only double flowers should discard seedlings with dark green foliage. Young plants should never be allowed to become rootbound in pots or flats. Stock grows best in a cool, moist temperature and in soil that is rich in available plant-food.

Strawflower   See Everlasting.

Sunflower

Giant sunflowers which often grow eight feet high or even more are fun where there is room and the setting is suitable. Several fully double forms, and a red-flowering kind are sometimes grown. For small gardens, there are hybrids with smaller flowers in red, yellow, and orange, distinctive markings, and twisted petals; these range in height from 2 to 5 feet. If space permits, these are worth considering.

Sweet Pea

Growing sweet peas successfully is a special hobby of many home gardeners who cherish the quantities of fragrant cut flowers they obtain. The Cuthbertson strain is widely planted, having been bred for heat resistance, as well as large ruffled bloom in a wide array of colors. Others include the Multiflora and Burpee's Giant Heat Resistant strain.

Sweet peas are not equally satisfactory in all parts of the United States. They flourish in cool climates; growth tends to weaken in extreme heat. In many parts of New England and in the Northwest, they are grown successfully through the summer months. Since sweet peas are grown primarily as cut flowers, they are best planted in rows in the vegetable plot, or where the brush or wire supports will not detract from the appearance of a well-planned garden. Deep planting in a well-prepared trench is the usual method.

If possible, dig a trench in the fall, spading it to a depth of 1½ to 2 feet and a foot wide. (Some gardeners have satisfactory results with trenches 12 inches deep.) When available, fill the trench with manure to a depth of several inches, then cover with rich loam. (Peat moss or compost may be substituted for manure.) Sweet peas thrive best in fertile soil that is moist but well drained. Sow the seed as early as possible in the spring, covering to a depth of 2 inches, and thin the seedlings to stand 6 inches apart. To soften the hard seed-shell, the seed may be soaked in water overnight. Or, seed may be sown in the late fall before the ground freezes. Cover it with soil to a depth of 2 inches and mulch the seedbed well after the ground has frozen hard. (In the South seed is sown from November to February.) Many gardeners start their seed indoors in flats during February or early March, then transplant the seedlings to pots, and place in a cold frame until it is warm enough to set the plants in their permanent places. When the seedlings have reached 6 inches in height, they need supports. Brushwood, 3 to 4 feet high, makes the best kind of support, or chicken wire may be used. Put supports in place when seedlings are 3 or 4 inches high. Booster feedings of liquid manure, plenty of water, and frequent picking of the flowers are essential to success.

Torenia   See Chapter 13.

Verbena—12"

For hot, dry situations, in rocky or sandy areas, even in poor soil, verbenas are most useful. They adapt well in containers also. By nature the plants are of trailing habit, serving admirably as ground cover. The color range is complete except for yellow, and the fragrant flowers, borne in clusters, are truly distinctive because many are marked with a contrasting eye in each tiny flower. Seed is offered in separate colors and in mixtures. There is also a compact strain 8 to 10 inches tall. Verbena seed is slow to germinate and needs an early start indoors. Set plants 12 to 15 inches apart and allow for them to spread to 2 feet. Practically all growers offer seedlings and small plants in pots.

Zinnia—6-36"

Zinnias rank in popularity with petunias and marigolds. The various forms range in height from 6 inches to 3 feet, and the blooms of some types may be an inch or more across, while others measure 6 inches or more in diameter. These are flowers beginners enjoy growing and results are almost always rewarding if zinnias are planted in full sun in garden soil of average fertility.

Tall-growers with the longest blooms include the Giant Dahlia-flowered, the California Giants, the Burpeeana Giants, the State Fair strain, and the Zenith Zinnias with their curious twisted petals. These are available in separate colors with named varieties in practically every color except true blue and vary from 2 to 3 feet tall, according to kind. Of medium height are the Cut-and-Come-Again, the Liliput or Pompons, and the Button type. Multicolored include Peppermint Stick with conspicuous stripes, the delightful Persian Carpet strain featuring small flowers rich in dark tones, and the dainty *Zinnia linearis* with narrow foliage and small yellow and orange fairly single, flowers. Dwarfest of all is the Thumbellina strain, producing small blooms on plants only 6 inches high. In addition, seedmen offer many novelties.

Zinnias are easily raised from seed, germinating in less than a week. For an early start, they can be sown indoors in plant bands or small pots. In the open, seed is not safely planted until all danger of frost has passed. Prepare the soil thoroughly and plant 2 or 3 seeds in each spot, allowing only the strongest seedling to develop. Transplanting is not always successful because of the slender taproot which develops from the beginning, but it can be accomplished if the seedlings are transplanted when they have formed two sets of true leaves. The distance between plants should equal one-half of the height of the strain being grown. Although not particular as to soil, they thrive in rich loam; full sun is essential for maximum bloom.

3

PROGRESSING
TO PERENNIALS

Ageratum, annual phlox, and snapdragon make a superb border

Petunias, verbenas, and flowering tobacco are noted for constant bloom

Dwarf dahlia   Dwarf marigold

Cleome or spider flower is available in pink and white

Dwarf Patient Lucy or Patience plant appears in many colors

Petunia Coral Cascade edged with Ageratum Blue Mist

Daylilies thrive with little care and make a spectacular display

Gas plant (Dictamnus) and bearded or German iris

Pinks are cherished for their color and fragrance

Phlox Miss Lingard produce several crops of pure white flowers

Perennials and annuals effectively combined for continuous bloom

Hardy phlox flaunts its bloom in midsummer

Azaleamums rate high for hardiness and free-blooming habit

❧❧❧ While annuals are usually the plants which most beginners set out in their gardens, hardy perennials are actually the backbone of any home garden. Once established, they appear and bloom each year. Perennials are attractive in a border, by themselves, or in a mixed planting that combines annuals and bulbs for season-long bloom. Not only are they effective in the foreground of a shrub planting, but they can be used to advantage in casual groups among evergreens or in rock garden plantings.

A perennial is a fleshy-stemmed plant that dies to the ground each winter and renews its growth from the base each spring. With reasonable care, it can be expected to grow and develop flowering stems from its roots over a period of years.

A considerable number of hardy perennials require little care, are not particular as to soil (provided that it is well-drained), and can be used effectively in large groups where a mass of foliage is needed, or as backgrounds for annuals, low-growing perennials, and bulbs.

Some, by virtue of their deep roots, vigor, and hardiness, are extremely long-lived. Among these are balloon-flowered, bleeding-heart, daylilies, false spirea, gas-plant, hardy asters, iris, Oriental poppies, phlox, plantain-lilies, the various sedums, and a host of others.

On the other hand, the hybrid strains of delphinium are apt to be short-lived. They are best grown from seed and treated as biennials.

To maintain healthy stock, certain perennials require frequent division. These include chrysanthemums, dianthus, Shasta daisies, and violas. Some perennials are essentially weedy by nature, and these are best confined to large gardens where space permits them to "take over." Among these are achillea, boltonia, evening primroses, false dragonhead, hardy sunflowers, widow's tear or spiderwort, as well as nearly all the sedums found in rock gardens. The beginner should be wary about accepting plants that a well-meaning neighbor may be eager to pass on. The fact that there are clumps to spare is not always a criterion of a

55

plant's value. The spreaders often choke out slower-growing, more desirable kinds.

Selecting and Placing of Plants

In choosing perennials for the home garden, consideration should be given to their foliage as well as to their flowers. The blooming period of most kinds is limited, but the leaves of many of the most desirable kinds last throughout the growing season. The ability of a plant to produce foliage of enduring quality that retains a fresh appearance even in dry weather is of prime value since its texture adds to the over-all effect.

As one turns the pages of any well-illustrated nursery catalog, the brilliant color plates and the striking descriptions can be somewhat bewildering. To be sure, the vividness of a color plate may be more intense than the plant actually appears in the landscape, for when any mass of color is photographed at close range, it is more brilliant than when seen at a distance. The flowers shown in catalogs may be deceptive also in that those used for illustrations are usually selected as outstanding specimens. However, with careful attention, many of these illustrations may be "duplicated" in home gardens.

Any clump of bright-flowering perennials properly placed in a garden can be twice as effective if it is given a suitable setting. Yet, to plant individual specimens of a dozen or more perennials without giving thought to their foliage, their time of bloom, and the brilliance of their color creates little more than a hodgepodge effect. Perennials planted in groups or drifts of 3 to 5 or more are more pleasing to the eye.

A succession of color with perennials is neither impossible nor impractical, if certain basic notions are kept in mind. Usually some annuals are needed once the high peak of perennial bloom has passed. From mid-July through September, annuals are at their best, and they can be used both successfully and effectively in combination with perennials to create continuity of bloom.

The perennial or herbaceous border has long been a traditional part of the American garden. It was originally adapted from the British Isles, where the climate is more ideally suited to the growing of various kinds of perennials in extensive borders than in many parts of America. Then, too, to be successful in distributing color masses and planning continuity of bloom, borders should be at least 7 to 9 feet wide and be accessible from both sides for easy maintenance. On most present-day properties, such a border is usually not practical. Therefore, only the best features of the ideal perennial border can be adapted to most home grounds; select those perennials which can be depended on to give a large and long-lasting display of bloom in relation to the space they require.

A bed or border with delphiniums and foxgloves in the background—interspersed with Canterbury bells and sweet William and edged with English daisies, pansies, and violas—is one of the most delightful effects imaginable in late June and early July. To the beginner who may not know, most of these latter plants are biennials (or best treated as such), requiring seed to be sown the previous year in early summer and plants grown on to flowering size. Next season, moved into their permanent places, they will bloom. After flowering, most have completed their cycle and must be renewed. The amount of effort required to achieve such a border is usually more than the beginner can cope with, and even experienced gardeners find it a challenge. These comments are offered primarily to guide beginners in adapting what they can care for to the space they have at hand. After all, to be successful, any gardener must take into consideration the limits of his space and the amount of maintenance possible.

If a border planting is contemplated, a rough plan to make placement easy and effective is basic practice. Using a convenient scale such as 1 inch equals 3 feet, plot the area. Then locate plants according to height: those for the background, middle area, and foreground. Rules for spacing as outlined above aid in determining the number of plants in each group. Balance can be achieved without making a severely geometric pattern. In fact, masses of each kind can be so arranged as to flow together in irregular drifts. Identify each unit with a key number. The key is a list containing plant names, number of plants, distance apart, and time of bloom.

When planning a new border, or replanting an old one, consider first the long-lived perennials mentioned in the opening paragraph. Add to the basic list favorite colors in hardy chrysanthemums. For extended bloom, choose such annuals as petunias, zinnias, blue salvia, snapdragons, and marigolds. As the border develops, other perennials can be added in spring or fall to fill gaps of bloom. Then, over a period of several years, a beginner may assemble a collection of hardy perennials suited to individual needs that will produce bloom from April through October.

How and When to Set Out Perennials

When the ground has lost its winter chill and is just dry enough to handle without getting the fingers sticky, it is ready to receive young perennials and biennials. If these are to be planted in small groups, prepare the soil by adding organic matter and a complete fertilizer mixed in the usual manner. The hole for each plant should be large enough to accommodate all roots, well spread out, without crowding. Cut back broken roots and any exceptionally long, stringy segments. Set crowns at the same level at which they grew in the nursery. Using both hands, firm the soil around the roots as the hole is filled in. When nearly level with the adjoining soil, fill the cavity with water, allowing it to drain away before adding the remainder of the soil. When planting is completed, the soil should be made level so that there are no low areas where water can stand after rains or sprinkling. A few perennials such as iris, peonies, and poppies are more exacting in their planting requirements; the methods for handling these are discussed separately.

Drainage is essential for the continual well-being of all perennials.

Spacing between plants to allow enough room for adequate development and air circulation for each plant is important. The general rule for spacing is half the mature height. Perennials that are slow growing and do not multiply rapidly may be set closer.

Moving Plants in Bloom

Despite careful planning, perennials are often placed in locations not well suited to their needs or where they do not look well with nearby companions. If precautions are taken, many can be moved in full bloom, particularly those with compact root systems. Among these are chrysanthemums, coral bells, false spirea, plantain-lilies, phlox, primroses, violas, and other shallow-rooted types. However, do not try it with balloon-flower, daylilies, gasplant, lupines, peonies, and other deep-rooted kinds.

Before digging, thoroughly soak the soil around the plant to be moved. Use a sharp spade to cut straight down on all four sides, then lift with as large a ball of soil as can be obtained. Place the plant in its new location. The shade provided by a fruit basket, long-stemmed brush, or lightweight cloth (suspended on stakes) and maintained for several days will give the plant an opportunity to become re-established with a minimum of shock. Do not allow it to dry out.

Subsequent Care

In one form or another, maintenance is a constant requirement with perennials, and some need more care than others. To keep perennials vigorous and productive, pick off dead flowers and remove as much of the remaining stems as possible. However, be careful not to cut buds appearing along the sides of the stems. A booster feeding with liquid fertilizer encourages new growth and improves the size of secondary bloom. If foliage is exceptionally dense, it can be thinned to allow for better air circulation.

Pinching. With the exception of bleeding heart, daylilies, iris, peonies, plantain-lilies, and poppies, most perennials are benefited by pinching out top growth. Remove the top inch or two of growth on each stem to induce side shoots for sturdier stems and maximum flowering. Sturdy stems mean less staking.

Thinning. Perennials which produce many stems from the base, such as Michaelmas daisies and phlox, may need to have some growth cut out to allow for air circulation.

Staking. Painted bamboo stakes tied with Twistems or raffia make the job of supporting heavy stems easy. Removing dead flowers and seed pods extends the bloom period of most perennials by allowing secondary buds to develop and keeps the planting tidy in appearance. Diseased and damaged foliage also needs to be removed.

Feeding. Booster feedings for perennials are often needed on thin sandy soils, since plant food is leached out quickly.

Mulching. See Chapter 18.

Watering. Adequate moisture is essential for perennials. The frequency of watering depends on the use of mulches and on weather conditions.

A Selected List of Dependable Perennials

The plants in the following list grow well in average garden soil. When special culture is required, it is indicated. Since practically all are well suited to full sun, no special mention is made of this fact in their descriptions. However, a considerable number of hardy perennials can be grown in varying degrees of shade. The relative amount of subdued light which the various kinds can endure is indicated by the following code:

LS (Light Shade)   SS (Semi-Shade)   DS (Deep Shade)

Flowering period as indicated by months refers to the appearance of primary bloom and the period during which secondary crops of flowers may be expected normally. It should not be interpreted to mean a continuous display of abundant color for any given kind. Rather, as with day lilies, if a goodly number of varieties is planted, continuity of bloom is assured. Average height (designated following the common name) may vary according to soil conditions and other factors.

Asters, Hardy   See Michaelmas Daisies.

Astilbe   See False Spirea.

Balloon-Flower—1½-2′—LS-SS   *Platycodon grandiflorum*
                        JUNE–JULY

Blue, white, or lavender cup-shaped flowers which may be single or double, according to the type grown, are borne in clusters. Glaucous foliage on sturdy stems which holds well throughout the season turns golden yellow in autumn. Deep-rooted, permanent, and dependable, the balloon-flower needs staking in shade unless the dwarf form, *P. mariesi* is grown. More easily grown from seed than divided because of its long tap roots, this old standby often self-sows.

Barrenwort—6″—LS-DS   *Epimedium species*

Good carpet plant. See Ground Covers, Chapter 11.

Bee Balm—2-3′—LS-SS   *Monarda species*
JUNE–AUGUST

The showy heads of red, pink, or lavender flowers (depending on the species) are loved by bees and hummingbirds. Several improved forms are listed in catalogs. A sturdy rapid grower with clean foliage, which is minty when crushed, this old-time native perennial is also known as bergamot. It spreads by underground stems and needs room. Well-suited to naturalizing, especially in moist locations, it provides abundant color in early summer. Increase by division in spring or fall.

Bellflower, Peachleaf—1½-3′—LS-SS   *Campanula persicifolia*
JUNE–JULY

Slender spikes of white or lavender flowers rise from tufts of peach-like, durable foliage. Bellflower forms clumps by underground stems and needs division and resetting every 3 years. Effective under trees and tall shrubs with ferns for a background, it is also a desirable border plant for accent.

Bleeding Heart—1½-2′—LS-SS   *Dicentra spectabilis*
APRIL–JUNE

The pink, heart-shaped flowers on graceful, arching stems make a notable display, but the attractive, glaucous foliage dies down in midsummer. It combines well with ferns and an underplanting of blue phlox, Jacob's ladder, spotted lungwort, and other spring flowers, including bulbs. It frequently self-sows and numerous small plants may be obtained, if the area around an established clump is left undisturbed until late spring. Look for seedlings and move them to desirable locations, since divisions of this perennial are more expensive than most kinds. See also Fringed Bleeding Heart.

Bloodroot—6-10″—SS-DS   *Sanguinaria canadensis*
APRIL–MAY

The dainty, single white flowers appear as the bold, deeply cut foliage is unfolding. An easy wilding to establish in mats with other native plants, it is well suited to naturalistic plantings and ground-cover use. The double form bears long-lasting peony-like blooms in miniature and is most pleasing in carpets of small-leaved English ivy. Divide roots in late summer.

Blue Phlox—15"—LS-SS   *Phlox divaricata*
MAY–JUNE

Drifts of blue or lavender flowers appear on slender stems at tulip time. Blue phlox forms dense mats spreading by underground stems and makes a refined ground cover. Divide plants after flowering and feed to stimulate growth. Few gardeners ever have too much of it. It is ideal for naturalizing.

Bugle-weed—4-12"—LS-SS   *Ajuga*

Useful carpet plant. See Ground Covers, Chapter 11.

Cardinal-Flower—3'—LS-SS   *Lobelia cardinalis*
JULY–AUGUST

Spikes of rich red flowers are carried on sturdy stems in stately clumps. This native is a prime favorite of hummingbirds. The foliage holds up well throughout the season. Although native to moist conditions such as stream-banks, it adapts itself well to fertile garden soil. Easy to raise from seed. Clumps need frequent division which is best done after flowering.

Christmas-Rose—1'—LS-SS   *Helleborus niger*
NOVEMBER–APRIL

Extensive advertising and false claims have misled many beginners about the true merit of this worthwhile plant. Welcome white flowers changing to pink with age, appear from November to April, depending on protection, size of the plant, location, and the ability to establish it. The foliage is evergreen, forming heavy clumps as the plants mature. Those offered by nurseries are usually small divisions, which require several years to develop sufficient size to produce abundant bloom. To enjoy the flowers to the fullest, protect with evergreen boughs or a simple frame covered with glass. A bushel box with the bottom removed and an old window sash will suffice. Well-drained humusy soil, not too acid, and a sheltered location are needed. Feeding with superphosphate induces better flowering. Also consider the Lenten-Rose, *H. orientalis*, which flowers in early spring. Neither is happy in summer sun.

Chrysanthemum—1-3'—LS   *Chrysanthemum species*
SEPTEMBER–NOVEMBER

Essentially sun-loving perennials but suitable for light shade, chrysanthe-mums bloom even in semi-shade if there is adequate direct light. There are many distinct types worth growing. The cushion mums or azaleamums are valued for their mound-like habit, early bloom, and exceptional hardiness. The single and double Korean hybrids are equally noteworthy for winter-hardy qualities. Various double forms include those with button-like flowers, pompons, and large decorative varieties. Others have spoon-like ray petals, and those called spider chrysanthemums are distinguished by thread-like petals.

Common practice is to divide clumps annually in spring, setting single-stemmed divisions a foot apart each way. Since this method often perpetuates nematodes, healthier plants result from rooted cuttings. These are taken in early May, selecting sturdy top growth 4 to 6 inches long. See Chapter 17 for procedure. Pinch plants hard two or three times during the growing season from May to August 1 for bushy growth and to avoid staking as well.

Because of their shallow root systems, chrysanthemums often winterkill due to heaving or as a result of standing water and ice. A slight slope assures good drainage for wintering. Cover with marsh hay, straw, or evergreen boughs after the ground has frozen hard. Roots of favorite kinds can be wintered easily in a cold frame, by lifting them after flowering and cutting off tops at soil level before replanting in the frame.

Columbine—1-3'—LS   *Aquilegia species*
MAY–JULY

The color range runs the gamut with these showy perennials, but the glaucous foliage has little value after midsummer. Well-drained soil is essential for longevity. Many species and strains including the McKana hybrids are easily raised from seed. Long taproots make division of clumps difficult.

Coral Bells—1½-2'—LS   *Heuchera sanguinea*
MAY–SEPTEMBER

The tiny pink, coral, or white bells (depending on the variety) appear in airy racemes on sturdy stems rising from compact heart-shaped foliage. Free-flowering, long-lasting, and showy, they are essential even in the smallest garden. Use them for borders, in drifts, or in broad masses for ground covers. Well-drained average soil, even gritty, suits them. In heavily acid soil, add lime annually. Divide every 3 years in spring or early fall.

Dame's-Violet—2-3'—LS-SS   *Hesperis matronalis*
JUNE–SEPTEMBER

The fragrant white, lavender, or purple flowers borne in loose panicles resemble those of hardy phlox. A good filler, often short-lived, but it self-sows and naturalizes readily. Effective among ferns and low shrubs, this old-time plant, also known as sweet rocket, is a desirable cut flower.

Daylily—2-5′—LS-SS   *Hemerocallis species*
MAY–SEPTEMBER

Trumpet-shaped flowers range from pale yellow through deepest red on sturdy stems (scapes), but each lasts only a day. Free-flowering and showy, there are hundreds of varieties offered by specialists, which make possible a continuous display of bloom from May through September. These big-scale plants with graceful arching foliage need ample room. Sturdy, drought- and disease-resistant, long-lived and dependable, daylilies require little care. They multiply rapidly and can be divided every 3 years. Plant in spring or fall; dividing can be done after flowering if desired. Not only adaptable to sun or shade, the common types can be used in hot dry places, even in poor soil, for naturalizing and on banks and slopes for ground cover. An individual clump may require 3 to 4 square feet of space.

Dwarf Anchusa—15″—LS-SS   *Brunnera macrophylla*
MAY–JUNE

Also listed as *Anchusa myosotidiflora*, the rich blue flowers, which appear with late daffodils and tulips, last several weeks. The foliage is large, coarse heart-shaped. Useful under shrubs as a cover plant, it self-sows readily, is hardy, long-lived, and requires little care. A few plants left to themselves provide a sizable colony in several years.

Evening Primrose—18-24″—LS   *Oenothera tetragona*
JUNE–AUGUST

Often listed as *O. fruticosa youngii,* this rather weedy perennial is valued for its bronzy-green foliage and yellow, cup-shaped flowers in early summer. Where space permits, it is desirable for its over-all effect. It spreads by underground roots, is hardy and long-lived.

False Spirea—1½-4′—LS-SS   *Astilbe species*
JUNE–JULY

Showy plumes of white, pink, or red, according to the kind grown. A wide range in the height of the varieties provides for striking massed effects in early summer. The fern-like foliage is durable and attractive except when allowed to dry out in dry weather, but even prolonged dryness does not kill plants. It prefers a moist, humusy soil, and is hardy, long-lived and desirable. Low kinds make attractive borders or edges. One of best perennials for shade, stock is easily increased by dividing every 2 or 3 years in spring or fall.

Forget-Me-Not—8"—LS-SS   *Myosotis species*
APRIL–JULY

Spring flowering favorite, the flower may be white, blue or pink with soft green foliage. Forget-me-nots thrive in moist soil and self-sow readily, but are well suited to average conditions. Most kinds sold are biennials, but their seeding habit give them an effect of permanence. Ideal companion plants for spring bulbs as ground cover, they are also good fillers among taller perennials.

Foxglove—4'—LS-SS   *Digitalis species*
JUNE–JULY

Most familiar kinds (*D. purpurea*) are those with white or pinkish-purple flower spikes. Improved forms, the Shirley and Excelsior hybrids have a wider color range including apricot. Foxgloves make dramatic showy spires of bloom in shady areas. All are biennials, self-sowing readily; some plants may live to bloom a third year. They may naturalize, creating impressive effects for a month or more in early summer.

Fringed Bleeding Heart—15"—LS-DS   *Dicentra eximia*
MAY–SEPTEMBER

Dainty pink or white heart-shaped flowers on sturdy stems appear in profusion above clumps of lacy foliage. Long-flowering, dependable, hardy, and easy to grow, it is one of the most adaptable perennials for the shady garden. *D. eximia* is native to the East Coast and a similar species, *D. formosa,* is common on the West Coast and named varieties are offered by many growers. Especially useful under shrubs and trees or among ferns and as a ground cover plant, increasing stock is no problem, since it self-sows readily; divide clumps in spring or fall.

Funkia   See Plantain-lily.

Gas-Plant—3'—LS   *Dictamnus albus*
JUNE–JULY

White or pink flowers in spikes standing above a shrubby mass of glossy foliage, they require 3 to 4 square feet per plant when established. Deep-rooted, long-lived, and dependable once established, gas-plant can be important in a group of perennials and requires little care. Transplant as seedlings or small container-grown plants, since big clumps are difficult to move, because of their heavy, deep-rooting habit.

Globe-Flower—1-2'—LS   *Trollius species*
MAY–JULY

The large buttercup-like flowers in varying shades of yellow and orange show to good advantage on sturdy stems. The attractive foliage retains its vigor and freshness in moist, humusy soil, but globe-flower is not well suited to dry conditions. Plants make sizable clumps; divide every 3 years.

Hardy Candytuft—1'—LS   *Iberis sempervirens*
MAY–JUNE

Snow-white flowers on a low shrubby plant with evergreen foliage, candytuft makes an excellent border, or it can be used in large drifts. A desirable ground cover plant because of its broad spreading habit and enduring foliage, it is particularly effective when interplanted with spring bulbs. There are several improved forms including one called Little Gem. Cut back hard after flowering to induce compact new growth. Plants can be divided after flowering or stock may be increased by cuttings.

Iris—6"-3'—LS   *Iris species*
APRIL–JULY

Not only are many distinct types of iris suitable for home gardens, but the number of varieties in several categories is ever on the increase. Bearded or German iris with its extensive color range stands at the top of the list. An individual bloom is composed of three upper petals or "standards" and three lower petals or "falls." The sword-like foliage remains decorative and attractive from spring to late fall. Dwarf iris (*I. pumila*) and the Intermediate hybrids have flowers and foliage of similar form but are low growing. Japanese iris (*I. kaempferi*) belongs in the spectacular class. With large flat blooms, rich in color and texture, it flourishes in moist, humusy soil, producing bloom in June and July. Siberian iris (*I. sibirica*) is distinguished by slender foliage and small purple or white flowers of distinctive form.

In addition, there are numerous worthwhile species including the Roof iris (*I. tectorum*), the Louisiana iris, the spuria hybrids, the bulbous types, the Vesper iris for summer bloom and others. The Crested iris (*I. cristata*) makes a most useful ground cover.

Bearded iris is best grown in full sun. Give it a well-drained location and soil of average fertility. Where acidity runs high, an annual side dressing with ground limestone scattered lightly around each clump in early spring is desirable. The most annoying pests are iris borer and rhizome rot. Clumps need dividing every 3 or 4 years, and this is best done after flowering through August so that the divisions are well established before winter. Late fall transplanting often causes plants to heave unless they are well mulched.

Dig clumps and shake all soil off the roots. Cut foliage back to 6 inches from the base of the rhizome (as the starchy root is called). Examine carefully for borer damage and decay, cutting out all damaged parts including old shriveled portions of the rhizomes. Select only healthy, firm divisions, resetting them in well-prepared soil. Plant singly or in groups, allowing 8 inches of space each way, and cover the rhizomes lightly with soil (less than an inch). The long string-like roots can be cut back to a few inches. Water to help settle the soil around the roots.

Jacob's Ladder—1'—LS-SS   *Polemonium caeruleum*
MAY–JUNE

This spring-flowering carpeting plant with its clusters of soft blue bells and lacy foliage would be a much more satisfactory ground cover were it not for its habit of becoming dormant in midsummer. Effective among ferns, it spreads and seeds readily and is easily divided in spring or fall.

Leopards-Bane—1-2'—LS-SS   *Doronicum species*
APRIL–MAY

Showy yellow daisy-like flowers rise from a crown of heart-shaped foliage. It flourishes in naturally moist, humusy soil making sizable clumps, but languishes where soil and heat are not to its liking. Divide every 2 to 3 years after flowering. There are several kinds of varying heights which are at their best in tulip time.

Michaelmas Daisies—1-4'—LS   *Aster species*
SEPTEMBER–OCTOBER

Hardy asters have considerable value for their welcome fall bloom. White, pink, lavender, or purple daisy-like flowers in panicles, range in height from 9 inches to 4 feet or more. There are dwarfs for edging or rock gardens, medium growing forms for combining with chrysanthemums, tall varieties for background use. Foliage of New England asters is often mildewed and is not outstanding, but plants are generally long-lived, hardy, and showy in flower. Frequent division every other year, and pinching back several times from May to early August keeps the growth of tall types compact and cuts down on staking. Thin heavy growth, allowing several stems for each clump, for better air circulation. Average soil is suitable, but they will take moist conditions, if well drained.

Monkshood—3-5'—LS-SS   *Aconitum species*
JULY–OCTOBER

Loose panicles of purplish flowers are borne in late summer and autumn on long, slender stems with delicately cut foliage. Give it moist, humusy soil in a shady situation and dig in superphosphate to improve flowering. Plants usually need staking. Monkshood is easily divided in early spring, and it usually requires a full year to become established before it blooms. The root is a source of a deadly poison.

Oriental Poppy—2-3′   *Papaver orientale*
MAY–JUNE

Not only the noisiest but the showiest of perennials when in flower, the common forms of Oriental poppies are notably long-lived and deep rooted. Scarlet, orange, various shades of red and pink, and pure white are available in named varieties. Allow ample space for each plant to develop (2 to 3 square feet), and provide companion plants to camouflage the short-lived foliage which begins to deteriorate after flowering. Drainage is essential to longevity. Plant in late summer or early fall when roots are dormant. Set the crown 2 to 3 inches below the surface of the soil and dig a hole deep enough for the taproot to be perpendicular. Container-grown plants can be set out anytime. Old clumps may be divided in late summer or plants may be increased by root cuttings at this time. To make cuttings, dig up the entire root; cut into pieces 3 to 4 inches long and plant with wide end up in pots or directly in the ground, setting pieces 3 inches deep.

Peony—2-3½′   *Paeonia species*
MAY–JUNE

Once established, the peony is one of the easiest, hardiest, and longest lived of all perennials. Although the flowering period is comparatively short, the foliage remains effective until fall when it continues to lend interest turning crimson and yellow. Varieties are legion in both single and double flowering kinds.

Full sun and a deep, well-drained, well-prepared location produce the most vigorous growth. Early fall is the ideal planting time. Obtain healthy divisions with 3 to 5 eyes (pointed reddish buds) and dig holes large enough to accommodate the roots without crowding. Place the roots so that the eyes are an inch below the soil level. Too-deep planting may result in sparse bloom.

When old, established plants are being divided and reset (every 15 to 20 years is not unusual), care must be taken in digging to loosen the soil thoroughly by deep digging all around the plant. Lift roots without breaking and divide with a sharp knife. Choose disease-free sections from the outer rim of the clump, with at least 3 to 5 or more large, plump eyes. Make clean cuts on the starchy roots, removing damaged or broken segments. Discard the central part of the crown. Sections of roots with even a single eye will eventually develop blooming-size plants. Healthy divisions may produce a bloom or two the first year after planting, or it may require two or more years for a creditable display, but peonies are worth waiting for.

Lack of bloom on established plants is a common complaint and may be attributed to several causes. Deep planting as previously mentioned, poor soil, root competition from nearby trees and shrubs, lack of sun, small divisions, unexpected spring freezes, or botrytis blight are typical conditions. All are correctable.

Phlox—2-3′—LS   *Phlox paniculata*
JUNE–OCTOBER

Phlox is the backbone of the hardy flower border in summer, and in its bright array rivals many of the showiest annuals. Name varieties include white, numerous shades of pink, red, lavender and purple, many with contrasting centers. An outstanding early white is Miss Lingard (*P. suffruticosa*) with glossy foliage that remains clean. There are varieties of moderate height and some that grow 3 feet tall as well as early, midsummer, and late flowering kinds. The chief drawback is foliage mildew which can be most unsightly. It occurs in humid weather and can be checked by dusting the leaves with sulfur or using a copper fungicide. Allowing clumps ample room for development and air circulation often circumvents heavy attacks of mildew. Given moderate care, including water in dry spells, division every three years (spring or fall), and adequate feeding, phlox is long-lived and most satisfactory.

Plantain-lily

See Ground Covers, Chapter 11.

Pinks—3″-18″—Zone 2-4   *Dianthus species*
MAY–JULY

Hardy pinks are for sunny places where there is ample lime in the soil. Sprawling perennials, appealing when in flower, they are a bit untidy afterward, despite their glaucous foliage. Several alpine forms make enduring mats of blue-green foliage, studded with pink, white, or red fragrant blooms. These are neat of habit, require little care, and give a softening effect to rough, rocky ground or in crevices between flagstones. Along paths, as edgings for border plantings, or in drifts, they are most adaptable.

Sweet William (*D. barbatus*) is a biennial. Often combined with Canterbury bells, foxgloves, and delphiniums, it usually lives on to bloom for two years or more. The showy flower heads produced on sturdy stems range in color from white to dark red and are pleasingly fragrant. The hardy border carnations, of hybrid origin, are not long-lived and best considered as biennials. For a top-notch performance with these delightfully fragrant summer flowers, considerable care, from feeding to staking, is needed. Easiest and hardiest of all are the cottage pinks (*D. plumarius*) which make generous clumps and are free-flowering and long-lived.

Most of the rock garden kinds are rugged enough for ground-cover use or ledge cover. The maiden pink (*D. deltoides*) makes a blue-green lawn about 3 inches high as it spreads over the ground, producing masses of bloom that range from white to deep red in June.

Average well-drained soil, even on the gritty side, and full sun are best for pinks. Too much plant food is no asset. Soil on the sweet side improved with lime is essential. Hard shearing after flowering and removal of seed pods stimulates compact growth. Pinks can be propagated by seed, cuttings, or division, but the latter is easiest for beginners. Set plants or divisions 10 to 12 inches apart.

Primrose—6-18"—LS-SS   *Primula species*
APRIL–JUNE

All the colors of the rainbow may be had if one is so minded. Species and hybrids vary in height and time of bloom from early April to late June. Primroses are denizens of shade, where soil is naturally moist and humusy, and hot sun is hard on them, especially if the soil becomes dry. Ideal for edgings or carpeting effects, they are well-suited to wild gardens even where boggy conditions occur. Divide every 3 years after flowering or grow plants from seed. Greatest losses occur when plants are neglected in dry summers.

Shasta Daisy—18"—LS   *Chrysanthemum maximum*
JUNE–OCTOBER

These glorified daisies, both single and double, usually pay their way with the bloom they produce, but they are not always long-lived in the colder parts of the Northeast. The best of drainage is essential as well as fertile soil. Sturdy, durable foliage and sturdy stems are typical of the majority. For the most part, the single forms live the longest. Many of the doubles and those with frilled petals, while most appealing, are not dependably hardy, a point to remember when ordering. Increase for named kinds is by division, but in early spring or early fall if plants are mulched.

Snakeroot—4-6'—LS-DS   *Cimicifuga species*
JULY–AUGUST

Stately white spires on sturdy stems rise above clumps of rather coarsely cut but attractive foliage. Dramatic effects can be achieved when snakeroot is used with false spirea in the foreground. Moist, humusy soil is best, but snakeroot will grow under average conditions and requires little care. Long-lived and hardy; increase is by division of the roots in early spring.

Speedwell—1-2′—LS-SS   *Veronica species*
JUNE–SEPTEMBER

Flower spikes may be blue, purple, pink, or white depending on the kind chosen. Clean and attractive with durable foliage, Veronica is a vigorous grower, usually neat in habit. Pinching makes stems sturdy and increases bloom. All are of easy culture in average soil. Increase is by division. Many kinds, including creeping sorts for carpet use, are inclined to be weedy except when used for ground cover.

Stonecrop   See Chapter 11.

Viola, Violet—8″—LS-SS   *Viola species*
APRIL–AUGUST

Violas are best described as short-lived perennials with blooms similar to pansies but smaller. The color range is wide with several good blues and purples, yellows, white, apricot, red, and bicolors. Treated as biennials, they often self-sow and naturalize making good filler plants as well as edgings. Frequent pinching and cutting back by taking long stems for cut-flower use, keeps plants trim.

Violets of many kinds are true denizens of shady places. Not all are weeds, as for example, Rosina, pink; Double Russian, a double purple; and several other named varieties. Many native kinds are ideal for naturalizing under shrubs and trees as ground cover. If left to themselves, they will run wild. Choose kinds with care to fill a need.

Virginia Bluebells—18″—LS-DS   *Mertensia virginica*
APRIL–MAY

A subtle combination of blue and pink is found in each flower cluster. True lovers of shade, with soft, glaucous foliage which adds to their appeal while it lasts, Virginia bluebells are for spring only, since the foliage becomes dormant soon after flowering. Roots are planted in autumn; once colonized, they self-sow. Moist, humusy soil suits them.

Wake-Robin—12″—LS-DS   *Trillium species*
MAY

Among the most notable of our native wildings for shady gardens, the great or snow trillium (*T. grandiflorum*) is valued for its white, three-pointed flowers that turn pink with age. Other species also of interest in wild gardens but not as showy. Plant roots (rhizomes) in fall, giving them moist humusy soil, slightly acid preferred.

Windflower—2-4″—LS   *Anemone species*
SEPTEMBER–OCTOBER

The fall-flowering Japanese kinds in white, pink, and purple tones of waxy texture flaunt their bloom on long slender stems rising from clumps of durable and attractive foliage. Not easy to establish, they require moist, well-drained soil with plenty of humus, a protected exposure, and are sensitive to summer dryness. Best transplanted in spring, they are slow in showing signs of life, and their locations need to be marked carefully. It is not practical to plant them unless their needs can be met.

Raising Perennials from Seed

Many perennials may be raised from seed, and most will bloom the second year if seed is sown early the previous season. This is an inexpensive way to acquire a representative collection of border plants which will flower from year to year. However, named varieties referred to as "cultivars" do not come true from seed, so these are propagated by divisions or cuttings (see Chapter 17). Examples are varieties of chrysanthemums, daylilies, iris, peonies, and phlox.

Some perennials self-sow in gardens when seed pods are allowed to ripen. These include balloon-flower, bleeding heart, columbine, coreopsis, dwarf anchusa, hollyhock, phlox (seedlings are usually unwanted magenta), pinks, speedwell, thermopsis, and many others. In late spring, they may appear near the parent plants or almost anywhere in the border. The easiest way to handle these volunteers is to move them to a sunny location, where they can be grown on for a full season in rows for easy maintenance. Later they can be given permanent locations. Kinds easy to grow from seed include:

Balloon-Flower	Forget-Me-Not	Primrose
Bellflower	Foxglove	Shasta Daisy
Blue Phlox	Golden-Tuft	Speedwell
Columbine	Hardy Candytuft	Sweet William
Dame's Violet	Larkspur	Thermopsis
Dwarf Anchusa	Leopards-Bane	Viola

Timing. Sow seed May 15 to June 1. Later dates are often recommended, but perennial seed sown early produces plants of sufficient size to winter over with a minimum of protection.

Procedure. Sow in a seedbed, using the method as outlined for "Sowing Annuals in the Open."

Transplanting. A well-drained location in full sun or light shade is essential. Prepare and fertilize soil and plant seedlings in rows spaced a foot apart, allowing 4 inches between seedlings. Handle as described earlier in this chapter.

General Care. After seedlings have become established, mulch to keep down weeds and conserve moisture (see Chapter 18). Aside from routine watering and weeding, no other care is required. Some gardeners prefer to winter perennial seedlings over in a cold frame, but this is not essential if the site is well drained. To assure ideal drainage in flat areas, it is good practice to raise a nursery bed 3 to 4 inches above the normal level.

Winter Protection. After the ground has frozen, a light cover of marsh hay, straw, or evergreen boughs (discarded Christmas trees) keeps plants from heaving.

Permanent Placement. Year-old plants may be set in permanent places in the spring or grown on for a second year.

Catering to Biennials

Biennials are among the most popular flowering plants for spring and summer gardens. Because they are often grouped with perennials, their precise life cycle is not always clearly defined. A biennial is a plant which normally requires two growing seasons to reach the flowering stage from seed, after which it produces seed and dies. Typical are pansies, English daisies, forget-me-nots, Siberian and English wallflowers, foxgloves, Canterbury bells, sweet William, and hollyhocks. (As with many perennials, biennials often self-sow, appearing close to the original planting or wherever the wind may carry the seed in the garden.) In addition, it should be noted that sometimes biennials live over to bloom a third and even a fourth year. This habit is characteristic of pansies, foxglove, sweet William, and hollyhocks, particularly where plants are grown in protected areas or when winter conditions are ideal. All are easily raised from seed.

Open Ground. For sowing seed, use the method described for hardy annuals. Planting dates: July 15 to August 1, for pansies,

English daisies, forget-me-nots. June 15 to July 1, for wall-flowers, foxgloves, Canterbury bells, sweet William, hollyhocks. Despite the fact that later dates are often specified, an early start is advisable in order to obtain plants large enough to assure bloom the second season. This is especially important with Canterbury bells and foxgloves.

Cold Frames. Where temperatures drop below zero and protective snow is uncertain, the gardener with a cold frame has an advantage. Seeds of biennials (or perennials, for that matter) may be sown directly in the frame, cared for there during their first growing season, and sheltered there over winter. The frame needs to be large enough to allow for transplanting the seedlings after they have germinated.

Transplanting. As soon as seedlings are large enough to handle, they should be moved from the seed bed. Pansies, English daisies, and forget-me-nots may be set in flats or beds, allowing 6 inches in each direction between plants. Hollyhocks, because of their taproots, are best given their permanent places at this stage, with 18 inches of space allowed each way. If beds into which seedlings are transplanted are raised 2 to 3 inches above the normal ground level, the drainage required for successful wintering will be assured. Excess moisture which sometimes collects in level areas, due to periods of alternate thawing and freezing, spells death for young plants. For this reason, a sloping area is a good site for biennials.

Feeding. After seedlings have become established, feed with liquid fertilizer (a handful of a complete fertilizer diluted in two gallons of water) or side-dress the rows by scattering thinly a complete fertilizer (low in nitrogen such as 5–10–5; see Chapter 16) and water it in. High nitrogen makes lush, soft foliage which does not winter well.

Winter Cover. After the ground has frozen hard, plants in the open ground need cover to prevent heaving caused by alternate periods of thawing and freezing, which are likely to occur in January or later. Use salt marsh hay, straw, or evergreen boughs, since these materials do not pack. Most tree leaves are undesirable because, by absorbing moisture readily, they tend to mat, causing damage to the crowns of biennials. This type of cover, known as a protective mulch, keeps the soil temperature even during cold weather and is removed gradually as the frost recedes in spring. Check local weather conditions before uncovering completely.

Cold frames are most satisfactory for winter protection of plants, but unless unusually deep, they need sash adjustment at intervals during warm weather in winter.

Spring Planting. Biennials can be moved to permanent places in beds and borders as soon as the ground can be worked in spring. If given a booster feeding of a complete fertilizer (see Chapter 16), they produce maximum growth and bloom. Removal of dead flowers and additional feeding produce a second crop of bloom on Canterbury bells, as well as the development of side shoots for more flowers on foxgloves and wallflowers. Hollyhocks and sweet William often live over for another year or two and bloom well, particularly if seed pods are not allowed to ripen.

Hybrid delphiniums, especially the selected named varieties, produce enormous spikes of bloom when well grown and seem to spend themselves in flower production. Although perennial by nature, frequently these delphiniums are not long-lived and are best handled as biennials.

4

GARDENING IN
WINDOW BOXES AND
CONTAINERS

❦❦❦ The age-old lure of green things growing and the joy of having a hand in nurturing them is seldom stifled even among dwellers in apartments which have no land for planting. A window box, a wooden tub, a large flower pot, or some makeshift receptacle—even a tin can—often serves the novice who would have a garden despite the limitations of his surroundings. Even with a minimum of direct sunlight, window ledges, terraces, porches, balconies, or fire escapes can provide settings for a single plant, a collection, or a miniature garden. Once the requirements of adequate drainage and fertile soil are met, the novice selects plants according to their light requirements and his adventure begins. Some beginners, determined to start from "scratch," sow seeds or obtain cuttings which they root in water or a soil mixture. However, the majority, eager for immediate results, start with potted plants.

Choosing the Container. For easy maintenance and sturdy growth, containers must be large enough to hold a sufficient amount of soil so that the roots of the plants will not dry out. Flower pots or containers less than 10 inches in diameter are usually not practical, although they can be used. The smaller the container, the more frequently it must be watered. Deep containers are preferable to shallow types. There are so many kinds of plant containers available in garden shops and nurseries that the choice is wide enough to meet the demands of the most discriminating gardener. Durability is a prime requisite. Any container chosen must be wide enough and heavy enough so that when filled with soil, it will not tip over in heavy wind. On the other hand, unless given a permanent place, the container should not be so large as to require more than one person to handle it. Sometimes, containers are made to order with wheels attached, or redwood platforms with attached wheels may be purchased for those that are to be moved occasionally.

To prolong their use, wooden containers need to be treated with a wood preservative inside and out before painting. Redwood containers last considerably longer if given treatment on both surfaces with a wood preservative. When the bottoms of

wooden containers rot, after several years of use, they may be replaced with hardware wire and lined with black plastic paper.

New clay pots (both the common and the fancy French and
Italian types) need to be thoroughly soaked before they are used
so that the porous clay can absorb an ample supply of water.
Otherwise, a dry clay pot absorbs water needed by plant roots
from the soil.

Metal and wooden containers with painted surfaces need to be
repainted every few years to preserve them and to enhance their
appearance. For this reason, those made of redwood or cypress
are often preferred since they take on a pleasing natural appearance as they weather.

Providing Drainage. Adequate drainage is as essential for
success as is good soil. Whether made of wood or metal, a
window box needs a three-quarter-inch hole in the bottom for
each foot of length. Additional holes can be made by boring or
punching. The same principle holds for tubs and other types of
wooden planters. Clay pots and most types of ceramic, plastic,
fiberglass, and metal containers are designed with openings in
the bottom or sides. To provide adequate drainage, cover each
opening with a flat stone or a piece of broken pot, concave side
down. Then add a 1-inch layer of broken pots, small stones, or
coarse gravel. To keep the soil from washing through, use a piece
of burlap or a layer of sphagnum moss to cover the drainage
holes. Containers without openings, especially those that are nonporous, demand special attention. Provide for twice as much
drainage material (such as crocks and pebbles) as recommended
for those with holes. Otherwise, during seasons of prolonged rain,
the soil becomes waterlogged, and results may prove disappointing.

Preparing soil. Fertile soil with the capacity to hold moisture is
a basic requirement for obtaining good results in any type of
planter. Adequate organic matter is needed in the soil for moisture retention, since soil in containers dries out quickly when
exposed to sun and wind. Plant food, absorbed by water in the
soil and made available to plants through their roots, is not
effective in dry soil. Prepared soil may be obtained from greenhouse or garden centers. Or, use the following formula:

> 2 parts garden loam
> 1 part (salt free) builder's sand
> 1 part peat moss, leaf mold, or prepared humus.

To this mixture add 1 tablespoon of bone meal for each 10-inch potful or a 5-inch potful of bone meal for each bushel. Bone meal supplies phosphorus and potash which plants require and is made slowly available when added in this way.

Planting. Moist, workable soil is the ideal medium for planting. Fill the container with enough soil to allow space for the root ball of each plant. Then set the plant or plants in place, filling the space around or between them with prepared soil. Firm the soil around the plants with your hands, using a stick or trowel handle to eliminate air pockets. Then soak the container thoroughly to settle the entire soil mass and eliminate any remaining air pockets. Additional soil may be needed. The soil level in any container must be at least an inch to an inch and one half below the sides of the container to allow for adequate watering and mulching.

Feeding. Container-grown plants respond readily to feeding with a complete fertilizer. Apply it every 2 to 3 weeks, following the instructions on the container. Fertilizer may be scattered on the surface of the soil and watered in or mixed with water. Foliar feeding is also good practice, and many gardeners are dedicated to this method. Various kinds of liquid plant food are available, including such materials as fish oil emulsion. Watering after feeding is essential to make plant food available to the roots. Beware of fertilizer overdoses, which usually produce an over-abundance of foliage at the expense of flowers. See Chapter 16.

Maintenance. Pinching plants to induce branching and removing dead flowers, and yellowing or damaged foliage are the essentials of maintenance. Occasional pruning to improve appearance and staking tall plants are other points to remember. In essence, container gardening, unlike planting in beds and borders, is a showcase procedure. Unkempt plants are sad to behold and not worth having.

Watering. While overwatering is practically impossible in gardens, soil in containers may become saturated during heavy rains, hence, the need for adequate drainage. Waterlogged soil prevents the movement of air which is essential to healthy growth. When the condition persists for long periods, roots decay and plants die. During hot and windy weather, most containers may require daily watering. If small containers are used, both morning and evening soakings may be needed. A mulch of crushed stone, pebbles, or wood chips—at least an inch deep—is a practical way of conserving moisture. To soak a container that has drainage openings adequately, enough water must be applied so that it drains at the base. Containers without openings need to be watered more carefully. It is far better to have container-grown plants show signs of wilting than to water too frequently.

Window Boxes. For uncounted thousands of plant lovers who reside in cities, window box gardening is the only means of growing plants. During the spring they may be filled with spring flowering bulbs, pansies, forget-me-nots, primroses, and others. Through the summer and fall months, geraniums, petunias, coleus, patient lucy, and a dozen other kinds of summer flowers are an unending source of pleasure. In late fall, chrysanthemums fill the bill, and during the winter cut greens and showy berries provide new variety.

Boxes vary in size according to the window, usually 2½ to 3½ feet long. Adequate depth and width are vital to good growth. A box at least 8 inches deep and 10 inches wide allows for enough soil and root space. An inch or two more in both dimensions is all to the good. Wooden boxes are preferred to metal because metal absorbs and holds heat during prolonged periods of hot weather. The soil, in turn, becomes warmer than is desirable for the plant roots. Materials used may be redwood, cypress, cedar, or white pine; boards at least one inch thick should be used. If the boxes are to be painted both the inner and outer surfaces need treatment with a wood preservative. Even if a natural finish is desired, treating the wood is important. A window box filled with moist soil and plants is sufficiently heavy to warrant sturdy support in the way of brackets and bolts or lag screws.

Drainage, soil preparation, watering, feeding, and maintenance are the same as for other types of containers.

Plants for Full Sun

Begonias, as discussed under plants for shady situations in this chapter, are equally adaptable for full sun.

Geraniums have universal appeal because of their sturdiness, free-blooming habit, and ability to thrive in summer heat. White and various shades of pink and red may be had at moderate prices. Although the common or zonal kinds are those most frequently grown, the ivy-leaved trailers are now more widely used than formerly and apparently flourish even in light shade. There are numerous fancy-leaved kinds with richly colored foliage and variegated forms which are particularly handsome. Among the scented-leaved geraniums are the rose, the peppermint, the lemon-scented, and a host of others. These are always the subject of delightful conversation and provide a continuous supply of nosegays.

Sweet-smelling herbs such as basil, parsley, marjoram, chives, fennel, dill, rosemary, nasturtiums, and others that thrive in hot, dry situations may be grown successfully in containers, providing a delightful kitchen-door garden with a minimum of care.

Lantana, in pink, white, lavender, yellow, and orange, makes a continuous display of bloom from late spring until hard frost. Although essentially a hot-weather plant, it produces woody stems and wilts quickly when allowed to become dry.

Petunias rank with geraniums as the most widely grown flowering plants for containers. Their wide color range, long season of bloom, and adaptability makes them particularly desirable. See Chapter 2 for the various types.

Many kinds of annuals can be used to advantage in containers. For easy maintenance, it is practical to select those which are fairly compact in form and under 2 feet in height; otherwise, staking may be necessary to keep plants from toppling over. Those worth trying include ageratum, lobelia, Madagascar periwinkle, marigolds—both the French and the dwarf African types —snapdragons, sweet alyssum, and verbena. Local growers offer these in small flats of a dozen and in pots.

Plants for Shade

Begonias—the wax or semperflorens type in pink, white, or red—combine effectively with such trailers as small-leaved English ivy, variegated wandering Jew, strawberry begonia, variegated vinca, German ivy, and others.

Begonia richmondensis is a handsome pink-flowered, semi-trailing form with clear blooms and richly textured, dark, glossy foliage which turns red in full sun. This is an ideal plant for hanging pots, window boxes, or other containers.

Tuberous begonias, both the small- and long-flowered types, make an impressive display when well grown. See Chapter 5.

Browallia, both the familiar blue and the white-flowering form, used separately or combined, is free-flowering and highly ornamental in summer. Its free-branching, open growth lends itself to all types of containers, including hanging pots and baskets.

Coleus, in all its tropical richness, makes a gallant display in a wide array of brilliant colors. There are also green and cream and chartreuse forms for those who prefer more subdued colors. The showy variety, Trailing Queen, is a good softener for the edge of containers.

Fuchsias, both the pendulous varieties and the upright growers, are among the handsomest of summer flowers for shady sites. Colors range from pure white to deep red-purple.

Patience Plant or Patient Lucy as described in Chapter 13 is most rewarding and the color range is wide.

Others well suited to shade include English ivy, tender types of ferns (holly, maidenhair, and Boston), black-eyed Susan vine, pansies and violets (for spring), grape ivy, Madagascar periwinkle, and dwarf boxwood. Local growers and specialists often feature a number of unusual tender plants which are well worth trying.

5

FLOWERING BULBS

From every standpoint, flowering bulbs are practically foolproof as far as assured bloom is concerned. Within each firm round bulb is a complete flower or cluster of flowers in embryo form. It is only necessary to slice a tulip in half from top to bottom to see this wonder of nature. The term *bulb* is used commonly to refer to various kinds of underground buds, stems, and swollen roots from which growth emerges. A true bulb is a subterranean bud made up of tightly packed leaves, arranged around a woody core from which stems emerge; roots develop from the base. Food for the development of the leaves, stem flowers, and seeds is stored within the bud. Examples of true bulbs include: tulips, daffodils, hyacinths, lilies, and others. The first three are composed of concentric fleshy layers of tissue or scales with a protective skin or tunic and are referred to as tunicated bulbs. The structure of a lily bulb is a series of overlapping scales attached to a stem but without a protective cover.

A *corm* is a solid underground stem containing plant food; leaves, stem, and flowers emerge from its top; roots develop from its base. Common examples are crocus and gladiolus. A *rhizome*, or rootstalk, may be compared to a side or lateral branch of a plant known as a stolon which creeps along the ground. Where it goes underground forming thickened starchy mass, it is known as a rhizome. Bearded iris and Solomon's-seal are typical examples. A *tuber* is an enlarged rhizome or underground stem containing plant food. A common example is a dahlia root. Despite these structural distinctions, the term bulb is commonly used in the trade and by gardeners in referring to all of these storage organs.

Spring-Flowering Kinds

To every gardener spring means daffodils, tulips, crocuses, and all the other kinds of bulbs that launch the beginning of each growing year. It is hardly trite to say that no planting, however small, is quite complete without at least a few of several kinds. Some such as daffodils, scillas, snowdrops, grape hyacinths, and

87

glory-of-the-snow are permanent, once planted and left undisturbed. These are the kinds for naturalizing. Crocuses, too, belong in this group, but somehow the squirrels, chipmunks, and rabbits find them to their liking, so they must be replanted frequently. For the most part, tulips and Dutch hyacinths last but a few years. Late autumn is the time for planting bulbs. Usually when spring comes, most gardeners wish they had planted more.

Hyacinths, Daffodils, and Tulips

Dutch Hyacinths. Most fragrant of all the spring-flowering bulbs, although a bit stiff and formal in appearance, hyacinths look their best in beds and borders or as edgings for shrubs, especially evergreens, Colors are blue, lavender, purple, pink, red, white, and soft yellow. Full sun and light, rich soil suit them best. A protected site brings earlier than normal bloom. Cover with 4 inches of soil and set bulbs 6 to 8 inches apart. Allow the foliage to ripen before removing it. Hyacinths are at their best the first spring after planting.

Daffodils. Growing daffodils is truly a fascinating adventure, especially when one has an ideal setting such as a meadow or an open woodland. The terms *daffodil, narcissus,* and *jonquil* are often used interchangeably and are confusing to beginners. Daffodil is the common name for the genus narcissus. When correctly used, jonquil refers to the small, fragrant yellow flowers of the rush-leaved kinds. These are not flowers to plant in formal beds. Rather, jonquils are happier, look their best, and thrive for years when naturalized and left undisturbed. In the small home garden, they fit well rising amidst ground cover, in shrub borders, or in grass areas where mowing can be deferred until the foliage has thoroughly ripened. There are more than 9000 daffodil varieties grouped in 11 classes ranging in height from 3 to 18 inches. The manner in which the various types are classified gives meaning to their display at flower shows where they are judged according to class. By selecting varieties from the various classes, blooms in yellow, white, or bicolors may be enjoyed for several weeks.

Selecting daffodils can be a pleasant diversion, and the 11 divisions need offer no confusion. Most popular of all are the Trumpet types. These may be yellow, white, or bicolored. The blooms appear, one to a stem, with trumpet or corona as long as or longer than the flaring perianth segments (the parts of the flower which surround the trumpet). Varieties are legion. The Large-cupped Narcissi are similar except that the cup or corona is smaller—one third but less than equal to the perianth segments. These are similar in color range to the trumpets. The small-cupped varieties are similar to the previous group, only with smaller cups. The double-flowered kinds with blooms, one or several to a stem, have a class to themselves. Triandrus hybrids usually bear two or three nodding or reflexed flowers to a stem, mostly white. These are delightful as are the bright yellow Cyclamineus hybrids with their long trumpet and reflexed collars or sepals. Rush-leaved foliage characterizes the Jonquilla hybrids. The Poets Narcissi have white perianths and small centers or eyes which may be red, orange, or yellow. They are usually the last to bloom. Many species and unusual small kinds for rock gardens are also available. Most catalogs offer daffodils according to class.

Full sun or light shade suits these versatile bulbs. The richer the soil, the better the crop. Light, fertile, well-drained loam suits them best, and daffodils are not averse to low-lying sites in wet land and along the edges of streams, providing they have ample drainage beneath and around them. Daffodils are long-lived and dividends great when the soil is prepared to a depth of 6 to 8 inches below the bulbs. Plant as early in fall as possible so that the roots have ample time to develop before winter. Set bulbs 4 to 5 inches deep and 8 to 10 inches apart. For naturalizing, a foot apart is better to allow ample space for increase. After flowering, remove dead blooms to prevent seed formation and allow the foliage to ripen completely so that when given a light pull it comes out easily. Feed with bone meal and superphosphate annually after flowering by sprinkling the mixture (four parts bonemeal, 1 part superphosphate) on the ground.

Tulips. The color and variety which tulips bring to home gardens may extend over a period of 5 to 6 weeks, if bulbs are selected from the various types offered in catalogs. Twenty-three distinct classes are recognized by the experts, but this fact need not confuse the beginner. Classification is needed primarily for judging varieties in flower shows.

Among the first to bloom (with or following crocuses) are the species, or botanical tulips, of which many are available in a wide range of colors. These vary in height from 3 or 4 to 18 inches. A few kinds flower in late spring. A goodly number are native to Turkistan and Persia, where winters are long and cold and summers are hot and dry. Species tulips are well-suited to naturalizing in shrub borders or in rock gardens. Generally, they are much more permanent than the hybrid tulips, when planted deep in a well-drained location. Outstanding among the species are varieties of the Waterlily tulip (*T. Kaufmanniana*) which average 6 to 9 inches in height. The long, tapering flowers, opening to form great flat stars, are pink, creamy white, rose, or red with contrasting edges on the outer surface. Perhaps the most spectacular of all are the Fosteriana hybrids, particularly the variety Red Emperor with its immense red blooms.

The early singles, with their huge, broad cups on sturdy stems, averaging 15 to 18 inches in height, together with the early doubles of similar height, appear when the large trumpet daffodils are in flower. These are followed by the cottage tulips, with their egg-shaped blooms on slender sturdy stems, and the lily-flowered varieties, with pointed petals.

The high point of the tulip season comes with the appearance of the

Triumphs, the Breeders, and the Darwins. These are long-stemmed, stately growers with colors that rival the rainbow. Since tulips have been extensively hybridized by the Dutch growers over a long period of years, it is often difficult to draw sharp lines of distinction between the various hybrids. Triumphs are characterized by broad-cupped blooms in bright colors, sometimes with contrasting edges and markings. However, these characteristics are not to be confused with the so-called "breaking" of tulips, a virus, spread by aphids, which causes flowers to become multi-colored with unusual feathering and flecks. The so-called "broken" tulips, which are listed in catalogs as Bizarre and Bybloemen are actually products of this disease. (Avoid planting these in gardens in conjunction with lilies, which are susceptible to this virus.) Blooms are often seen in old Dutch paintings.

Most of the Breeders are in shades of rich bronze, deep red, and purple. These sought-after colors are all the more striking when grouped with tulips of lighter color, particularly the yellows which tend to accentuate the richness and depth of color so characteristic of breeder varieties.

The Darwins seem to have their own rainbow, limited only by the skill and imagination of the hybridizers. Purity of color, immense size, sturdy stems, and exceptional height—to 30 inches or more—have contributed greatly to the stature of this deservedly popular group. The nodding stems of the parrots, with their shaggy heads of wavy-petaled flowers, sometimes bowed down in heavy rains, are curious and intriguing, both in color and in form.

Finally, there are the late-flowered doubles or Peony-flowered tulips. These are receiving considerable attention from home gardeners because of their superbly formed flowers.

Striking contrasts and combinations can be achieved in planting these various groups, either in solid masses, or in combination with low-growing perennials, in the foregrounds of shrub borders or perennial plantings. When ordering tulips, consider the succession of bloom that can be achieved.

Tulips are for sunny situations. Set the bulbs 6 inches deep (2 inches deeper in light, sandy soils) and the same distance apart. Planting time extends from early October until the ground freezes hard. They are especially effective when planted in groups of three, five, or more of a single color, or in drifts. For the most part they are short-lived. The first year after planting, they make a superb display, but their performance during the second and third spring is usually uneven. Deep planting allows for leaving the bulbs in the ground rather than removing them after the foliage has ripened. In this way, annuals can be planted without disturbing the bulbs. Lifting, curing (allowing foliage to ripen thoroughly before it is removed), and storing bulbs for replanting in the fall is a tiring chore. Each season after flowering, bloom heads and stems should be removed to prevent the formation of seed pods and the foliage must be allowed to ripen completely; otherwise the new bulbs that form will not develop to blooming size for the following year. Buy clean, healthy bulbs from reliable dealers.

The Little Bulbs

Crocuses that bloom in spring are of two distinct groups. (There are autumn-flowering kinds, also.) The Dutch crocuses, producing large, cup-like flowers in blue, lavender, purple, white, and yellow grow to six inches. Species crocuses—the wild forms native to the Mediterranean regions and Asia—are the forerunners of spring. These are lower in habit with smaller flowers which often brave cold, wintry blasts to show their color in some protected part of the garden. Usually, some species bloom before the Dutch varieties by as much as a month, depending on location. Crocuses literally fit well in many parts of the garden, popping out of ground cover, in drifts along the edge of shrub borders, or naturalized in grass or in the rock garden.

Snowdrops (*Galanthus*), bearing little white flowers with greenish markings suspended on stems 3 to 5 inches tall, are happy companions for all the other little bulbous treasures that bring us renewed hope each year.

Scillas or squills, as they are commonly known, produce tiny blue or white bell-like flowers on short stems a few inches tall. They, too, are for naturalizing everywhere there is space, and increase they will by seed, making welcome sheets of blue.

Glory-of-the-snow (*Chionodoxa*) came to us from far off Asia Minor. Its bluish lavender flower with a white eye borne on slender stems is a joy. Like scillas and snowdrops, once established, they seed and spread.

Grape Hyacinths (*Muscari*) send up foliage in autumn which often becomes ragged at the tips by spring when the spikes of blue, bell-like flowers appear in tight clusters on stems 4 inches or more tall. There is a white variety; several species with larger flowers than the common type are available also. These stately little flowers have many uses in the garden and frequently are combined with daffodils and early tulips.

Then there are the winter aconites, the windflowers, or anemones, tiny bulbous irises, spring star-flower, fritillarias, dogtooth violets, and several others.

Culture. The little bulbs need covering of 2 to 3 inches of soil in the average garden. Where soils are light and sandy, 4 inches is not too deep. For naturalizing, space the bulbs 4 to 6 inches apart to allow for increase; set closer for immediate massed effects. Bulb planters or bulb trowels make the job easy. After flowering, allow foliage to ripen completely before removing or cutting with the mower. The leaves must mature by turning yellow to produce a new bulb. Many set seed which is scattered by the wind.

Growing Lilies

Most novices may not realize that lilies are much easier to grow than formerly. They are best considered as hardy perennials with an elaborate root system composed of a bulb and fleshy roots. In the past, aside from diseased bulbs, much of the failure experienced in growing lilies was due to the fact that the roots attached to the bulb were cut off before shipment. Hence, the bulb had to make a complete new root system. With sufficient food stored within its scales, it was able to bloom successfully the first year after planting, but usually it became greatly weakened after flowering and disappeared. As a result, lilies were considered temperamental and fell into the category of expensive luxuries. During the past twenty years, American lily growers have created new strains of hybrids, which are reliably hardy, disease-free, and shipped with roots intact.

More than 200 garden and greenhouse flowers embrace the name *lily* as part of their common names. Many are not even members of the lily family, but in some way resemble or suggest the lily form. The waterlily belongs to the genus *Nymphaea;* the climbing lily is *Gloriosa,* while the daylily, *Hemerocallis,* is a member of the lily family. Lilies are noted for their fragrance and valued as cut flowers. The shorter the stem is cut, the better chance the bulb has for renewing itself. This is a point to remember when tempted to cut too many blooms with long stems. Lily flowers vary in shape and include trumpets as with the Easter lily, turks-caps as with the tiger lily; in addition there are cup-like, bowl-like, and star-shaped flowers. By selecting from the various species and hybrid strains, lilies may be enjoyed from late spring until late fall.

The Coral Lily (*L. pumilum*), with its dainty turks-caps and its yellow companion on wiry 2-foot stems, is well suited to the rock garden or the foreground of a perennial border. It blooms in late May and June. The Fiesta hybrids, on 3-foot, sturdy stems, follow in June, displaying yellow, orange, and red turks-cap flowers.

The Madonna Lily (*L. candidum*) flowers with June-blooming delphiniums and climbing roses. Often these are not a success in home gardens, either because they are too deeply planted or the bulbs become diseased. However, when clean stock can be obtained, few garden flowers are more delightful than the stately white Madonna lily bearing fragrant clusters of waxy, white bloom on 3- to 4-foot stems. Plant bulbs as early in September as possible, covering them with a mere inch of soil.

Mid-Century Hybrids grow 2 to 3 feet tall and produce large flower clusters which may be of the upright candlestick type, or reflexed on stiff stems 2 feet or more tall. These are practically foolproof, extremely hardy, and make large clumps in a few years. Colors vary from orange-red to cool yellow and make a spectacular show from mid-June through early July.

The Regal Lily, reliable and notably hardy, and its hybrids on nodding stems 2 to 4 feet tall, comes in late June. This is the lily that gave gardeners new courage more than half a century ago. Easy to raise from seed, thriving with little or no attention, hybridizers have found it invaluable.

Olympic Hybrids are large-flowered trumpet lilies with white, pink, or yellow blooms pleasingly arranged around the stem, like a great candelabra, and growing 3 to 5 feet tall. The Green Mountain hybrids are valued for their greenish overtones.

Aurelian Hybrids are characterized by short, bowl-shaped trumpets with petals which flare and recurve to produce flowers of great size and beauty. Colors range from white to various shades of yellow. Stems are sturdy, growth vigorous. These fit nicely into the middle or background of a planting and are greatly enhanced by such shrubs as rhododendrons, azaleas, and other broad-leaved kinds. In this group we find the Golden Clarion strain, which might well be considered the Regal yellow lilies. In addition to their rich coloring, they are noted for their delightful fragrance. Those included in the Heart's Desire hybrids range from white to yellow-orange, with deeper throats. The Sunburst hybrids have narrow petals which are distinctly recurved and richly colored. Pink Olympics are usually listed separately, because of their distinctive coloring, a deep fuchsia.

The Showy Speciosums in white, pink, and red make their appearance, as the season progresses, characterized by distinctive spotting and penetrating fragrance. These make superb cut flowers and are equally desirable for corsages. The Goldband lilies with their great broad petals, contrasting markings, and bands of gold emanating from the center are particularly worthwhile. Well-established bulbs produce three to a dozen blossoms or more, and stems may reach 4 to 5 feet in height, but they are often fickle. Crosses between the speciosum, the goldband, and other lilies have produced a fascinating new race for midsummer bloom. Nor are these all the treasures to be found among modern hybrid lilies. There are many more.

Lilies will grow in any average garden soil that is *well drained*. Fertility is not nearly as vital as drainage, since plant food can be added when the soil is prepared for planting. A slight slope is an ideal planting site where drainage is a problem. Give lilies a location in full sun or light shade, preferably where the lower part of the stem can be protected from the heat of the sun. Lilies planted among rhododendrons, azaleas, and low-growing evergreens are given the stem shade they enjoy and a good setting as well. Ground covers, shallow-rooted annuals, and perennials are good companions for the same reasons. Growers ship the bulbs in late fall, usually in plastolene bags to keep the bulbs firm and the roots from drying.

Planting time extends from October until the ground freezes hard. Prepare soil thoroughly to a depth of 10 to 12 inches beneath the bulbs, mixing with it a scant handful of steamed bone meal for each bulb. Set bulbs 4 to 6 inches deep, measuring from the top of the bulb; the larger the bulb, the deeper it can be planted. When the bulb is positioned, spread the roots and pack soil around them, cover the bulbs and mark their locations. Mulch and avoid cultivation, see Chapter 18. After flowering, allow the foliage and stems to turn yellow and become soft.

Summer-Flowering Kinds

Summer-flowering bulbs are a source of pleasure for their bloom and the exotic effects which they create in the garden. They are ideal for temporary garden effects or for the summer place, since they require little care and can be stored over the winter in a frostproof place for replanting the following year. All the kinds described are tender (except where noted) and must not be planted in the open until all danger of frost has passed. Some are true bulbs, others corms or tubers, but all are commonly referred to as bulbs. In general, prepare soil to a depth of 6 to 8 inches beneath the specified planting depth.

When frost has nipped the foliage, dig the bulbs, shaking soil from the roots and allow to dry for a week before storing in a frostproof location. Those requiring warmer temperature are indicated. Label named varieties before storing.

Acidanthera

Acidanthera is an awkward name for one of the most delightful and fragrant members of the gladiolus family. Unusually delicate in form, the white petals are marked with red-purple, and the buds and blooms are most distinctive as they appear on sturdy 2- to 3-foot stems. Plant in full sun, spacing the corms 4 inches apart in groups of three to five, and cover with 3 inches of soil.

Basket-flower

Basket-flower, or ismene, resembles the amaryllis in form and the greenish-white trumpets which rise from strap-like foliage are usually about 18 inches tall. Like all the amaryllis family, it needs shallow planting in a sunny location. Barely cover the bulbs, spacing them a foot apart each way. For satisfactory bloom the following season, the bulbs must be stored over the winter at a temperature of at least 50°F.

Begonias, Tuberous-rooted

Begonias, Tuberous-rooted. Of all the bulbous plants that flower in summer, none can rival the tuberous-rooted begonias for their free-flowering habit and their adaptability to shade. They are easier to grow than most beginners realize. Tubers already started may be purchased from local growers at planting time, but it is easy and much less expensive to start your own indoors.

Plant them indoors 6 to 8 weeks before they are to be set out. Use flats, small boxes (at least 3 inches deep), or bulb pans filled with a mixture of 2 parts of thoroughly moistened peat moss and 1 part sand. Press the tubers, concave side up, into the mixture, allowing 2 inches between them each way, and water well. Place them in the basement near the heater (60 to 65°F. is ideal). When growth starts, bring them into normal daylight, since growth becomes spindly if they are kept in the dark too long. As soon as plants have developed several leaves, pot them in 6-inch bulb pans.

For potting, use a mixture of equal parts of compost or well-rotted manure, peat moss, and fertile garden soil. To each bushel of this mixture, add one 4-inch pot of steamed bone meal. If soil is on the heavy side, add enough sand to make it crumbly. As you pot the tubers, keep as much of the starting mixture as possible on the roots and set them no deeper than the first planting. After potting, water the young plants thoroughly to settle the soil. Occasional spraying of the foliage is also desirable, but keep them out of sun until the leaves have dried off, because water-spotting disfigures foliage permanently. To avoid waterlogged soil, watering should be done carefully until plants are well established.

Tuberous-rooted begonias are especially tender, and must not be set out until all danger of frost has passed and the ground is thoroughly warm. For best results, the soil mixture in the garden should be similar to that used in potting. Where root competition of shrubs and trees is a problem, pots can be sunk in the ground up to their rims. Never allow plants to dry out, because drought affects growth, foliage, and the size of the blooms. If watered in the morning, there is less chance for mildew to develop. Plants kept in pots or tubs on terraces require constant watering. Feed begonias with liquid fertilizer (low in nitrogen) every 3 or 4 weeks. Too much plant food results in lush growth, causing plants to topple over during heavy rain; staking may be required.

Few pests trouble tuberous begonias—except slugs and snails, which can be controlled with poison bait or by hand picking. Stem rot attributed to manure occurs occasionally, but is seldom serious. The most challenging disease affecting the plants is powdery mildew, which disfigures the foliage seriously. Control with Captan, or a similar fungicide. Badly infected plants should be destroyed to prevent the spores from spreading. When growth has been cut down by frost, cut it off at the soil level, dig the tubers and allow them to dry off for several days. Store over winter in dry sand in a frostproof place, 40°F.

Caladiums

Caladiums. Fancy-leaved caladiums are ideal for shady parts of the garden and are grown for their richly colored, tropical foliage, but they are sometimes grown in full sun. The blooms are insignificant and should be removed. They can be started indoors, but if not given plenty of bottom heat, they are slow to root and sprout. Use flats or bulb pans filled with a mixture of equal parts of garden soil, sand, and peatmoss. Moisten it thoroughly and barely cover the corms when planting. Place them near a heater or radiator so that they get maximum bottom heat. The dry roots are usually shriveled and lifeless in appearance, but as long as they are firm to the touch, they will grow. Once roots have developed and buds have broken, give them ample light. Exceptionally tender, they cannot be set out until the soil is thoroughly warm, about the same time as tomato plants. Space 12 to 15 inches apart each way and cover with an inch of soil. Humusy soil suits them best, and a mulch of peatmoss conserves moisture. Water thoroughly during dry spells and feed occasionally. Dig tubers before hard frost and store over winter in a temperature of 60°F.

Calla lilies

Calla lilies, white, yellow, and pink-flowering kinds, can be grown in full sun or part shade, provided the soil is on the moist side and rich in organic matter. The white-spotted foliage of the yellow variety is attractive throughout the season. These natives of the tropics need an abundance of water. Cover with 3 inches of soil and space them 12 to 18 inches apart.

Cannas

Cannas, usually thought of as Victorian bedding plants, are back in favor again. Their tropical foliage and exotic blooms are strong points in their favor, and the new hybrids, which range from soft yellow to deep rose, average 3 feet in height, making them desirable for small gardens. They can also be grown in tubs, provided they are kept well watered. Give them soil with plenty of organic matter and an abundance of water in dry weather. Plant in full sun, spacing the roots 18 inches apart each way, and cover with 4 inches of soil. For an early start, set the roots in deep boxes in a warm basement and cover with thoroughly soaked peat moss 4 to 6 weeks before planting out.

Dahlias

Dahlias are planted when all danger of frost has passed. Examine stored tubers and cut them to single divisions using a sharp knife. Buds appear at the junction of the neck of the tuber and the stem of the previous year's growth. There is no point in planting an entire clump of tubers when one will suffice. If purchased from a garden center or a dahlia specialist, one firm tuber with one or more eyes is the usual method of selling them. Whether setting out named varieties or tubers saved from last year's seedlings, the practice is the same. In feeding dahlias, avoid fertilizers high in nitrogen, since they tend to produce foliage at the expense of flowers. Space dwarf kinds 18 inches apart each way; tall varieties require 2 to 3 feet between plants. Cover tubers with 3 inches of soil, giving them full sun and a well-drained location. Many home gardeners prefer the small-flowered single and double kinds. These are treated as annuals and started from seed indoors 8 weeks prior to planting time, or they may be purchased already started. In late fall, tubers of favorite colors can be dug and stored over winter to flower the following year.

Gladiolus

Gladiolus. Probably the best known of all summer-flowering bulbs in home gardens, gladiolus are more commonly grown in rows in the cutting garden than for landscape effects. Yet, the miniature types are well suited for border use, combined with annuals and perennials or in the foreground of a shrub planting. There are five distinct classes based on the size of the individual florets, and the flower stalks range in height from 1 to nearly 6 feet, depending on the type and variety grown.

Few bulbs are easier to grow, provided a start is made with healthy corms that have been treated for thrips, which are tiny pests. They disfigure foliage, causing silvery streaks as well as deforming buds and flowers. They are controlled with DDT, dieldrin, or malathion by spraying or dusting, and, as a protective measure, corms are dusted with 5 per cent DDT before storing.

Plant corms in full sun, 5 inches deep and the same distance apart; planting 1 or 2 inches deeper is desirable in light sandy soils. Successive plantings made at intervals, beginning as soon as the soil is workable, provide for a succession of bloom. Rotation of crops each year is good insurance against disease. Tall exhibition kinds may need staking, but deeper-than-normal planting helps to correct this problem.

Dig in late fall, remove all growth to the top of the corms, allowing them to dry off. Separate old, withered corms from those newly formed and inspect for disease before treating with DDT. Store in ventilated bags in a frostproof place. The small cormels can be segregated and planted the following year to increase stock of favorite varieties. Growers grade corms according to size, a point to remember when buying them. Bargain offers are sometimes not bargains but simply small-size corms.

Lilies

Lilies. Although fall is the ideal time to plant lilies, bulbs are sold for spring planting also. Stored over winter at cool temperatures with their roots attached, they are offered in plastolene bags, packed in peat moss to keep the scales firm and roots from drying out. Plant as soon as the soil is workable, or start in pots indoors and transfer to the garden later. For culture, see previous section of this chapter. After setting out, mark the bulbs' locations to avoid damaging emerging growth, which may require 2 weeks or more to break through the soil.

Montbretias

Montbretias resemble miniature gladiolus in flower and foliage. Plants average 18 to 24 inches in height, and the color range is pale yellow to orange-red. The delicately shaped flowers are diminutive and graceful and well suited for flower arranging. Plant in full sun in groups of five or more, spacing 4 inches apart and covering the corms with 3 inches of soil.

Summer Hyacinths   *Galtonia candicans*

Summer Hyacinths (*Galtonia candicans*). These grow to 3 feet in height, producing spikes of white, bell-like flowers loosely arranged on sturdy stems surrounded by glaucous, strap-like foliage. They make pleasing accents in the border, are good cut flowers, and hardy from Philadelphia south. Set in groups of three to five in a sunny location, spacing them 8 inches apart, and cover with 4 inches of soil.

Tigridias

Tigridias have gladiolus-like foliage and spectacular flat blooms on 2½-foot stems, ranging from pale yellow to bright red with contrasting blotches. Plant them in full sun, 6 inches deep.

6

FLOWERING SHRUBS

❧❧❧ For decorative effects in the garden, we depend on various kinds of flowering shrubs. At first glance, their value seems·to rest in the blooms they produce, but these are, at best, of fleeting value. Rather it is their foliage, habit of growth, disease resistance, ultimate size, fall color (if any), fruit-producing habits, and the over-all landscape effect which they provide that give flowering shrubs their true merit.

Many of the big-scale shrubs, such as forsythia, lilacs, mock orange, weigela, hydrangeas, the various viburnums, and others, develop to considerable size, unless pruned frequently. This fact must be borne in mind when selecting and placing them. Otherwise, they soon outgrow their allotted space, and may even dwarf the house or the rest of the planting. On small home grounds, these shrubs are best relegated to boundary line or border use to provide a pleasing display in season as well as a screen or hedge. All flowering shrubs require periodic pruning. If the task must be performed frequently to achieve proper scale, it soon becomes burdensome. The solution is initially to select the right shrub for the right place.

Today, low-slung houses offer all gardeners, beginner and veteran alike, a challenge to select those shrubs which will remain in scale with contemporary architecture. Shrubs need to be chosen as one would choose furniture for a room. For example, the Burkwood viburnum (*V. burkwoodii*) and the fragrant snowball (*V. carlcephalum*), both of recent introduction, are tailor-made for small gardens. In fact, they are admirable replacements for the old-fashioned snowball, once popular. Both average 6 feet in height, with large heads of pale pink to white fragrant blossoms. Their foliage is attractive through the summer, and both contribute their share of autumn color.

The list of shrubs that follows is by no means a complete one, but represents examples of those suited to the needs of the small property owner. Heights designated are those of mature specimens allowed to develop without pruning of any kind. In most instances, size is controlled easily by pruning. (See Chapter 20; also Hedges, Chapter 12.)

Alpine Currant *Pieris floribunda*

See Chapter 12.

Andromeda—3-6′—Zone 4 *Pieris japonica*

One of our truly notable broad-leaved evergreens, the mountain andromeda is native in mountainous areas from Virginia to Georgia and is often referred to as mountain fetter-bush. Mature plants range in height from 3 to 6 feet, but are easily kept lower by pruning. Because of moderate rate of growth and broad-spreading habit, it makes an ideal dwarf shrub or groundcover, best suited to a place protected from the wind. The showy spikes of white bloom are held upright and appear in early spring. Conspicuous flower buds add to its winter beauty. Particularly useful for combining with rhododendrons, azaleas, and other broad-leaved evergreens, it makes a tasteful underplanting for dogwood, sourwood, and other high-branched trees.

Japanese andromeda (*P. japonica*) is upright in habit with glossy foliage and pendulous racemes of white flowers in early spring. The new foliage unfolds with reddish-bronze coloring in spring and similar coloring shows on the flower buds which develop in late summer making this broad-leaved evergreen appealing in every season. Plants grow to 6 feet in height and spread as wide, but can be kept smaller by pruning.

Well-drained, acid soil with plenty of organic matter produces good growth. Andromeda can be grown in sun or shade; in fact, it can endure considerable shade, producing lush growth, but fewer flowers than when grown in full sun. Stock is increased by cuttings and, occasionally in home gardens, by layering (see Chapter 17) of the lower stems. Side branches close to the soil can be induced to root by pinning them down.

Arctic Willows See Chapter 12.

Azalea—3-9′—Zones 4-5 *Azalea species*

Of all the flowering shrubs, azaleas provide the most spectacular pageant of color for spring gardens. There are many kinds from which to select, so that continuity of bloom is assured for 8 to 10 weeks. The bloom of an individual plant will last from 10 days to 2 weeks or more, depending on weather and moisture conditions. For the most part, the plants are compact in habit or can be controlled by pruning so that they require comparatively little space for the display which they provide. All are valued for their attractive foliage, and many have brightly colored leaves in the fall. Azaleas make excellent backgrounds and settings for low-growing perennials, annuals, and bulbs. They are effective as specimen plants when placed where they can be admired from all sides. Frequently, they are combined with needle or broad-leaf evergreens in borders and foundation plantings. Decorative shrubs that flourish in full sun or partial shade, flowering is most profuse where an abundance of direct light is available. The native kinds fit well in wild gardens. The heights specified are those at maturity, but in most gardens they are kept at desired heights by pruning.

Azaleas are closely related to rhododendrons. In fact, botanists make no distinction between the two groups of plants, classifying them under the genus rhododendron, but horticulturists designate them separately.

The Korean azalea (*A. mucronulatum*) produces its rosy-purple, crepe-like blooms on upright, slender plants when forsythia is in flower. In autumn, the foliage changes to yellow to crimson. 6 to 8 feet.

For vividness and brilliance, few azaleas can rival the intense cerise coloring of the Hinodegiri, a mound-shaped evergreen form, literally covered with bloom in mid-May. It is seen to best advantage when placed against a background of evergreens or grouped with white-flowering kinds. 4 feet.

Ranging from salmon to vermilion and making a shapely plant as it matures, the Torch azalea (*A. obtusum kaempferi*) is one of the best-loved of all. Because of its rich coloring, which fades quickly in bright sun, it needs light shade where its brilliance shows to best advantage. 6 feet.

Of all the hybrid strains, few can compare with the Mills hybrids, which are distinctive for their individual flowers, measuring 2 inches or more in diameter, and the extraordinary color range varying from pale yellow to orange-red. Most of the plants offered by growers are seedlings, and they are best selected when in flower. As they get older, they tend to produce considerable dead wood, but usually send up vigorous growth from the base. Unfortunately, they are subject to borers. 6 feet.

One of the most satisfactory of all is the semi-evergreen white-flowering Snow azalea, usually sold as *A. ledifolia alba*. As plants develop, they take on a broad-spreading habit and flowering is exceptionally heavy. Notably hardy, it is a "must" in a collection of any size to separate the more brilliant colors, or for its own beauty. 3 feet.

The Ghent hybrids are valued for their fragrant flowers in sizable clusters. There are single and double forms, and the color range is extensive. 6 to 10 feet.

Roseshell azalea (*A. roseum*) produces bright pink, fragrant blooms and is well suited to wild gardens. 9 feet.

In late spring, the Flame azalea (*A. calendulaceum*) makes a brilliant display with its intense orange coloring and attractive foliage. Although the flowers persist well in full sun, they last even longer in light shade. Many hybrid forms are paler than the type, and others of greatly improved coloring are offered by growers. 9 feet.

In addition to these azaleas, there are many notable hybrids some of which blossom in mid-June. Others produce their flowers over a 6-week period from late April through early June. The best way to get acquainted with the extensive range of color, beauty, and form offered by the great azalea tribe is to visit a well-stocked nursery when they are in flower.

Plants obtained as balled and burlapped specimens or container grown are easily transplanted at any time during the growing year. Azaleas thrive in acid soil. Allow each shrub ample space for development and provide a generous supply of leaf mold or thoroughly moistened peat moss and topsoil at the bottom of the hole. Set plants at the same level they grew in the nursery. Mulch with peat moss, pine needles, wood chips, or oak leaves to conserve moisture. Avoid cultivating around the roots.

Barberry   See Chapter 12.

Beauty Bush—6-10′—Zone 3   *Kolkwitzia amabilis*

Beauty bush, a comparative newcomer to American gardens, has become widely known in recent years. The soft pink flowers borne in graceful sprays, the clean, attractive foliage, and the curious seed pods are among its assets, together with a graceful, fountain-like habit of growth. Often this shrub becomes ungainly due to lack of pruning, but it can be cut back hard to induce new growth from the base. Unusually hardy, it endures hot, dry situations, and it is at its best in full sun. Its dense growth makes a good windbreak. Given ample room to develop, it will produce a most attractive specimen. Skillful pruning will keep it any desired height, ranging from 4 to 10 feet.

Beauty bush can be grown from seed, but cuttings from a specimen of good coloring assures one of true stock. Most nurseries and garden centers offer it.

Blueberry—10-12′—Zone 3   *Vaccinium corymbosum*

Blueberry bushes grow wild in the natural landscape over a large part of the eastern United States and have many attributes as desirable ornamentals. The clean, glossy foliage, dainty bell-shaped flowers, delicious blueberries, and rich autumn coloring of this picturesque twiggy shrub total up to a high score for any plant. Blueberries grow in various types of acid soil, often in sandy and rocky ground, close to the coast. They endure a fair amount of shade and can be combined with a wide variety of native shrubs for naturalistic effects.

Blueberries thrive in acid soil; where there is plenty of humus, growth is usually exceptional. Even in thin soils, when fed with acid-type fertilizer, they develop into impressive shrubs. Full sun or part shade suits them, and they are known to endure considerable dryness, but, in dry summers, the quality of the fruit is not as good. Collected stock is offered by some nurserymen, and the heavy-fruiting cultivated kinds are available from most growers and garden centers, balled and burlapped or container grown.

Bridal Wreath   See Spirea.

Bush Honeysuckle—4-9′—Zone 3   *Lonicera species*

Shrubby forms of honeysuckle, although fairly commonplace, are both attractive and useful in home gardens. They produce rapid growth for hedges and screens and make good specimen plants. A few kinds self-sow to the point of becoming naturalized. Flowers are notably fragrant, and fruits, red or yellow, are decorative and welcomed by the birds. Honeysuckles are at their best when they have plenty of room; when constantly pruned, they may become ungainly unless old wood is removed to the base.

Bush honeysuckle is not particular as to soil and does its best in full sun, but will take a fair amount of shade. Easy to grow and seldom troubled by pests, it is truly a low-maintenance shrub. Increase is by cuttings.

Butterfly Bush—4-8′—Zone 4   *Buddleia davidii*

Butterfly bush and summer lilac are popular names for buddleia, one of the showiest of the summer-flowering shrubs. Plants vary in height depending on the way in which they are pruned and the severity of the winter, which may cause dieback to the ground. However, it is fast growing and free flowering, and the fragrant blooms are produced in long, graceful spikes often with a contrasting orange eye. Varieties include white, pink, mauve, purple, and red.

Full sun, a well-drained location, and average garden soil suit their needs. Prune hard when new growth appears in spring since all bloom is produced on the current year's wood.

Cinquefoil—6″-3′—Zone 2   *Potentilla species*

Many of our native plants, overlooked here at home, had to be sent overseas before American gardeners learned to appreciate them. Among them are several of the shrubby cinquefoils, which in their improved forms now appear in the color pages of our leading nursery catalogs. They are called buttercup shrubs, an apt name for these compact masses of fern-like foliage topped with quantities of single, yellow blossoms in summer. In the wild, they have long been considered little above the rank of weeds.

The cinquefoils thrive in hot, dry situations, have clean and attractive foliage, and are ironclad in their hardiness. As ground covers and for general ornamental use, they provide not only good foliage but attractive bloom as well, particularly in summer.

Cotoneaster—1-8′—Zones 4-6 *Cotoneaster species*

The delicate tracery of the twigs, and their fan-like branching habit are notable characteristics of these sprawling shrubs. When seen protruding through the snow, or viewed in the barren winter landscape with the sun glistening on the bright berries, they become all the more appealing. For the most part, cotoneasters are broad-spreading plants of ample proportions, requiring adequate space for full development. What is more, they can be pruned with ease, and kept within bounds while still retaining their graceful, fountain-like habit.

Cotoneasters are ideally suited for hot, dry situations on banks and slopes exposed to the wind. Skirting the top or base of a wall or among rocks, where they can develop their broad-spreading habit and free-branching growth, they are particularly decorative. They are deep-rooted, useful as soil binders for ground cover. Combine the low-growing kinds with spreading junipers, or use an occasional plant in a bank of pachysandra or myrtle. Cotoneasters grow well in part shade.

They are subject to several pests, including fireblight, scale, lace bug, and red spider, which disfigure their appearance and defoliate the plants. These troubles can be serious, if not kept under control; they detract greatly from the appearance of these ornamental plants, causing dieback as well as defoliation. Sprays for the control of all these pests are effective, but they must be applied at the proper time.

Cotoneasters may be grown in any well-drained soil, even of poor quality. Although full sun is best, they can be expected to make satisfactory growth in part shade, but fruiting is usually sparse. Since plants of any size seldom can be moved successfully, they are offered by nurserymen in containers, which are easily transplanted at any time during the growing season. These shrubs respond readily to feeding, making considerable growth each year, but they will develop satisfactorily with little or no care. The usual method of increase is by cuttings.

Daphne   See Garland-Flower.

Deutzia—3-9′—Zone 4 *Deutzia species*

Deutzias are tough shrubs and fairly rapid in growth, displaying mostly white single or double flowers. Slender deutzia, which makes a broad mound of attractive foliage to 3 feet, with pale pink or white bloom at tulip time, is well suited to small gardens.

Tall growers include the showy Pride of Rochester with long spikes of double white bloom, a big-scale shrub to 8 feet. Others are *D. elegantissima*, 4 to 5 feet tall, with delicately fragrant pink flowers and *D. kalmaaeflora* with bloom of pale pink coloring similar to mountain laurel on 3-foot plants.

Full sun and average garden soil are the simple requirements of these sturdy shrubs. Annual pruning keeps them shapely. Slender deutzia may be increased by division; the other by cuttings.

Dwarf Shrubs   See list for Hedges, Chapter 12.

Euonymus—6'—Zone 3   *Euonymus alatus*

For the most part, these are shrubs of considerable size. Some are tree-like; others are evergreen sprawling shrubs, ground covers, and vines. See Chapter 11 for these. For the average home garden, as specimen, or hedge plant, *E. alata compactus* is the most desirable. It is comparatively slow growing, averaging 5 feet in height often spreading even wider as it matures, but may be kept lower by annual pruning. By nature, it is compact, tidy, and especially well suited to hedge use. Attractive foliage which turns a brilliant red in autumn, equally colorful fruits, and cork-like ridges on the stems which have special appeal in winter are the assets of this worthwhile shrub.

Full sun or light shade and ordinary soil suits euonymus. Actually, it can endure considerable shade but under this condition the leaf color is not nearly as vivid. Extremely hardy, it requires no special attention; hedges require very little shearing. Propagate by cuttings.

Firethorn—10-12'—Zone 4   *Pyracantha coccinea*

A top-notch shrub, notable primarily for its showy fruiting habit, firethorn is one of the most adaptable of ornamentals, lending itself to many uses in the garden. The small, white flowers appear in clusters in May, followed by greenish berries which turn red or orange in late summer making a splendid display until the birds get hungry. Plants are heavily clothed with small oval leaves of fine texture, and the stems are distinctly spiny.

Mature plants may grow 15 to 20 feet tall, spreading as wide if allowed to. Most home gardeners prefer specimens 5 to 6 feet high, pruning to keep plants natural in appearance. Firethorn can also be used as an informal hedge, valuable for its dense growth and thorny stems which make it a useful barrier. When trained espalier fashion by selective pruning, it can be treated as a woody vine for walls and fences, providing highly decorative tracery. During severe winters, the partially evergreen foliage and tip growth may burn and show signs of dieback, but such damage seldom is serious. However, this shrub is subject to scab and fireblight. Both of these diseases need to be controlled before the infestation becomes serious.

Several varieties and a number of selected forms are available. The variety *P. coccinea lalandi* has decidedly orange fruit. Government Red is bright red. A yellow-fruited form, a dwarf kind known as Lowboy, and several other selected forms are in the trade.

Average well-drained soil suits this plant, which belongs in full sun for best results, particularly fruiting. Plants are not easily moved even when balled and burlapped, because of the heavy, sprawling root system which they develop. Consequently, nurseries and garden centers offer container-grown specimens of modest size which are easily handled at any season of the year. Once set out, they make rapid growth, spreading as wide or wider than their height. Constant pruning is necessary to keep firethorn within bounds. Where winters are normally severe, avoid exposed locations. Even when considerable dieback occurs, new growth is produced from the base.

Flowering Almond—4′—Zone 4   *Prunus triloba*

An Oriental flowering shrub of more than ordinary beauty, the dwarf flowering almond is one of those cottage garden bushes that remains a favorite nearly a century and a half after its introduction. Both single and double-flowering forms in pink and white are commonly grown. The blooms appear along the twiggy stems in May to brighten spring gardens. The beach plum (*P. maritima*) and the Manchu cherry (*P. tomentosa*) commonly grown in sandy soils are related species.

Full sun and average garden soil are its simple requirements. It can be increased by cuttings.

Flowering Quince—6′—Zone 4   *Chaenomeles lagenaria*

Japanese Quince—1-4′—Zone 3   *Chaenomeles japonica*

For generations quince bushes and lilacs have framed dooryard plantings along much of the Atlantic seaboard and inland as well. Sometimes seen as hedge plants but more frequently as great specimens, together with flowering almond, wisteria, and strawberry shrub, they seemed to belong near the front door or by the side entrance to the house. Flowers, appearing in May, were bright red or orange, and these big shrubs often outgrew the space provided for them, reaching 6 feet in height and often spreading twice as wide. Furthermore, their spiny stems made them difficult to prune.

New dwarf forms, 1 to 4 feet tall, valued for their dense, twiggy growth, have largely replaced the taller types. Their assets are glossy foliage and a wider color range, including several good pinks. The spiny stems give them value for checking traffic where it is not wanted. These shrubs sucker as they develop and make suitable cover plants and soil binders for slopes and level areas where this type of growth is needed. The Alpine flowering quince is usually less than 1 foot tall, with bright orange flowers in spring. Knaphill and Rowellane are hybrids of recent introduction, reaching 2 feet or more, with flowers in the bright red range.

Ordinary garden soil and full sun suit the flowering quinces. They are easily propagated by root division or by pulling the suckers apart.

Forsythia—3-9′—Zone 4   *Forsythia species*

Forsythia are among the commonest and most popular shrubs planted over a large part of the United States. There are many kinds available, and some have greater merit than others. Golden bells, as they are often called, fill a variety of needs in all types of gardens. They develop rapidly into shrubs of ample size, require considerable space, and are reliably hardy and disease free. The foliage is pleasing throughout the growing years, and some forms are conspicuous for their autumn coloring. The flowers which are among the earliest to appear in spring, range from pale primrose to bright yellow.

Ordinary soil in sun or partial shade is all that forsythia requires. It is drought resistant and makes a deep and heavy root system, once established. Pruning after flowering requires the removal of old canes and shortening of new growth.

Garland-Flower—12″—Zone 4   *Daphne cneorum*

Sometimes tantalizing to grow successfully, because the foliage suffers from winter burn when not protected, garland-flower or rose daphne, is nonetheless, one of the most delightful of all dwarf shrubs. The fragrant, bright pink flowers, borne in clusters above narrow evergreen foliage rise from a sprawling mound. If adequately pruned, this low shrub can be tidy in habit and highly decorative.

Garland-flower, a native of the European Alps, is actually reliably hardy but, in most gardens, it needs protection from the winter sun. Evergreen boughs put on after the ground freezes provide the required shade. It thrives in full sun in well-drained, humusy soil that is not highly acid. Increase is easy by layering; cluttings are more difficult.

Hydrangea—3-20′—Zones 4-5   *Hydrangea species*

Hydrangeas are free from serious pests and of easy culture. There are kinds for sun and shade, a climbing form for use on walls, ledges, and banks—as well as tender types, sometimes grown in tubs or in the open ground with protection in cold climates. All have rather coarse foliage and big-scale flowers. Yet, when given a suitable setting among evergreens and deciduous shrubs, hydrangeas have notable landscape value.

French hydrangeas. The double-flowered hydrangeas grown by florists for spring trade are hybrids of *H. macrophylla*, native to Japan. Frequently referred to as French hydrangeas since many varieties were developed in

France, they are also called hortensias. Many have proved hardy in sheltered locations, even in the colder sections of the Northeast. However, all require protection in areas where winter temperatures drop below zero for extended periods.

When severe dieback occurs, plants produce little or no bloom the following season, since flower buds are formed at the tips of the previous season's growth. However, by skillful pruning, by mulching heavily after the ground freezes, and wrapping plants with burlap, roofing paper, or similar protection, the plants survive for long periods and make spectacular displays of bloom from midsummer to early autumn. In coastal gardens from Cape Cod south, where French hydrangeas have proved hardy with little or no protection, they are featured in dooryards and sometimes in extensive plantings. For porch and terrace use, they are particularly effective when planted in tubs and other large containers. With the present enthusiasm for container gardening, French hydrangeas are attracting well-deserved attention.

Varieties include red, pink, white, and blue flowering forms. However, true pink or red varieties change to blue when grown in acid soil. This fact should be borne in mind when selecting varieties and planning color schemes. Furthermore, he quality and intensity of true blue varieties is governed by the degree of acidity. Since pale or sickly blues are seldom desirable, acidity can be increased easily and quickly by applying a scant handful of acid-type fertilizer around each plant and watering it in. Alum and aluminum sulphate are sometimes used for this purpose. These procedures are also used to obtain a rich blue with pink varieties. When pink varieties are planted in acid soil areas and good-quality pink flowers are desired, lime must be added to the soil. The presence of lime in acid soil makes the aluminum insoluble, thus preventing a change to blue.

Since blooms are produced on year-old wood, pruning must be done thoughtfully. Immediately after flowering, remove dead blooms and stems, cutting back to sturdy new growth. Also remove any weak stems and undesirable growth to improve the appearance of the plant. New basal shoots are the source of next year's flowers. In the colder parts of the Northeast, some gardeners avoid all pruning—except the removal of flower heads—until spring. If heavy pruning is resorted to late in the growing season, followed by heavy watering and feeding, new growth developing may not have sufficient time to harden before winter, with the result that flower buds are likely to be killed.

Well-drained garden soil suits the various kinds of hydrangeas. The macrophylla varieties respond to periodic feeding and require considerable water in dry weather, particularly when flower buds are opening. They retain their color better and longer when grown in part shade. As previously discussed, winter protection should not be overlooked. Tubbed specimens are stored in frostproof cellars during the winter and require only enough water to keep them from drying out. Where winters are mild, they can be stored in the open in a protected place. All types may be propagated from cuttings.

Hypericum   See St.-Johnswort.

Japanese Holly—1-3′—Zone 4   *Ilex crenata varieties*

During the past few decades, Japanese hollies have become exceedingly popular. Because of their dwarf habit, compact growth, rich evergreen foliage, and distinctive forms, they fit a variety of uses on the home grounds. Since they differ considerably in appearance in foliage and in the color and size of their fruits from the red-berried hollies, they are discussed separately.

The original form of Japanese holly (*I. crenata*), introduced a century ago, develops into a sizable shrub 18 to 20 feet high and wide at maturity, but such specimens are rarely seen. Rather it is the selected dwarf forms that fit the needs of present-day landscaping. These are kept at the desired size by pruning and shearing. Slow-growing and compact, the smooth, leathery, box-like foliage of Japanese holly is one of its most rewarding features. Neither the tiny white flowers nor its black berries are of particular significance.

Stokes variety, Green Cushion, Green Island, and others such as *I. crenata nummularis, I. c. microphylla,* and the Kingsville holly are typical of the improved forms available. Because of their moderate rate of growth, pleasing texture, and mound-like habit, they rank high as desirable plants for landscaping. Then, too, they are excellent where low maintenance is essential and as substitutes for boxwood where it is not reliably hardy.

Japanese holly needs fertile soil on the acid side incorporated with plenty of peat moss or leaf mold. Balled and burlapped or container-grown specimens are easily handled. They can be set out at any time during the growing seasons. Plants can be increased by cuttings, using a rooting hormone powder to hasten the development of roots.

Leucothoë—3-6′—Zone 5   *Leucothoë Catesbaei*

One of the most graceful and decorative of all our broad-leaved evergreens, leucothoë is a truly outstanding, low-growing, native shrub. The arching habit of the branches, the lustrous quality of its foliage, which has few rivals among garden plants, and the waxy white, lily-of-the-valley-like flowers, borne in clusters on the underside of the leaves, are other assets. This is a plant of year-round beauty and of particular value in winter, because of the bronzy tones of its foliage. It can reach a height of 6 feet, but is not often seen that tall in the Northeast. There winter has a way of pruning it by killing back the growth, but it breaks from the base readily and is greatly benefited by pruning. Flower arrangers usually keep their plants in prime condition, with the result that its underground stems spread, making it a most effective ground cover. It is especially effective when planted with rhododendrons, azaleas, and other acid-loving plants. A variegated form with highly colored foliage in shades of red and creamy yellow has been introduced in recent years. It is decidedly showy and surprisingly hardy.

Good garden soil, on the acid side, rich in humus, is needed to grow leucothoë successfully. It grows in sun or shade, but is less apt to suffer winter damage in shady locations. A mulch of peat moss and pine needles or oak-leaf compost benefits it greatly, since it is shallow rooted. It can be increased by dividing the roots or by cuttings.

Lilac—12′—Zone 3   *Syringa vulgaris*

The common purple and white lilacs are garden heirlooms along the Eastern seaboard and inland as well. They seem to be most suitably placed when they appear to be growing out of the foundation of an old home. Today, the preference is for the French hybrids, both single and double varieties notable for their large florets and flower clusters and their rich coloring—purple, pink, red, and white.

Beginners and experienced gardeners are often puzzled because lilacs are slow to flower. The common white and purple forms may require 7 or 8 years before bloom appears in quantity. However, grafted specimens of the French hybrids usually flower much sooner.

Lilacs should be pruned after flowering and the flower heads removed. Bloom is produced on the previous season's wood, and this fact should be borne in mind if it becomes necessary to do a drastic job of pruning to improve the shape of a plant. Suckers at the base of lilacs often present a problem. If too many are allowed to develop, blooms on older branches will be lessened, since some of the plant food derived from the soil is absorbed by the developing suckers. Grafted plants of the French hybrids often produce suckers, and these should be cut out as soon as noticed. Some dealers offer plants grown on their own roots, and these are preferred.

Mildew, scale, and an occasional borer are the pests common to lilacs. Mildew, which causes an unsightly grayish cast on the leaves, is more prevalent during wet summers but causes no serious harm. Sulfur dust or Mildex can be used as a means of control.

Scale, when prevalent, can be most annoying. It appears like a crust on stems and spreads rapidly if not checked. Badly infected branches should be cut out and burned. A miscible oil spray applied before the buds break in spring is the usual control. Borers, easily recognized by telltale piles of sawdust on the ground in early summer, can be wormed out with wire. Then plug holes with borer paste or soap.

All lilacs need time to become well established, and plants do best in full sun. Well-drained garden soil free of competition from the roots of trees and other shrubs is also essential. They persist in considerable shade, making an abundance of suckers but few blooms, since lilacs prefer sweet or alkaline soil. A generous sprinkling of ground limestone applied every two years is essential.

Magnolia   See Chapter 7.

Mentor Barberry   See Chapter 12.

Mock-Orange—3-9′—Zone 4   *Philadelphius coronarius*
JUNE

Appropriately named, the mock-oranges with their squarish, white single flowers accentuated by clusters of yellow stamens are as delightful as the blossoms of the orange. For the most part, they are good background shrubs, tall and broad-spreading, but a few are low growers. The foliage is coarse, and the shrubs themselves are without distinction. Numerous varieties are available, including some with double flowers, small and large single-flowered varieties, and a yellow-leaved form. Choose thoughtfully the variety you plant with an eye to its use and its place in the garden.

Full sun or light shade and average garden soil suits them. Since mock-orange bloom on old wood, prune each year after flowering.

Mountain-Laurel—8-10′—Zone 3   *Kalmia latifolia*

Perhaps the best-loved of all native flowering shrubs is mountain-laurel, but it is not always seen at its best in gardens or in public plantings. All too often, it is planted in exposed areas where it suffers windburn in winter. Most of the plants available are collected stock that has been dug in the wild, cut back hard, and lined out in nursery rows for several years. This is the ideal way to handle mountain-laurel, and unless one is familiar with the methods of moving native plants, it is a mistake for the beginner to collect this shrub from the wild. In its native setting, mountain-laurel is found in sun and shade but is most floriferous in full sun or where it has high shade.

When combined with rhododendrons, azaleas, various broad-leaved and needle evergreens, its long, oval evergreen leaves make a pleasing contrast in form and texture. It is a delightful plant for the wild garden. Bloom is light pink fading to white, or a rich, deep pink approaching red; the crinkly, roundish flowers being formed in clusters. Many old stands of mountain-laurel are preserved in parks and on private estates, where the plants have taken on a picturesque, leggy, tree-like habit with age.

Mountain-laurel is an acid-soil plant and benefits greatly from a soil rich in organic matter. As with rhododendrons, azaleas, and others, soil preparation should be thorough with plenty of peat added. Mulching is good practice to conserve soil moisture. Avoid windswept and exposed locations which cause serious winter damage to the foliage. Propagation is by layering of young shoots, careful severance of separate stems from old clumps, or from seed.

Pieris   See Andromeda.

Potentilla   See Cinquefoil.

Privet   See Chapter 12.

Pyracantha   See Firethorn.

Red-Osier Dogwood—7′—Zone 2   *Cornus stolonifera*

Red-osier dogwood and the yellow-twigged form are native shrubs of more than ordinary value, especially for moist soil or low, boggy areas. Yet, they can be expected to do well even under ordinary growing conditions. White flowers in flat clusters, white fruits in late summer, and bright red or golden yellow twigs in winter, according to the type planted, make this shrub a distinct asset in the landscape. Allow it plenty of room in which to develop, for this is a shrub of generous proportions, stretching to 7 feet in height and spreading much wider when left to itself. It is a good soil binder, because of its heavy root system and habit of increasing in size by underground stems. The color of the twigs, especially when the sun shines on them, greatly enlivens the winter landscape.

Plants are offered by most nurserymen and require no special care. Additional plants may be obtained from cuttings or dividing the roots. Pruning keeps them within bounds in sun or shade.

Rhododendron—3-20′—Zones 3-5   *Rhododendron species*

There is something majestic about rhododendrons in flower—the superb form of the individual blooms and the dramatic effects created by masses of blossoms—that excites a desire to grow as many as space allows. The year-round attractiveness of the foliage and its rich texture are other assets not to be overlooked. Among the most permanent of woody plants, rhododendrons may well be considered garden heirlooms.

In choosing suitable kinds and colors, thought as to placement and the plants used as companions for them is important. Also the ultimate height and spread of each specimen or group needs to be considered.

Rhododendrons are at their best in some shade for part of the day. High shade provided by tall trees, which do not offer root competition, is ideal. Although rhododendrons can be expected to flourish in full sun, windswept areas should be avoided, as well as hot, dry spots or southern exposures against buildings or walls where they suffer badly from the effects of winter sun. Where space is limited and there is no planting alternative, rhododendrons can be protected from winter sun by the use of evergreen boughs, straw matting, or a wooden framework covered with burlap or slats put on after the ground has frozen hard. The point is to keep the plants cool, since the effects of alternate thawing and freezing are harmful to the roots and the plant as a whole.

The north side of a building is most satisfactory, provided there is adequate light. Home gardeners faced with a heavy growth of trees can provide suitable settings for these shrubs by thinning top growth and removing lower tree branches to increase the amount of light. Because rhododendrons have a compact and shallow root system, their growth is impeded by encroaching roots of other plants that consume the plant food.

An acid soil is the basic requirement for all broad-leaved evergreens. In areas where this type of soil prevails there is no problem. Specially prepared acid-soil fertilizers containing organic nitrogen are readily available at garden shops and nurseries; these preparations should be used according to the instructions on the package.

Lack of acidity is usually indicated by pale green to yellow coloring in the leaves, contrasted by darker veins. A lowering of acidity may be caused by alkaline water from the local supply, drainage from walls in which plaster has been used, limestone outcroppings, rubble left in the soil by builders, or types of fertilizer producing toxic salts.

Although aluminum sulfate is widely used and commonly recommended to increase acidity, it can produce a toxic condition in the soil. It is safer to apply ordinary dusting sulfur, scattering a quarter of a pound around an average-sized rhododendron and watering it in. Supplement with acid-soil fertilizer. Too much sulfur can injure plants, but scattered at the rate of one-fourth pound per square yard will do no harm. Apply sulfur on a dry day, and do not allow any of it to coat the foliage. If this occurs, be sure to wash it off, since it tends to burn the leaves, especially in the presence of sun.

Like most plants, rhododendrons need good drainage. In low areas where water collects and in heavy soils, plants show an unhealthy condition of growth. If drainage is a problem, dig holes twice as wide and deep as needed for proper planting and fill in six inches of coarse gravel. Also plant the shrubs high.

Because they are slow to propagate, rhododendrons are more costly than other types of flowering shrubs. Plants purchased are usually 12 to 24 inches high and sometimes smaller. In preparing the holes for planting them, remove the soil from an area twice as great as the root-ball will require. Use moist peat and top-soil for planting. If leaf mold or compost is available, it should be used generously.

Set the plant at the same level it was growing in the nursery. Eliminate air pockets in the soil with water, gradually filling in soil. Form a slight basin to catch water until the plant is established. Avoid firm tamping with a shovel handle or your feet; rather, pack the soil with your hands so as not to damage the root system. Newly set plants should be watered at least twice a week under ordinary conditions. Spraying the foliage also helps to lessen transpiration shock.

The simplest and most effective way to conserve moisture around rhododendrons is to mulch them, using pine needles, peat moss, or oak leaves. Wood chips or sawdust to which nitrogen has been added are also practical. Once planted, they require little care except for an annual feeding in early spring with acid-soil fertilizer.

Many beginners are unsuccessful with rhododendrons because they continually cultivate the soil around them. This is a harmful practice, since it damages the tiny, fibrous roots which are close to the surface. An adequate mulch (1-inch deep) will help to keep them thriving. Deep planting also kills many.

Among the most annoying pests that attack rhododendrons during late spring and summer are lacebugs, insects approximately an eighth of an inch long with lace-like wings. Evidence of their presence is a mottled, grayish appearance on the upper side of the leaves. Spray with nicotine sulfate or malathion, hitting both sides of the leaves.

Another pest is red spider, which causes the leaves to turn reddish-brown with tiny white webs on the under surface. This tiny insect is a mite, best controlled by such preparations as aramite or ovotran. Spray when the plants are in flower and again once or twice.

The Catawba rhododendron (*R. catawbiense*) and its hybrids are most commonly planted. Mature plants grow 6 feet or more in height and when mature spread to even greater proportions. Frequent pruning (after flowering) keeps them at the desired size. Individual flowers are large and are borne in sizable clusters. They range from white through pink, to lavender, purple, and red.

Rose   See Chapter 8.

Rose Daphne   See Garland-Flower.

Rose-of-Sharon—15′—Zone 4   *Hibiscus syriacus*

A tree-like, summer-flowering shrub, it makes a lively display in August when shrubby bloom is scarce. The large, hollyhock-like flowers, single or double, range from white through lavender, purple, and pink to red. While mature specimens may reach 12 to 15 feet, if left to themselves, this shapely shrub is easily pruned to keep it within bounds. Shrubby althea is another common name for this Oriental native, which is sometimes used as a hedge.

Full sun and good garden soil produce the best results. Feeding and hard pruning result in large flowers. Young plants often prove questionably hardy in severe winter climates. Japanese beetles have a special fondness for it, since it flowers when they are active. Increase is by cuttings of named varieties. The common kinds frequently self-sow.

Shrub Roses   See Chapter 8.

Spindle-Tree   See Euonymus.

Spirea—2-6′—Zone 3 *Spiraea species*

From May through July and even into August, some form of spirea can be found blooming in gardens. Although widely planted and, for the most part, common, the various kinds have strong eye appeal and flower abundantly with little or no care. They are easy to grow, pest-free, and require only a deft hand with the pruning shears to keep them free of dead wood and ungainly growth. Some are useful for garden backgrounds, others for hedges, and still others as specimens. White flowers are welcome in any garden, and there are many among the spireas.

Garland spirea or foam-of-May (*S. arguta*) flowers at daffodil time, even before the lacy foliage appears. The tiny white blooms appear on slender branches that arch gracefully. Specimens may reach 5 feet but are easily pruned lower. There is also a dwarf form. The true bridal wreath (*S. prunifolia plena*) with its graceful sprays of white buttons grows to 8 feet if allowed to, but can be kept much lower. In autumn, the foliage takes on vermillion tones. Vanhouttei: spirea, often called bridal wreath, is the heaviest bloomer of them all, producing fountains of white flowers often 6 feet tall in late May. Anthony Waterer is the variety name for a deep pink, flat-clustered kind (*S. bumalda var.*) that begins to show color in late June and produces bloom for a month or more on 2-foot stems. There are a number of other spireas, less commonly grown, which are of interest for large gardens.

Full sun and average garden soil are sufficient for the spireas. Prune to eliminate dead wood and keep the plants shapely and vigorous. Increase is by cuttings or division of the roots.

St.-Johnswort—18″—Zones 4-6 *Hypericum species*

The St.-Johnsworts are showy, low-growing shrubs found native in various parts of the United States and Europe. They have soft, light green foliage and thrive in full sun, but make a good display in a fair amount of shade. Showy, yellow tassel-like blooms appear over a long period in summer, and plants require no special soil or attention. Some kinds are known to rock-garden enthusiasts; others are collected by those who grow dwarf shrubs. They make good ground covers of varying heights and are most adaptable as well as decorative, but some forms cannot be counted on for hardiness in areas of prolonged sub-zero temperatures.

Well-suited to sandy soils in full sun or light shade, these plants are listed by many nurseries throughout the country. Container-grown plants are easy to plant at any season of the year. Stock may be increased by cuttings, segments of the rooted stems, division, or seed, according to the types grown.

Summer Sweet—9′—Zone 3 *Clethra alnifolia*

Summer sweet and sweet pepperbush are popular names for this summer-flowering shrub, which is found native along the entire Eastern seaboard. It is easily recognized by its showy spikes of fragrant white flowers in late July, followed by clusters of small black seeds resembling peppercorns, hence the name sweet pepperbush. These are decorative for dried arrangements. The foliage takes on yellow and orange coloring in autumn. A true denizen of the seacoast, it is often found close to the shore in great masses growing with the seaside rose and other wildings. It spreads by underground stems and makes a dense mass of roots, giving it value as a soil binder. While enduring dry soil, it is sometimes found in moist places. Although summer sweet grows to 8 to 9 feet, it can be kept much lower by pruning.

Summer sweet grows in ordinary garden soil in sun or shade, but the better the soil, the more luxurious will be the growth. Plants are available from many nurseries. Clumps can be divided to increase stock.

Tree Peony—2-5′—Zone 4 *Paeonia suffruticosa*

Although tree peonies have been growing in America for more than a century and a half, they remain among the most uncommon and choice shrubs in our gardens. The name *tree peony* refers to the woody stems as contrasted with the herbaceous type listed under perennials. Old plants of the tree peony often develop a miniature tree-like aspect. They are slow to propagate and thus costly, as flowering shrubs go. Plants range in height from 2 to 5 feet, according to age and variety. During the past decade, several specialists have featured them at leading spring flower shows, thereby increasing the demand for these ornamentals the beauty of which is rivaled only by the fragility of their blooms.

Superb in color, form, and texture, the flowers range from pure white to darkest red, sometimes measuring 10 inches or more in diameter. A few have delicate yellow coloring. Distinct varieties are numerous; many carry poetic Japanese names. Since lists and descriptions can be bewildering, it is wise to choose varieties when they are in flower. Some growers offer container-grown plants which can be set out immediately. The glaucous, broad-lobed foliage makes a dramatic contrast with that of the simpler leaves of many garden plants.

White Cascade petunia is ideally suited for containers

Pots of pink geraniums bracketed to a fence

Fuchsias thrive in shady sites when watered and fed frequently

Coleus, patient Lucy, and English ivy thrive in shade

Scented-leaved geraniums, basil, parsley, and lavender cotton lend contrast to the colorful geranium blossoms

Ferns along the shady side of a house

Trillium, lily-of-the-valley, wild geranium, and other wild flowers
combined with ferns are well suited to shady situations

Mountain laurel, ferns, and bloodroot provide pleasing foliage texture

Semperflorens or wax begonias and coleus lend rich color effects to shady situations

Pachysandra, a useful ground cover, serves admirably in this approach planting. Wilson rhododendrons flank the entrance

Ferns and hardy ivy ground cover thrive in shady spots

Fall planting is the usual practice, but container-grown plants may be set out at any time during the growing season. High shade is preferable to full sun, since the blooms flag quickly in heat. Prepare holes deeply and thoroughly with the best of garden soil, thoroughly mixing an ample supply of humus and a handful of ground limestone with the soil. Perfect drainage is essential, and a permanent mulch around the roots is desirable, beginning with initial plantings. Ambitious amateurs enjoy raising plants from seed. Commercial growers produce their stock by grafting or division of the roots.

Viburnum—6-30′—Zones 2-7   *Viburnum species*

Viburnums are sturdy shrubs, valued for their vigor and hardiness. They are notably decorative in flower and fruiting habit, and the foliage of most kinds remains clean and attractive throughout the growing year. For the most part, they are big-scale plants which lend themselves admirably to mixed borders and screen plantings, as informal hedges, and as specimens.

Some kinds can endure considerably more exposure than others, particularly wind and salt spray. Among them is arrow-wood (*V. dentatum*), 12 to 15 feet tall with white flowers, blue fruits, and foliage which turns glossy red in autumn. Most adaptable and not particular as to soil, a position in sun or shade suits it. Equally sturdy, withe-rod (*V. cassinoides*) contributes a similar display of beauty, but the fruits are much more interesting, since they range from green through yellow, red, and black as they ripen. A shrub of moderate height, it grows about 6 feet tall.

One of the best known of all the viburnums is the European Cranberry-bush (*V. Opulus*) which grows to 10 feet or more. The white, flat flowers borne in May are followed by clusters of red fruits in autumn. There is also a handsome, yellow fruiting form. Even more showy in every way is the Doublefile viburnum (*V. tomentosum mariesi*) with a distinctly horizontal branching habit. The flat, white flower heads, red coloring of the foliage in autumn, and brilliant red fruit add to its value. Plants average 6 to 7 feet, often spreading as wide to make decidedly spectacular specimens. This shrub is much more desirable than the snowballs which we grow commonly.

Given adequate preparation of soil at planting time and average care, the viburnums can be counted on to make a creditable appearance over a period of years. The only pruning required is the removal of branches to retain a pleasing form. Most nurseries and garden centers offer them. All can be propagated from cuttings.

Weigela—6′—Zone 4   *Weigela species*

A number of weigelas are grown in gardens for their late spring bloom. Named varieties in white, several shades of pink and red, along with a form having variegated foliage are frequently seen. Typical plants are fountain-like in habit, 4 to 6 feet tall and spreading to even greater width. The trumpet-shaped blooms appear in clusters among somewhat coarse foliage. In the small garden, it will be found that weigela often takes up more room than can be spared.

Full sun or partial shade and good garden soil meet its needs. Pruning keeps plants trim. Dieback, which occurs when winters are severe, sometimes damages flower buds. Increase is by cuttings.

7

FLOWERING
AND SHADE TREES

❧❧❧ There are several ways of considering trees for ornamental use and shade on the home grounds. A typical approach is to discuss favorite kinds and evaluate them from the point of view of foliage, flowers, and shade value, but listing their merits is only part of the story. Growth requirements including exposure, aspect when mature, the pests that are likely to affect them, and the over-all size of the mature tree are also of vital importance.

Another question to ask is how fast a particular kind of tree can be expected to grow. Soil requirements for most trees are easily met. Methods of planting, fertilizing, and staking usually pose no problem. The task is to pick the most suitable tree possible for the location you have chosen.

Unlike most flowering shrubs and evergreens which can be transplanted and moved about with comparative ease, trees once planted are not as easy to move. Thus the location chosen is important.

On the average home grounds, where space is limited and trees are desired, careful thought is needed in their selection. How tall will it grow and how wide will it spread are the first two questions to be answered. Fortunate indeed is the homeowner who acquires a property with existing trees to create a setting for his house and garden. However, this type of situation is not commonplace, as it once was.

Today, most of our trees desired for the home grounds must be planted. The right tree in the right place adds immeasurably to the setting of your grounds. It can be placed to frame the house or make the front entrance more inviting. Or, it can provide a background to set off the house. Trees make shadow patterns on lawns, too, lacy or dense, depending on the type planted. In any case, both the trees and the house should be "fittin to be settin there," as an old Cape Codder once expressed it.

In spring or late fall, when trees are leafless, it is easy to observe the basic structure of their branches and twigs. It is an ideal time to do essential pruning to improve their form and general appearance. In some instances, flower buds may be removed in the process. However, the ease and speed with which necessary pruning can be done now is far more vital than the loss of a few flowers. Here are some practical points to consider in pruning and caring for trees.

1) Study the tree carefully before any branches are removed.
2) Evaluate your tree from the point of view of its natural habit of growth.
3) Select limbs to be removed with an eye to balance.
4) Remove all dead, bruised, or broken branches.
5) Make clean cuts without defacing the bark on the main trunk.
6) Paint all scars with tree paint.
7) Use sharp, well-oiled tools to insure clean cuts.
8) Where branches near the base are dense and create undesirable shade on the ground below, some of them may be removed to allow more light for grass, ground covers, or low growing shrubs beneath the trees.
9) Feeding trees with a complete plant food pays dividends. Apply plant food according to printed directions on package.
10) Professional help in pruning trees is a sound investment, especially when climbing is required. All too often, inexperienced amateurs do irreparable damage to trees and to themselves through accidents.
11) Beware of the fly-by-night sales approach which is usually unreliable. Any licensed arborist carries proper identification and complete equipment; he uses a truck with the firm's name clearly lettered on the side.
12) Certain trees such as birches, elms, hawthorns, and others usually need periodic spraying to control pests which disfigure the foliage. This fact should be borne in mind when choosing new trees for your home grounds.

The romantic, almost nostalgic appeal of a weeping willow is the reason for many mistakes in landscape plantings. In a proper setting, one where the soil is naturally moist and there is ample room for development, few trees are more picturesque at various seasons of the year than the weeping willow.

Its trunk, gracefully arching branches, and pleasing foliage are attributes of distinct merit. Yet, a willow is out of place on a slope where it becomes easy prey to the wind, or on high ground where there is not sufficient moisture to supply its greedy roots. But plant a willow in a suitable location, and it will be a source of pride for many years.

Maples, on the other hand, are trees of surprising adaptability. They often grow under trying conditions. When given good soil, they flourish, often to the point of creating more shade than is desirable. Then, too, maples often crowd out other types of desirable plant material growing in close proximity to them. But they can be pruned and thinned to allow needed light in areas beneath their branches. Most kinds can endure considerable dryness and general neglect.

In autumn, the maples provide a color pageant that has few rivals. Furthermore, there are many types and kinds of maples, but most gardeners know only the common ones. Consequently, there are in many communities an overabundance of sugar, Norway, and silver maples. There is a need to plant more of the showy Crimson King maples, the various types of Japanese cut-leaf maple, the Amur maple, and others.

The list of trees that follows includes a selection of the popular kinds which are frequently planted by home gardeners. In addition, there are several which are less well known and deserve to be more widely planted. However, the list is by no means comprehensive, for such is not the scope of this book.

American Elm   See Elm.

Beech—60-90'—Zones 3-4   *Fagus genus*

Even when small, the various forms of beech hold strong appeal for the home gardener, who is attracted by the richly textured foliage and the general aspect of the young tree. They are superb ornamentals that are suited to large properties where their true form can develop. Some spread as wide as they are high. It is a mistake to plant a beech on a small lot, since it will eventually outscale the house and its surroundings. In addition to specimen use, they are most adaptable for clipped hedges. The American beech (*F. grandifolia*) is not as widely planted as its European relative (*F. sylvatica*), which is highly valued for its distinctive varieties. These include the copper, the purple, the fernleaf, the cutleaf, and the weeping beech.

Beeches need well-prepared soil with plenty of organic matter. They are heavy feeders and respond to annual applications of fertilizer. Full sun or light shade suits them, and the site chosen should be ample for their normal development. Hard pruning induces dense, well-shaped growth.

Birch—15-80′—Zone 2 *Betula species*

Both the paper birch and the weeping birch have wide appeal for gardeners and especially for beginners, but they are not always wise choices. Both need careful handling in transplanting, several sprayings to control birch-leaf miner, and moist soil. The paper or canoe white birch usually grow in clumps producing several stems. Its white bark which peels in thin layers, graceful twigs, and attractive foliage contributing a generous display of golden yellow in autumn are the chief assets of one of the handsomest of our native trees.

Weeping birch (*B. pendula*) is of European origin. Of high ornamental value, unfortunately it is short-lived and dies back at the tip, due to attacks of the bronze birch borer. Several varieties of distinct habit are available. Gray birch (*B. populifolia*) also has white bark conspicuously marked with black triangular patches and usually produces a clump of several stems. Although picturesque in habit, it, too, is short-lived.

Owners of suburban property with natural stands of birch—or even a few trees—are fortunate in owning them, if they are willing to give them the required maintenance. Pruning of damaged and diseased branches, control of borers, and a program of spraying to check birch-leaf miner are essential. Otherwise, these handsome ornamentals may present a sad appearance in summer. Birches are found in thin, dry soil and in moist locations in the wild. When cultivated they thrive in good garden soil. In the cooler parts of the country, spring planting is preferable.

Chinese Dogwood   See Flowering Dogwood.

Crab-Apple   See Flowering Crab-Apple.

Dogwood   See Flowering Dogwood.

Elm—100′—Zone 2 *Ulmus americana*

The American elm is without a peer for shade, ornamental effects, and longevity but, in recent years, the inroads of insect attack and disease have wiped out many of our noblest specimens. Hope of re-establishing this tree is based on the resistance shown by young trees and a program of good maintenance and systematic spraying. The most serious pest of elms is the Dutch elm disease, a fungus spread by the elm bark beetle. A virus, phloem necrosis, is also a threat. All elms are subject to attack, but several resistant forms of the Dutch elm are being planted as well as the Augustine elm, a variety of the American elm.

A heavy feeder, the elm is well suited as a lawn or street tree. It grows well in any well-drained soil in full sun or light shade. Stock is increased by seed and grafting.

English Hawthorn   See Washington Hawthorn.

Flowering Cherry—10-25′—Zone 4-5   *Prunus species*

These are the glamour trees of spring, so greatly admired and enjoyed for their abundant bloom. The notable collection sent to Washington, D.C., by the mayor of Tokyo, more than 50 years ago, has inspired planting the flowering cherries in gardens and parks and along streets in many parts of the country. They belong to the genus *Prunus* which includes almonds, peaches, and plums, both those grown primarily for their fruit and the ornamental types. Flowers may be single or double, ranging from deep pink to white according to kind. Fruits of the ornamental kinds are few and of no consequence. The bark of cherries is smooth, shiny, and dark red in color like the scales which enclose the flower buds. Species and varieties include several distinct sizes and forms, among them pendulous types. Tent caterpillar and borers are their chief pests. Hardiness is a factor to consider in the colder parts of the country, and success in many cases is determined by proper feeding and watering.

Name varieties of various kinds are numerous, but, with the exception of specialists, most nurseries carry only a limited number. The Kwansan cherry, a variety of *P. serrulata,* is one of the most popular. Double, deep pink flowers are borne in pendulous clusters on a round-headed tree of upright habit which reaches 15 to 18 feet when mature. It fits well in the small garden.

Flowering cherries thrive in moist fertile soil. Plant only healthy young specimens, choosing varieties on the basis of known hardiness and obtain plants from reputable growers. They are neither cheap nor in large supply. Staking or guying is vital until the roots are well developed. Hard pruning makes sturdy trunks, which are essential to support the heavy branching habit of many kinds. In regions where winters are severe, feeding is best done before June 1 and artificial watering should be terminated after September 1 to allow growth to harden sufficiently before winter. Mulching to keep the soil temperature even is sound practice.

Flowering Crab-Apple—6-30′—Zones 2-4   *Malus species*

Among the crab-apples, there are so many handsome varieties that it is an easy matter to obtain one or several well suited to the average home grounds. Rich in flower color, they range from white to dark red with single or double bloom. Heavy flowering occurs every other year, as a rule. Fall fruiting may be yellow or red. Pleasing in aspect, with durable foliage, crab-apples rate high in the list of small trees. Heights vary from 6 to 30 feet, according to species or variety, and forms may be round headed, pyramidal, broadly columnar, broad spreading, or pendulous. Hardy and long-lived, they are generally better suited to many home grounds than magnolias and other exotics. With crab-apples, it is important to choose carefully the type that is needed for a specific location and place it thoughtfully, since established specimens are not easily moved, because of their wide-spreading root systems. As the trees develop to maturity, they can be pruned high to give the same pleasing effect that old apple trees create on a place.

Give crab-apples a well-drained location, preferably in full sun. They are reliably hardy, relatively pest free, drought resistant, and require no special care. Many growers offer them container-grown, which makes transplanting easy. It often takes them several years to become sufficiently established for heavy flowering and fruiting. With all the varieties, occasional pruning to improve form is important.

Flowering Dogwood—25-30′—Zone 5   *Cornus florida*

Chinese Dogwood—20′—Zone 5   *Cornus Kousa*

Undoubtedly, the Eastern flowering dogwood (*Cornus florida*) is one of the best-loved flowering trees in America. Ideal in every respect, it averages 25 to 30 feet in height and often spreads more than half as wide. It has distinctive foliage and flowers, rich autumn coloring, decorative fruits, and a pleasing horizontal branching habit. During the winter, conspicuous gray buds are borne on the gracefully upturned twigs. The showy white "flowers" which unfold with the late daffodils and long-stemmed tulips are not true flowers, but rather modified leaves, known as bracts. Close examination reveals that the small, greenish, inconspicuous centers of each four-petaled blossom are the true flowers. In early autumn, the foliage assumes a variety of rich red tones, interspersed with dull green; the showy red fruits which ripen at this time remain to delight us as long as the birds leave them undisturbed. The pink-flowering form is equally ornamental and desirable, but, sometimes, does not flower as heavily as the white until acquiring considerable age.

A month after the Eastern flowering dogwood blooms, the Chinese dogwood (*Cornus Kousa*) comes into flower. Blooms, which appear after the foliage has fully matured, are cream colored with distinctly pointed bracts and remain on the branches for two weeks or more. It can be grown as a large-scale shrub or pruned at the base to develop as a small tree, eventually reaching 20 feet in height. Highly valued for its rich autumn tints, it bears curious raspberry-like fruits which are unusually attractive.

Full sun suits it best. A striking tree, it deserves to be enjoyed more widely.

Dogwood is being widely propagated by nurserymen and is best transplanted in spring, the earlier the better. Fall planting is not always successful, especially where winters are severe. Full sun or part shade suits it. While dogwood tolerates fairly dense shade, flowering is usually sparse. A well-drained location and good garden soil are essential, but avoid windswept sites. It is a good plan to wrap the bark of a newly transplanted tree to reduce transpiration and to anchor it by guying. Give it ample water until well established and also during long, dry spells. An annual feeding with acid soil fertilizer pays dividends. Be on the lookout for borers, which can be troublesome at times. If the telltale evidence of sawdust is discovered near the base of the tree, examine the bark carefully where the hole is located; then use a wire to worm out the borer and fill the opening with coarse soap or the specially prepared jelly used by tree surgeons.

Ginkgo, Maidenhair-Tree—100′—Zone 3   *Ginkgo biloba*

An ancient tree long cultivated in the Orient, the ginkgo is valued for its picturesque form and fan-shaped foliage which turns a rich golden yellow in autumn. Slow-growing when young, it needs pruning of ungainly branches. Only male trees should be planted, since the female form produces plum-like fruits which have a most objectionable odor. A fastigiate form of columnar habit, it is being widely planted as a street tree. Gardeners with an eye to the future favor the ginkgo for its vigor and disease resistance.

It can be grown in a variety of soils with ease and requires little or no special care except pruning, as mentioned, to improve its form.

Golden-Chain Tree—20′—Zone 4   *Laburnum Watereri*

This graceful ornamental tree, broadly columnar in form, bears pendulous clusters of yellow, pea-like flowers in late spring similar to those of wisteria which flower at the same time. An ideal tree for small gardens, it needs hard pruning to develop a sturdy trunk and to induce heavy bloom. Often it is not long lived, but since growth is rapid, it is easily replaced.

Plant in moist, fertile soil in sun or part shade. Young trees are shallow rooted and need to be carefully staked or guyed when set out.

Hawthorn   See Washington Thorn.

Honey Locust—60-100′—Zone 3   *Gleditsia tricanthos*

The common honey locust is a sturdy tree of great beauty, but it has several drawbacks for the home grounds. However, for clean growth, lacy shade, and graceful habit, the improved forms of the honey locust, notably

the thornless Moraine and the Shademaster locusts, are in a class by themselves. Few shade trees are more adaptable to the home grounds or for street
use and offer less competition to grass. Adapted to hot, dry situations or part
shade, they flourish in various types of soil and the sturdy branches are
seldom damaged by the wind.

The Moraine locust (*G. tricanthos inermis*), with its round head and
somewhat irregular curving trunk and branches, matures as a vase-shaped
tree. Rubylace has dark red leaves. The growth of Shademaster, more
upright than that of the Moraine locust, is a pronounced straight trunk.
Sunburst Thornless locust is especially conspicuous when the new foliage is
unfolding because of its golden-yellow coloring, but this novelty needs to be
planted with discretion. Skyline, distinctly pyramidal in form, has dark green
foliage.

Average soil suits all these varieties, which are reliably hardy, but young
trees are shallow-rooted and need to be carefully guyed or supported with
iron pipes until well established. Easy to transplant and fast growers, especially in fertile soil, all need to be cut back hard for several years after
planting to develop strong trunks. In recent years, the Moraine and the
Shademaster locust have been widely planted to replace the American elm.

Japanese Maple   See Maple.

Laburnum   See Golden-Chain Tree.

Little-Leaf Linden—30-50′—Zone 3   *Tilia cordata*

A handsome shade tree of rounded, pyramidal form which shows its dense
foliage character even as a young tree, the little-leaf linden is ideal for lawn
use if space is available. An added feature is the sweet fragrance of the small
creamy flowers which appear in early summer. Slow-growing and notably
hardy, it is easily obtainable.

Lindens can be grown in full sun or part shade, and ordinary soil suits
them. It is a good tree for exposed situations, enduring wind and salt spray
with ease.

Magnolia—12-25′—Zone 4   *Magnolia species*

Magnolias have much to offer in the way of spectacular bloom and
unusual fruits, in picturesque branching habit, and in their over-all appearance in the garden. Those most frequently seen in cold climates flower early
in spring. They are best enjoyed when given a somewhat exposed location,
which delays flowering. Otherwise their bloom time is shortened by late
frosts and the chill winds of the season. They make excellent lawn specimens
and combine well with low-growing evergreens, azaleas, and a wide variety
of ground covers.

Earliest to bloom is the Star magnolia (*M. Kobus stellata*) with large, white, lacy, star-like flowers borne on densely branched, mound-like trees which more often look like great shrubs. Old plants may grow to 15 feet or more in height and spread as wide, but the Star magnolia is rather slow in growth and usually averages 10 to 12 feet. Blooms of the Merrill magnolia (*M. loebneri*) are similar, but the plant is distinctly upright in habit and broadly columnar in form. Many other species well worth growing are not offered by numerous growers. The Saucer magnolia (*M. Soulangeana*) follows with its great white cups, splashed pink or purple on the outer surface, according to the variety planted. Low-branched and sometimes shrub-like in aspect with several stems emerging, it attains a broad pyramidal habit with age. Several varieties are available, including *M. Soulangeana Lennei* with rich red-purple outer petals. Mature specimens average 20 to 25 feet.

Magnolias are thin-barked trees and should not be transplanted in the fall. Early spring is the best time to move them. Give them full sun and the best soil preparation possible in a well-drained site. These trees resent pruning, since the bark does not heal readily once it has been cut. Control the general aspect of each specimen by removing young tender growth that may prove undesirable. Allow ample room for any magnolia set out on the home grounds.

Maidenhair-Tree   See Ginkgo.

Maple—25-90′—Zone 2   *Acer species*

Maples are useful and desirable shade trees on the home grounds, provided that they have adequate space to develop. However, they are gross feeders, robbing the soil of plant food and moisture, so that grass is not easily grown beneath them. The invading roots offer strong competition to shrubs, ground covers, and perennials planted in adjacent areas. Once established, they make rapid growth, and most kinds are of dense, branching habit, creating heavy shade. Although maples can be controlled as to size and thinned periodically to allow sunlight to filter through, the task is one of constant pruning and expense. These facts should be considered when planting maples, for there are many other desirable shade trees better-suited to small properties. Where maples are desired and space is limited, consider the Amur, the Japanese, the Paperbark, and other small-scale species.

Maples grow best in full sun, but will tolerate a fair amount of shade and are not particular as to soil. Allow ample space for development and choose carefully the kind best suited to a given property and proper placement.

May Tree   See Washington Hawthorn.

Moraine Locust   See Honey Locust.

Mountain-Ash—30'—Zone 2   *Sorbus Aucuparia*

One of the showiest of ornamental trees—both in flower and fruit—the mountain-ash or rowan tree has long been a favorite. Large flat clusters of white flowers appear in spring, followed by conspicuous clusters of orange fruits which turn red as they mature in early fall. With the passing of summer, the compound foliage assumes reddish tones. Upright in habit, this tree makes a striking effect in the landscape and is widely planted on small properties. Several selected forms are offered by nurserymen, including one with yellow fruits.

Full sun or light shade suits it, and the soil requirements of mountain ash are easily met. Be on the lookout for borers near the base; if not controlled, they cause serious damage which may kill the tree. Also several leaf-eating insects can be annoying.

Paper Birch   See Birch.

Paperbark Maple   See Maple.

Pin Oak—40'—Zone 3   *Quercus palustris*

Oaks are favorite trees for a number of reasons. Sturdy, long-lived, picturesque in form and attractive in foliage at all seasons, oaks would be more widely planted if success in moving them were more certain. Many kinds have long taproots which make transplanting difficult. However, the pin oak, which makes a striking pyramidal tree, produces a mass of fibrous roots and is fairly easy to handle. The fine-textured, glossy foliage assumes rich scarlet coloring in autumn and often remains through part of the winter, changing to brown tones. Ideal for a lawn, where space is available, it can be pruned high, or the branches may be allowed to sweep the ground.

The pin oak prefers a moist, acid soil, reacting quickly when an alkaline condition is present: its leaves become yellow-green, giving the tree an unhealthy appearance. Feeding with an acid-soil fertilizer is beneficial. It is important to obtain young specimens with well-developed root systems and stake them carefully until well established.

Washington Hawthorn—30'—Zone 3   *Crataegus phaenopyrum*

Washington thorn or hawthorn is a distinctive and pleasing small tree, broadly round headed when mature with slender zigzag branches of thorny habit. Its white flowers borne in large clusters in May are followed by scarlet-orange berries (or haws as they are commonly referred to), which blend superbly with the richly tinted autumn foliage. During spring and summer the foliage is light, glossy green resembling that of the gray birch. For general garden use, this is the best of the hawthorns.

Red, pink, and white-flowering varieties of English hawthorn or May tree (*C. Oxyacantha*) are widely planted because of their heavy flowering habit and showy effect. Perhaps the best known of all is Paul's Scarlet. Mature specimens average 15 feet in height, spreading widely. Unfortunately, the leaves may drop in late summer, leaving the branches bare; also, it is subject to attacks of the woolly aphis. Because it is frequently susceptible to fireblight and cedar-apple rust, it is a mistake to plant English hawthorn unless it can be adequately maintained. For these reasons, the Washington Hawthorn is preferable.

Sturdy and of easy culture, it flourishes in average garden soil. Give it a full sun or light shade. Fireblight is best controlled by cutting off and burning all diseased parts. Cedar-apple rust, which usually occurs when red cedars are found nearby, is most effectively handled by not planting English Hawthorn. See Chapter 19.

Weeping Birch   See Birch.

Willow—30-40′—Zone 3   *Salix species*

Perhaps no ornamental tree is more closely linked with sentiment than the weeping willow. All too often, it is planted without considering the site, the soil best suited to it, or the rapacious root system which it develops. Willows thrive in moist soil and, because of their rapid growth and soft brittle wood, are easily damaged by wind. They belong in low-lying or flat areas near ponds, streams, and lakes. In gardens where there is space to spare, they serve as superb focalpoints or as background for a planting. Ample space is needed to enjoy the characteristic weeping habit of the branches. Avoid locations near drainage systems, since the roots seek water and clog pipes.

Willows require no special care. They propagate readily from cuttings placed in water or inserted in moist sand.

Planting Trees and Shrubs

Since trees and shrubs are planted for permanent effects and, in most instances, expected to remain where they are placed, thorough soil preparation is essential. Many trees with long taproots penetrate the soil deeply as they establish themselves. These require adequate plant food for a good start as well as those with a compact mass of fibrous roots. The root systems of shrubs are similar in their root development and food requirements.

Nurseries usually offer deciduous trees and shrubs either bare root, as balled and burlapped specimens, or container grown. Bare-root material is most safely handled in early spring before growth breaks, or in late fall as it approaches dormancy. At other seasons of the year, balled and burlapped specimens (or those container grown) make transplanting easy. All evergreens are handled in this manner. The burlap used for balling is usually thin and open-meshed; it need not be removed when planting. In fact, while handling and planting a tree or shrub, care must be taken not to break the earth ball around the roots. Such injury causes the soil to become loose, thereby harming the tiny feeder roots.

When setting out plant material bare-root, keep the roots well covered during the process of planting. Since tiny feeding roots, exposed to sun and wind, dry out rapidly, keep them wrapped in moist burlap, or plunge the roots into a bucket of muddy water until plants are actually set in the ground. Before planting, remove broken and bruised roots as well as those of unusual length, using sharp pruning shears to make clean cuts. Dig holes large enough in width and depth to accommodate the root system without crowding; set the crown at the same level at which it was growing in the nursery. (The soil level is usually apparent on bare-root material.) The remainder of the procedure is the same as for balled and burlapped specimens, which is discussed next.

For a balled and burlapped plant, dig a generous hole, allowing for at least twice the width and depth of the root ball. After excavating, fill the hole half full of the best available topsoil or compost, or a mixture of both. Evergreens—both the needle types and the broad-leaved kinds as well as all types of azaleas— are benefited by lining the hole with moistened peat moss. Mix 2 to 3 handfuls of a complete fertilizer with the soil to provide the food needed to get roots off to a good start. Cover with an additional inch or two of topsoil so that the roots do not come in direct contact with the fertilizer. Set the top of the ball of earth level with the surrounding soil surface. As soil is filled in around it, tamp firmly with the end of a spade handle or use your feet for the purpose. Water thoroughly to eliminate air pockets and to settle the soil generally around the ball. Leave a depression around each plant for subsequent watering and to obtain the full benefit of rain. Mulching newly planted shrubs and trees is sound practice. See Chapter 18.

Once planted, top pruning is usually necessary, especially if the plant is heavily branched, or if growth is tall and ungainly. This practice is advisable for bare-root material and balled and burlapped plants as well. Cutting back the top growth of deciduous shrubs and trees at least one third is sound practice; it induces heavy root growth and improves the general form. It should be remembered that constant exposure to wind results in excessive transpiration of moisture from both stems and leaves, placing more than normal demands on a newly planted shrub. Each and every leaf gives off moisture, thus reducing the leaf area at planting time helps to check the loss of water in a plant.

Freshly planted evergreens are benefited by watering the foliage frequently as well as the roots, especially if winds are strong and temperatures unseasonably high.

Tree trunks may be wrapped with heavy paper or burlap to reduce transpiration. This practice involves labor but is good insurance, particularly on windy sites.

The importance of thorough and frequent watering for newly transplanted shrubs and trees, especially during prolonged dry spells, cannot be overstated.

Staking or guying big shrubs and all trees is also vital to success in establishing them in exposed areas. (All wire used should be encased in pieces of rubber tubing where it comes in contact with branches and main stems.) Careless handling of this procedure may result in serious damage to woody stems as they are blown against stakes, particularly when stems rub against the rough surfaces of pipes used as supports.

8

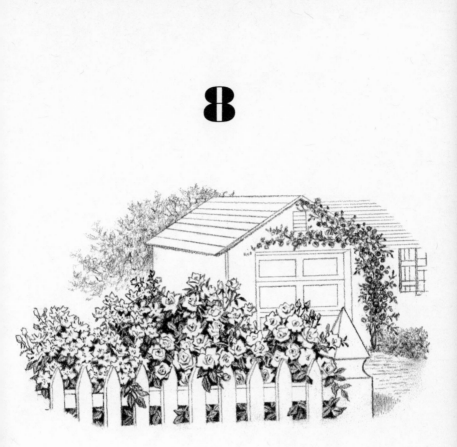

ROSES

❦❦❦ No gardener, beginner or ardent enthusiast, needs to be reminded of the beauty of the rose, the joy of gathering the blooms for indoor decoration, or planting them to fill a garden with color and fragrance from rose-time to frost-time. So much has been written about the uses and the countless varieties of hybrid teas, floribundas, grandifloras, climbers, miniature roses, and the various old-time varieties that it is superfluous to dwell on these aspects. All of these are hybrid forms, the result of crossing and recrossing hybrids and species or wild types. Growers propagate them by budding (see Chapter 17). They require frequent pruning, spraying, and feeding to produce maximum bloom; in addition, the hybrid teas need protection where the winters are severe.

Hybrid Teas

Varieties of these everblooming roses, ranging from white to dark red, are legion. Space plants 15 to 18 inches apart, except for Peace and its hybrids which require 2 feet each way. Flowers are usually semi-double or double, but there are good, single types also. For specimen blooms, disbud leaving one bud to a stem. Because hybrid teas require considerable care, they are best grown in groups or separate beds. Good air circulation is a deterrent to disease.

Floribundas

These everblooming forms, which produce single or double flowers in clusters or pyramidal heads, are valued for their free, everblooming habit, their vigor and hardiness—except in severe or unseasonal winters. Space plants 18 to 24 inches apart each way. Floribundas are ideal for shrub borders or dwarf hedges.

Grandifloras

This group of everblooming hybrids bears double flowers of hybrid tea size in clusters typical of the floribunda bloom habit. Space plants 18 to 24 inches apart each way. Generally, their cultural requirements are as exacting as hybrid teas.

Hybrid Perpetuals

The name of this class is confusing since plants produce one big splash of bloom in June; a few varieties give spasmodic performance in late summer

139

or fall. Plants make sturdy, long-lived shrubs, reaching 4 to 6 feet in height. The large, double blooms of many are notably fragrant. Cultural requirements are the same as hybrid teas without the continuity of bloom. Space plants 3 feet apart.

Climbing Roses

Paul's Scarlet Climber and the everblooming Blaze are typical of this group. Some flower once in a season, while others have everblooming characteristics. All need support and tying, or the support of suitable wooden or wire fences or trellises. Some are notably hardier than others. The climbing hybrid teas are tender in cold climates and require protection. Those with small flowers in clusters are known as Ramblers. Others which bear large flowers and grow 6 to 8 feet tall are referred to as Pillar roses. For creeping and trailing varieties see Chapter 10.

Tree Roses

These are hybrid teas grafted on rugosa stock. They need considerable winter protection in areas where temperatures dip below zero.

Shrub Roses

On the other hand, there are the shrub or species roses. Some are true wild forms, while others have been selected and improved by hybridizing but retain the vigor and sturdiness of the original wild types. These more rugged kinds are useful for shrub borders and hedges, as specimens, or for naturalizing. They are of prime value for their vigor, hardiness, freedom from disease, and easy culture. As such, shrub roses are useful for exposed situations, in mixed plantings where a minimum of maintenance is essential, and they deserve to be more widely planted. Varieties suited to hedge use are discussed in Chapter 12.

How to Plant and Care for a Rose

Choose a well-drained site in full sun. Dig a hole twice as wide and deep as the span of the roots. Roses send their roots deep into the soil, hence the need for deep preparation. In the bottom of the hole, place a generous shovelful of organic matter, which may be moist peat moss, chopped sod, compost, or well-rotted cow manure. These humus builders aid the plant in developing its feeding roots. Add two or three handfuls of dried cow manure, or one of a complete fertilizer. Mix these ingredients thoroughly with topsoil and other material in the hole.

Unwrap the rose plant, removing it from the moist fiber material surrounding the roots. Cut off any damaged parts and set it in the hole, holding it in position with one hand while filling in soil around the roots with the other. As the hole is filled, stamp the soil with your feet to eliminate air pockets.

In placing the plant, set the knot or graft union at least an inch below the surface of the bed. Water thoroughly and "hill up" or mound the soil around the stem to a height of 8 inches. This practice keeps the stems and buds from drying out before the roots are established. Scatter the mound after the buds break into leaf.

Once planted, prune back all damaged stems to live wood and shorten unusually long canes to 10 inches. If a number of roses are packed in one bundle, protect the roots from drying out by covering them with moist burlap until they are ready for planting. Better still, place them in a bucket of muddy water.

Pruning Established Roses. Types which produce bloom on new wood (hybrid teas, floribundas, and grandifloras) usually need hard pruning in early spring. Use sharp shears and make clean cuts. Remove all dead and bruised canes, cutting back to live wood. Allow about a half inch of stem to remain above the top bud on each cane. Then shape plants for evenness of height and an open center for good air circulation, removing canes that rub against one another. Some gardeners cut back growth to within 6 inches of the ground (low pruning). Others prefer to start the season with plants a foot or more in height (high pruning), depending on the amount of winter injury that has occurred.

With the exception of ramblers, climbers bloom on year-old wood. In spring, remove only dead and bruised canes and shorten those of ungainly appearance. Additional pruning is best done after flowering, by removing only such amounts of old wood as are necessary for the appearance of the plants and to keep canes within bounds.

Ramblers are pruned after flowering, taking out to the base of the plant all canes that have flowered.

Other types of roses need only such pruning as the general shape of the plants require and to remove dead wood.

Feeding. Assuming that the soil has been carefully prepared prior to planting time, newly set roses require no feeding until early summer, after the first splash of bloom has faded. Use a complete fertilizer, scattering it lightly around each plant without touching stems or foliage. Work it in with a small hoe and water thoroughly. Established plants are fed in the same way, twice— often three times—during the growing season. Give the first application after pruning in early spring, the second just before first flowering, and the third 6 to 8 weeks later. Feeding after August 1 encourages new growth, which frequently does not mature before winter and results in winterkill.

Mulching. Mulching roses in early spring reduces maintenance for the entire growing season and conserves moisture. Buckwheat hulls, peat moss, and other materials are desirable. See Chapter 18.

Autumn Care

Fall is often the best season of the year for hybrid tea roses, particularly from the point of view of color. The floribundas and grandiflora hybrids also perform well at this time. True, they are a joy in June when their vigorous young growth unfolds and blossoms are numerous, but hot weather makes them short-lived. Usually, bloom in July and August is not of top quality, and Japanese beetles make short work of buds and flowers. However, with the approach of autumn, these groups of roses regain their vigor and can be counted on to flower until hard frost. A rose in November is the choicest and most welcome of all.

Avoid Fall Pruning. Fall is also a season to give rose bushes special care. It is far better to obtain all the bloom possible on new growth. After heavy frost, tall and unruly growth can be removed along with any of the canes that might interfere with hilling-up of the soil around plants for winter.

Check on Blackspot. If blackspot or any other disease has been a nuisance, gather up all infected foliage and burn it. This practice prevents spores from hibernating in the soil or mulch and infecting next years growth.

Avoid Late Feeding. Some home gardeners make the mistake of feeding roses in late August or early September. This is poor practice: late feeding induces soft new growth which is bound to be winterkilled.

Tie Climbers. Most climbing roses produce an abundance of new growth from the base of the plant during summer and early autumn. New canes often protrude, taking up space and sometimes becoming a nuisance by catching in clothing. Tie them to their supports, and prune out excess growth that cannot be tied back without breaking it.

Cut Sucker Growth. Sometimes rose bushes that have shown poor growth during the summer produce several vigorous shoots from the base at this time of year. Examine these rapidly growing canes carefully, since they may be developing from the understock on which the rose is grafted. First note the point of union, usually a rough knob on the main stem near or below the soil surface. Shoots which develop below the graft should be cut off at the ground.

Fall Planting. Container-grown roses of all kinds can be planted safely until the ground freezes. At this time of year, garden centers and nurseries offer surplus stock at reduced prices. Often it is possible to obtain bushes at moderate prices.

From mid-October on, rose growers ship roses bare-root for fall planting. These plants are approaching dormancy and should be planted as soon as they are brought home. However, they must be hilled up with soil before the first hard frost.

Some gardeners make a practice of ordering new roses each fall, burying them in trenches so they can be planted as soon as the soil is workable in spring. This is sound practice for the colder parts of New England, especially with the hybrid tea varieties.

Winter Protection. Deep snow is the ideal kind of protective blanket for roses, but when it is an uncertain quantity, hybrid teas and grandifloras need additional protection. Beware of old stable manure, leaves, and various mulching materials, because they cause more harm than good. Hilling up soil around each plant in late fall before a hard freeze protects those portions of the canes that are covered. A cover of evergreen boughs over "hilled up" roses helps to keep the ground frozen, and shades exposed canes. The soil must be removed as soon as possible after the ground thaws in spring.

Controlling Rose Pests

Specialists who recommend spraying or dusting at 10-day intervals with an all-purpose mixture of fungicides and insecticides are approaching the problem of control from the preventive angle. It is much more practical to protect roses and keep them growing vigorously than to attempt to combat insects and diseases once they have made a headway. Pests that attack roses fall into several classifications. There are sucking insects, such as aphids, which take the life out of young growth; various kinds of chewing insects, such as beetles and rose chafers; and diseases, such as black spot, mildew, canker, and rust. Under normal conditions no gardener should expect to be visited by all these pests, but there are seasons when some are more abundant than others.

Aphids

Legion in variety, these are familiar even to most beginners. They collect on buds and young growth, often in great numbers, ranging in color from green to red and black. Damage consists of sapping the strength of new growth, and some kinds transmit diseases. Control them with a contact spray such as Black Leaf 40, Lindane, or any of the all-purpose sprays.

Leaf-hoppers

These pests are well named, since they pop about taking the sap from the lower surfaces of the leaves and disfiguring them with a whitish, mottled effect. Control with contact sprays as described above.

Red spider

So tiny in size as to be invisible to the naked eye, the red spider's damage is evident by a cobwebby effect on the underside of rose foliage. This tiny pest is a mite which can be dispersed with a strong spray of water or a miticide, such as aramite. All-purpose rose sprays are effective.

Thrips

These are also tiny in size and discolor flower buds, damaging them permanently. Since they work their way inside the blossoms, they are hard to reach. With badly infested plants, all buds and blossoms should be cut off and burned. Spray plants thoroughly with an all-purpose rose spray.

Rose midge

This is a midsummer pest which lays eggs on the foliage and buds, causing them to be distorted in appearance. Destroy infected parts, and use an all-purpose spray.

Rose chafer

Actually a fancy name for the rose bug, this pest can be controlled by hand picking or an all-purpose spray.

Japanese beetles

These widespread pests are especially partial to roses; the damage they do needs neither description nor elaboration. Hand picking not only destroys them but their progeny. The most effective control is to spray all turf lawn in early spring to kill the grubs before they emerge. See discussion in Chapter 15 under Lawn Pests.

Black spot

When serious, this fungus can be most discouraging, since it causes plants to be defoliated and, in any case, badly disfigures foliage and the general appearance of the plant. Spores are carried over winter in the soil or in lesions on the canes. Some gardeners are seldom troubled seriously, but this disease thrives in moist, humid weather, and often appears spontaneously. It can be caused by watering roses in late afternoon so that the foliage remains wet overnight. Mulching is a great help, since it prevents the spores from being washed onto the leaves in rainy weather. Dust or spray with Ferban or an all-purpose rose preparation. Many gardeners prefer dust to control black spot.

Mildew

This attacks many kinds of plants, causing a thin, grayish coating to appear on the leaves and stems. It thrives in humid weather, where air circulation is poor, and when temperature changes are sudden. The old-fashioned rambler roses are particularly subject to mildew, and gardens in which roses are grown in quantity can be kept much healthier if ramblers are not included. Dust with Ferban or Captan.

Brown canker

Causing purplish spots on the canes, brown canker lives over winter, promoting growths on the plant's stems and later on the foliage. Control is best achieved by cutting and burning all infected parts. Since the spores thrive in moist winter conditions, roses should be mulched with a material that dries quickly. Old manure used to mulch roses seems to develop conditions which encourage the development of canker.

Rust

Producing orange spots on the under sides of the leaves, rust causes the upper surfaces to become yellowish. Destroy all infected parts and spray with sulfur.

9

EVERGREENS

❦❦❦ Evergreen trees and shrubs lend eye appeal to a planting at every season of the year. They give the home grounds, particularly the areas adjacent to the house, a finished appearance. When carefully selected, properly place and spaced, and given an average amount of care, they are among the most permanent of plants. They can be allowed to grow naturally with occasional light pruning to enhance their appearance, or they can be clipped in a variety of ways for formal effects. With heavy pruning and thinning, many kinds can be kept at desired heights over a period of years without materially altering their natural form. Some are notably fast growers while others by nature remain low and compact.

In selecting evergreens for specific places on the home grounds, thought must be given to their mature size, both height and width. Otherwise, fast-growing kinds soon develop such proportions as to grow out of scale with their surroundings. For example, a row or a group of spruces may be most attractive when the plants are 3 to 5 feet high, but they soon take on the aspect of forest trees and outscale a small house. On the other hand, one or several Hicks or Hatfield yews thoughtfully placed may be kept within bounds by pruning, whereas spruces are not amenable to such treatment.

Evergreens fall into two broad groups: the narrow-leaved types or conifers—such as pine, hemlocks, and yews—and the broad-leaved types—such as rhododendrons, andromeda, ink-berry, and others. Most conifers have narrow leaves referred to as needles, and some have scale-like foliage such as the arborvitae, false cypress, and the junipers. Fruits of conifers are cones, or in the case of yew, a plum-like fruit with the seeds encased in a fleshy cover. Most broad-leaved kinds are distinguished for their showy flowers which develop typical seed pods. All of them have highly ornamental foliage, and some—such as holly and firethorn —are grown primarily for their showy fruits.

Some shrubs, for instance, firethorn and a number of the cotoneasters, are evergreen in mild climates but semi-evergreen in areas where winters are severe. In sheltered parts of the home

149

grounds, they may retain their true evergreen character, while in exposed areas they often shed a considerable amount of foliage in winter—a point to remember.

Despite their year 'round eye appeal, both needle-type and broad-leaf evergreen shed foliage after or while new growth is developing. Mature needles on yews, pines, hemlocks, and others turn yellow and drop. Similarly, the foliage of rhododendrons, azaleas, andromeda, hollies, and other broad-leaved kinds becomes yellowish and falls to the ground. Unaware of this natural function of growth, gardeners often become alarmed and get the notion that plants are dying. The denser the foliage on an evergreen, the greater the amount of shedding that can be expected.

The following list includes a representative number of those commonly grown. Most of the broad-leaved kinds are included in Chapter 6, Flowering Shrubs, because their bloom habit gives them special merit in this category. A number are described in Chapter 11, Ground Covers. Several have prime value for hedge use. Hence the reason for numerous cross references.

Andromeda   See Chapter 6.

Arborvitae   *Thuja species*

Commonly grown because they are comparatively inexpensive, arborvitaes are fast-growing, easily propagated evergreens. The scale-like leaves are arranged in fan-like form. Since heavy snow causes the branches of the pyramidal forms to separate, they need annual shearing and topping to strengthen the stems. Tieing the branches at intervals is another way of retaining the desired symmetrical form. Some kinds burn badly in windswept areas, and arborvitaes are not well suited to poor soils. Typical forms include the narrowly pyramidal kinds, the Globe arborvitae, and a number of varieties with variegated foliage. These latter need to be used with discretion, since some are gaudy in appearance and are not particularly pleasing when used in quantity. Arborvitaes can be used as specimens, in groups for accent, or as a hedge. But there are many other evergreens which are superior in every way. In most instances, unless varieties are carefully selected, they do not prove to be sound investments for the small property.

Arborvitae, one of the easiest of all evergreens to grow, is at its best in full sun. When grown in shade, it becomes thin and ragged. Moist, well-drained soils produce the best specimens; on dry soils, they are not particularly satisfactory.

Azalea   See Chapter 6.

Boxwood   See Chapter 12.

Cotoneaster   See Chapter 6.

Daphne   See Chapter 6.

English Ivy   See Chapter 10.

Euonymus   See Chapter 6.

Evergreen Privet   See Chapter 12.

Fir   *Abies species*

Firs and spruces are often confused, because they are similar in form, foliage, and general aspect. When the needles of the fir drop, the leaf scars that remain are flat and circular, whereas those of the spruce are rough and stubby. Fir retains its needles much longer when cut, giving it greater value than spruce for Christmas tree use. However, spruces are adaptable to wider use in gardens than most kinds of fir, since they endure heat, soot, and city conditions better. Firs are best suited to country and suburban gardens, where the soil is rich, well-drained, and moist, and the air clean. They are happiest in high elevations. In addition to a graceful habit of growth, with needles or rich green, sometimes grayish, their showy cones are held erect, another distinguishing feature.

Among the firs best suited to gardens on the East Coast are the Concolor fir (*A. concolor*), Fraser fir (*A. Fraseri*), Nikko fir (*A. homolepis*), and the Veitch fir (*A. Veitchii*). None of these are as common as the spruces, and usually they are not cheap.

Best-suited to sunny locations, preferably in situations free from smoke and soot, firs grow well in moist, well-drained garden soil, rich in organic matter. Allow them ample space for development, bearing in mind that they are forest trees.

Firethorn   See Chapter 6.

Garland-Flower   See Chapter 6.

Hall's Honeysuckle   See Chapter 11.

Hemlock   *Tsuga species*

Two kinds of hemlock are frequently grown in gardens, the common or Canadian (*T. canadensis*) and the Carolina (*T. caroliniana*). They are easily distinguished, since the needles of the Carolina hemlock are borne around the stems, whereas those of the Canadian are on a flatter plane. Both are highly ornamental as specimens, or for hedge use in sun or shade. The Carolina species has proved to be far better suited to city conditions than its Canadian relative. These evergreens can be sheared for a variety of formal effects and kept at any desired height, or they may be allowed to assume their natural graceful habit.

Give them well-drained soil and average care, using the pruning shears to control growth as desired. Hemlocks are seldom happy in windswept locations where growth is usually sparse, and needles are easily windburned, which causes them to fall quickly and produces dead wood in considerable quantity.

Holly—2-40′—Zones 3-7   *Ilex genera*

American holly (*I. opaca*) is a tree of open woods and fields, often found growing in sandy, stony soil. Holly devotees have spared no effort to study the needs of this plant for garden use and have selected a number of varieties that are outstanding for the quality and quantity of their fruits; these have been named. This handsome, broad-leaved ornamental is slow growing and requires considerable care until it reaches 4 to 5 feet in height. However, container-grown plants make it easy for present-day gardeners to grow holly with a minimum of loss. Once established, it develops into a trim, pyramidal specimen. Like other members of the genus, American holly has leathery foliage which endures considerable exposure to wind and even to salt spray but, in cultivation, it is more safely placed in a protected location.

The small, white flowers have little decorative value, but the success with which they are pollinated, mostly by bees, determines the quantity of showy red fruits that may be expected in autumn. Male and female flowers are borne on separate plants. It should be remembered that in gardens where only a few hollies are grown, plants of both sexes need to be in close proximity for heavy pollination. Some growers sell grafted plants that produce both staminate and pistillate flowers. For the development of fruits, good culture is essential since a weak plant cannot be expected to produce an abundance of well-developed berries.

Although American holly is sometimes found in sandy and gravelly soil, it is best planted in well-prepared holes where the best of drainage is assured, using ample amounts of humus under and around the roots. All hollies need acid soil. Evergreen fertilizer or cottonseed meal, applied in early spring, provide balanced feeding for all types. Mulching hollies is sound practice. Pruning after new growth has developed is essential for shapely trees. Prior to new growth's development, however, shedding of mature foliage begins, so that there is a period in late spring when the plants are not at their best in appearance. Several insects plague holly, among them the holly-leaf miner, which if not controlled, seeriously disfigures the foliage. See Chapter 19.

English holly (*I. Aquifolium*) has proved hardy as far north as Cape Cod, and it flourishes near the sea as it does in the British Isles. In the South, the Northwest, and in California many outstanding varieties are grown in gardens and on holly farms for use as specimens and hedges, as well as for the Christmas trade. Its glossy foliage gives this tree great distinction at all seasons of the year. There are many selected forms available, including some with white-edged foliage. It is hardy from Zone 6 south.

Inkberry   See Holly.

Ivy, English   See Chapter 10.

Japanese Andromeda   See Andromeda (Chapter 6).

Japanese Boxwood   See Chapter 12.

Japanese Holly   See Chapters 6, 12.

Japanese Spurge   See Chapter 11.

Juniper   *Juniperus species*

Junipers, some tree-like, some broad-spreading shrubs, and others of prostrate habit, are dominant features of the coastal landscape of the eastern United States—both in gardens and in the wild. These picturesque evergreens are sturdy and vigorous, lending an enduring richness to plantings.

The red-cedar (*J. virginiana*) is a narrowly pyramidal tree, often of picturesque appearance when twisted by the wind. Its glaucous foliage and dark blue berries are of special appeal in winter. Several improved forms of red-cedar are widely planted.

Among the tall-growing shrubby forms, the Pfitzer juniper is the most widely planted. It makes a sizable specimen with broad-spreading branches of blue-green foliage. There are several selected forms of compact habit, which are often better suited to small properties. Among the most useful of the shrubby types are those used as ground covers. See Chapter 11.

Junipers are for hot, dry locations in full sun and should not be planted in shade where they languish. Average soil suits them, and they are frequently planted in poor soil. Under these conditions and given annual feedings with evergreen fertilizer, they make amazing growth.

Korean Boxwood   See Chapter 12.

Leucothoë   See Chapter 6.

Mountain Andromeda   See Andromeda (Chapter 6).

Mountain-Laurel   See Chapter 6.

Myrtle   See Chapter 11.

Pachistima   See Chapter 11.

Pachysandra   See Chapter 11.

Periwinkle   See Chapter 11.

Pine   *Pinus species*

Since they are not particular as to the quality of soil in which they are planted, many kinds of pine are grown in home gardens where there is room to accommodate them. Actually there are enough native kinds found in various parts of the United States to satisfy most needs but, the Scots pine, the Austrian, and the Japanese black pine are adaptable to poor soils by the sea and inland. However, all pines when grown on better than average soil usually make notable specimens. Because there are so many species, they are generally described with relation to the number of needles in a bundle or unit along the stems and at the tips. Some make rapid growth, others are fairly slow in maturing.

Familiar native kinds include the Eastern white pine, the Jack pine, the red pine, the pitch pine, and others. The Dwarf Mugo pine (*P. Mugo Mughus*) is widely planted in gardens for its compact habit. In its typical form, it develops into a small tree, known as Swiss Mountain pine. However, the dwarf form is ideal for ground cover use and as a low-growing specimen in hot, dry locations.

Pines can be grown in any well-drained soil in full sun and require no special care once established. If seedlings are planted, they are greatly improved by annual pruning to induce dense growth.

Rhododendron   See Chapter 6.

Spruce   *Picea species*

Handsome evergreens, spruces are extensively planted in home gardens, but often in the wrong places. Most beginners are attracted to small specimens of blue spruce and plant them where they can be admired at close range, sometimes under windows—areas which they soon outgrow. They make attractive lawn specimens—particularly the Colorado or blue spruce—and need ample space in full sun to develop the true beauty of their symmetry. Spruces are similar in appearance to firs, and the characteristics which distinguish these two are noted under the description of firs in this chapter. There are several outstanding species and selected forms of spruce; all are worth growing where space permits.

Full sun and average garden soil are their simple requirements. Spruce gall and spruce mite are sometimes annoying pests; once discovered, these pests need to be controlled immediately less they injure growth which greatly detracts from the beauty of the spruce.

Vinca   See Chapter 10.

Wintercreeper   See Chapter 10.

Yew   *Taxus species*

Few evergreens are better suited to the average home grounds than the various forms of yew. They are valued for their rich, dark-green foliage, their showy, red fruits and their pleasing appearance at all seasons of the year. In sun or shade, they can be used for entrance and foundation plantings, as ground cover on level areas or on slopes, as specimens, or for hedges (see Chapter 12).

Typical forms include the Japanese yew (*T. cuspidata*), a broad-spreading tree-like shrub that will grow to 30 feet or more, unless controlled. The pyramidal form, called *T. cuspidata capitata,* makes a handsome cone-shaped specimen, growing to 40 feet or more. However, both can be pruned annually to remain at a desired height and width. There are many selected forms of dwarf habit available, among them the varieties *densa* and *nana.* Hicks yew (*T. media Hicksii*), which makes a columnar specimen, and the Hatfield yew of broader aspect are valued for their upright growth.

Yews can be grown successfully in average, well-drained garden soil in sun or shade. Organic matter incorporated with the soil and an annual feeding with evergreen fertilizer benefit them greatly.

10

USEFUL

ORNAMENTAL VINES

❧❧❧ Hardy vines are woody plants with one or several stems that require support for normal development. Some produce herbaceous growth which dies to the ground each winter and, in the case of perennial kinds, renews itself each spring. Many of those treated as annuals in cold climates are perennials in warm ones. Vines climb in several ways: by tendrils (extensions of stems or leaves that coil around whatever support is available to them), by self-twining of leaf or stem, or by small pad-like disks at the ends of the tendrils. Other vines need to be tied to keep growth tidy.

Beginning gardeners frequently plant hardy vines with little or no thought to the ultimate effects which may result from poor choices. Woody vines offer a quick and easy solution for creating shade and camouflage, as well as a softening effect on fences and walls. Yet, the extent to which they are used effectively and at the same time kept within bounds requires a knowledge of the various kinds. Many are notoriously rampant in their annual rate of growth. Consequently, arbors, trellises, pergolas, cedar posts, and other suitable supports used to hold vines up need to be of sturdy construction and firmly set in cement to withstand heavy wind and seasonal storms that occur. On the other hand, some of our hardy climbing plants rate at the top of the list among garden ornamentals. As with the selection of trees and shrubs for the home grounds, the right plant for the right place is of vital importance in selecting vines.

In lieu of a rock garden, striking cascading effects can be achieved with showy flowering types to enhance the appearance of outcropping rocks or ledges. Those of rapid growth, suitable for camouflaging fences and retaining walls, may be allowed to spill over on the ground of adjoining areas for cover. Vines are sometimes desirable for softening the walls of brick, stone, and stucco houses, but careful choice is required when they are used on wooden structures. All too often, tendrils work their way under clapboards and shingles or entwine themselves on gutters and blinds, creating costly maintenance jobs.

Climbing plants may be utilized as ground covers in large

159

areas where they have ample room to develop. Their prime value is that of rapid cover for banks and slopes where the grade steepness makes upkeep a problem. Many are sturdy, deep-rooted types adapted to wind and exposure and requiring little care. In addition, they have merit as soil stabilizers, since a number of vines spread by underground roots or produce roots along their stems, preventing erosion. Evergreen kinds such as bear-berry, myrtle, English ivy, and euonymus are among the most desirable of ground covers for tailored effects.

In addition to their decorative foliage, the showy blooms of such vines as the large-flowered clematis, honeysuckles, morning-glories, the climbing hydrangea, and others, add materially to their value. Fragrance is also an asset of jasmine, clematis, and nasturtiums. Trailing varieties of roses make the most spectacular display of all, and many varieties do double duty with showy hips in the fall. Conspicuous fruits of striking color are characteristic of bear-berry, clematis, bitter-sweet, porcelain ampelopsis, and others.

As previously mentioned, not all vines are satisfactory on small home grounds. Those that climb by tendrils and trailing stems usually prove to be a nuisance, since they encroach on shrubs and trees, creating a tangled mass of growth. This fact must be carefully considered before planting any of the more vigorous kinds listed below. For example, Hall's honeysuckle is a rampant grower that frequently becomes a serious nuisance, unless carefully restrained. Similarly, despite its showy fruits in autumn, bitter-sweet may prove to be more of a detriment than an asset. Large areas covered with rapid-growing vines make ideal seedbeds for weedy trees and shrubs, not to mention a host of troublesome weeds.

The following list of vines includes those commonly planted.

Bear-Berry   See Chapter 11.

Bitter-Sweet—10-20′—Zone 2   *Celastrus scandens*

A tough native vine, much admired for its colorful fruit, bitter-sweet can cause woe to any gardener who plants it without knowledge of its persistence, vigor, and deep-rooting habits. In the right place, it can serve as good cover for rocky areas, rough ground, a wall, or a bank or slope where erosion is a problem. It is effective on a sturdy fence if quick cover is needed, provided that the vine is kept within bounds by frequent, heavy pruning. Otherwise, it forms a tangle of growth with sturdy, rope-like stems that twine around shrubs and trees, often killing them.

Bitter-sweet grows in almost any kind of soil, in sun or shade, and is hardy in the coldest parts of the country. For fruit, plants of both sexes are needed. Seeds are carried by the birds; these germinate readily, making bitter-sweet a vine of distinctly weedy habit. Once planted, it is not an easy plant to eradicate.

Boston Ivy. See Virginia Creeper.

Clematis—6-20'—Zone 5   *Clematis species*

Among climbing plants, clematis may be said to rival the rose in the beauty of its flowers. Wherever there is a fence, a trellis, an arbor, a post, or a wall that afford sun at least half the day, usually a spot can be found for one or more varieties of clematis. They can be trained on wire or formal trellises for architectural effects, or allowed to clamber at will. As they reach out for the sun, the leaf-stems entwine themselves around whatever support they can find. In addition to showy blooms, the silky seed pods are highly decorative in late summer and autumn.

The large flowered hybrids will make excellent pot plants. Support them with heavy stakes of wood or wire, or provide an ornamental trellis on which to display their beauty.

Combined with climbing roses, clematis hybrids make charming color combinations, especially when pale pink, white, or yellow roses are used with the various blue, purple, and mauve varieties. Cedar or metal posts planted with several varieties of clematis provide dramatic accents in perennial and shrub plantings. For camouflaging tree stumps, unsightly fences of wood or wire, or allowed to scramble over stone walls, these vines have few peers.

Most kinds flower on new wood (except as noted), so that serious winterkill does not affect the current season's bloom. Except for the removal of dead wood, little pruning is necessary until the plants are well established, usually after the second year. Then they can be cut back to a foot in early spring, before growth starts.

Fertile, well-drained soil on the alkaline side with a moist root run suits clematis. The roots and lower stems prefer shade with top growth in the sun for at least half the day. Prepare the location with care. Dig a generous hole, 18 inches deep and 6 to 8 inches wide, and fill it with a mixture of the best available topsoil at hand and humus. Either compost or thoroughly moistened peat moss will suffice. To this mixture add a generous handful of a complete fertilizer and, if the soil is acid, a handful of ground limestone for each plant. These ingredients need to be thoroughly incorporated with the soil.

When setting out plants, dormant or pot grown, place them so that the crown is 2 inches below the soil level. This practice allows additional growth to develop below the surface of the soil, also providing insurance in the event that the top growth is killed back by wilt. It is claimed that shallow planting is a cause of wilt. When the crown is set below soil level and wilt occurs, new shoots often develop below the infected area. All diseased parts should be removed and burned, and the soil should be treated thoroughly with a fungicide such as ferbam. This practice is recommended also if replacements are required for the same location.

After planting, tie the stem to a stake as well as to some suitable support on which the vines can climb. A collar of hardware wire placed around the stem at the ground level protects it from bruising. All reputable growers purposely ship clematis with a stake attached to the stem. The weakest part of the clematis vine is the stem itself; when bruised, it can easily be infected by insects or disease.

Actually, clematis is no more demanding in its fertilizer requirements than other flowering plants. It often persists despite considerable neglect but responds readily to feeding. When plant food is scattered around the plants, it should be watered in so as not to damage the basal stems. Where soils are known to be strongly acid, annual applications of ground limestone are desirable.

To provide a moist root run for clematis, mulch plants with peat moss, buckwheat hulls, marsh hay, or any convenient material available. At least an inch of peat moss or buckwheat hulls is needed to retain soil moisture. Since the roots spread considerably once plants are established, mulch an area at least 2 feet in diameter around the stems of each plant. Organic fertilizers and dried animal manures incorporated with mulching materials make plant food available as plants are watered or rain supplies the needed moisture.

Climbing Hydrangea—30'—Zone 4   *Hydrangea petiolaris*

Long-lived and exceedingly handsome, the climbing hydrangea deserves to be more widely planted. Where there is space, a rocky slope needing cover, an outcropping of rock, or a ledge in need of softening, this vigorous summer-flowering vine may well be the answer. When planted near a brick, stone, or cement wall, climbing hydrangea eventually takes over and spreads widely, making a richly textured bank of foliage and flowers.

Give the climbing hydrangea good garden soil and a sunny or partially shaded location. It is extremely hardy, drought-resistant, and relatively free of serious pests. Container-grown plants are easy to handle.

English Ivy—4-10"—Zone 4-5   *Hedera Helix*

English ivy has a multitude of uses on walls, fences, rocks, and other types of support; it is also much utilized as a ground cover. When trained espalier fashion on stone or stucco walls, the distinctive pattern of the leaves shows to good advantage. Less common forms grown in containers are often featured on terraces and patios.

Like pachysandra and myrtle, it is one of the most versatile ground covers in gardens here and abroad. The typical form of English ivy, so common everywhere, with its long, trailing stems, is ideal for northern or western exposures on banks, slopes, or level ground where other plants are not easy to establish and an evergreen cover is desired.

Many selected forms are grown in various parts of the country, some hardier than others. The ideal ivy is one that endures wind and winter sun without burning and can be grown in practically any type of soil. To most people, ivy is ivy, so long as it has the typical leaf, but there are major differences. Baltic ivy (*H. Helix baltica*) has generally proved to be quite hardy—even under difficult conditions—and is widely planted, but during severe winters in the Northeast it does not always prove itself.

Ivy is easy to root from cuttings, or trailing stems with roots may be used. Some gardeners prefer to use hairpins or other means to peg down long trailers, so that they will form roots. Wherever roots develop, pieces can be cut from the main plant and started anew. This is one of the great joys of growing ivy and one of the reasons for its widespread popularity, as well as the fact that it can increase its ground-covering capacity with great rapidity.

Most forms of English ivy are hardly suited to full sun, and this point should be borne in mind when planting it. Use other plants in sunny locations.

Hall's Honeysuckle   See Chapter 11.

Honeysuckle—10-30′—Zone 3-4   *Lonicera species*

Fragrant and colorful, climbing forms of honeysuckle contribute generously to the summer garden and are valued for their rapid growth and hardiness. Since they withstand dry conditions and wind, they fit admirably into the planting schemes of coastal gardens. Best known of all is the trumpet honeysuckle, *L. sempervirens,* native from Connecticut to Florida and west to Texas. It climbs by means of wiry stems and, although the foliage is not impressive, the bright, orange-to-coral tubular blooms are spectacular. These are borne in clusters and make an impressive show through the summer months. There are varieties with red and yellow blooms as well.

Soil of average fertility suits these vines, which thrive in sun or part shade, and they require no special care. Constant pruning, which keeps them within bounds, encourages new growth from the base. Plants can be increased by cuttings. Aphids are the chief pest of the climbers.

Silver Lace-Vine—3-30′—Zone 3   *Polygonum Aubertii*

Popular for the late summer and fall garden, the silver lace-vine presents a memorable display when the delicate masses of fragrant, white flowers make their appearance. It is a rampant grower, covering large areas in a single season by means of twining stems. The leaves are not particularly attractive, but it is valued highly for its bloom, which creates billowy effects for a month or more. It is particularly striking when allowed to cascade over walls, rocks, and high fences. A good plant for hot, sunny locations, it endures wind and exposure with ease and is extremely hardy and disease-resistant as well.

Not particular as to soil, silver lace-vine is a deeply rooted, woody plant that requires no special care or attention, except for constant hard pruning to keep it within bounds. This treatment is often necessary each fall or early spring, except where it is needed to cover extensive areas quickly. Plants are easily started from cuttings.

Virginia Creeper—50′—Zone 3   *Parthenocissus quinquefolia*

Brilliantly colored, autumn foliage is the chief asset of Virginia creeper. Also known as woodbine, it is one of the relatively few climbing plants that can be expected to thrive almost anywhere, with little or no care. Even though a commonplace climber, it has eye appeal in every stage of its development. Useful for screening and softening walls and fences, it accomplishes its task quickly. It clings best to rough surfaces by means of root-like holdfasts and also makes a good ground cover. The five-parted leaves are purplish in spring, changing to dull green in summer, and terminating in a brilliant display of red. Clusters of deep blue fruits appear in the fall.

Related species include Boston ivy (*Ampelopsis tricuspidata*) with large, grape-like leaves of glossy texture which turn yellow, orange, and scarlet in autumn. Bluish-black fruits. A widely known variety—miniature Boston ivy (*A. tricuspidata Lowii*)—is valued for its small foliage, less than an inch in length, which changes color with the seasons and makes delicate tracery.

Although these vines grow best in moist soils, they soon take hold in most any type of soil, sending their roots deep. They endure sun, dryness, and wind, are reliably hardy, and can be grown successfully in shade as well. All are propagated by cuttings or bits that root readily with soil contact.

Weeping Forsythia   See Chapter 6.

Wintercreeper   *Euonymus Fortunei*

Evergreen forms of euonymus, commonly called wintercreeper, are excellent climbers and ground covers as well. Extremely hardy and vigorous, they maintain a fresh, attractive appearance throughout the year. Unfortunately, they are subject to scale insects, which require considerable spraying to eradicate. If neglected, these scaly pests spread rapidly, causing plants to lose their foliage and eventually die. Apparently, euonymus scale is more inclined to affect plants on walls in hot, dry locations than when it is grown as a cover plant. When present, the scale spreads to other plants such as pachysandra, English ivy, and bitter-sweet.

Its deep-rooting habit makes it a good soil binder. For covering banks and slopes, for clothing rocky areas, under shrubs and trees, and as a lawn substitute in the shade, wintercreeper is most valuable. It responds to shearing and clipping for tailored effects. On stucco, brick, and stone walls and on tree trunks as well, it clings readily by means of aerial roots, referred to as holdfasts, creating a richly textured surface.

Common wintercreeper (*E. Fortunei*), sometimes referred to as *E. radicans,* is the toughest and most vigorous of evergreen vines. There are many varieties, since it tends to produce foliage variations known as sports. Some are valued for their colorful fruits, others for variegated foliage or deeper color in autumn.

Any well-drained soil is satisfactory for this sturdy evergreen which thrives in sun or shade. Propagation is by division, pieces of the rooted stems, or by cuttings which root easily in sand and peat. To control euonymus scale, spray in early spring with a dormant oil spray. Cut out and burn badly infected growth. Crawlers emerge from scales in late May and again in late August. Use malathion as directed on the container.

Wisteria—25′—Zone 4   *Wisteria sinensis*

Wisteria, known for its vigor, longevity, and attractive bloom, needs little praise, but it requires determination and a pair of sharp pruning shears to keep it within bounds, so that on the small place this highly ornamental vine can be used to advantage on a fence, a trellis, or a pergola. Sometimes it is allowed to scramble over a ledge. However, it is a mistake to allow wisteria to be grown too close to wooden structures, since the twining stems quickly work their way under clapboards, shingles, and exterior trim, or between the slats on blinds, often causing considerable damage. By hard pruning, begun when the plants are young, wisteria can be kept to a single upright stem and grown in tree or shrub form. This treatment is most satisfactory for small gardens.

Two distinct species are grown in gardens: Japanese wisteria (*W. floribunda*), which has pendulous racemes of bloom, ranging from 1 to 3 feet, and Chinese wisteria (*W. sinensis*) with much shorter racemes 7 to 12 inches in length—by far the more common. However, considering that the Japanese species with its extremely long blossoms needs a special kind of setting to show itself to full advantage, Chinese wisteria is generally more adaptable in the average garden. Tree and even shrubby forms of wisteria are sometimes effective, but they require considerable pruning to maintain these forms.

Although of easy culture, wisteria is sometimes sparse in its bloom, to the great disappointment of those who plant it. "What can I do to make my wisteria bloom?" is a question often asked. Top pruning—cutting back new growth hard and continuously from late spring until midsummer—sometimes helps to induce flower buds. Or, root pruning may bring the desired results. A trench a foot or more in depth is dug around the base of the plant, 2 to 3 feet from the trunk (depending on its size). Use a sharp spade, plunging it into soil to sever as many roots as possible. Superphosphate is commonly used to increase flowering of certain woody plants. A generous handful dug in around a small trunk or 2 to 3 pounds for each diameter inch of trunk on an old wisteria plant is the usual method. Superphosphate is best applied immediately after normal bloomtime, since flower buds develop in early summer. In some instances, there are plants that apparently do not respond to any of these treatments.

Wisteria is long lived, deep rooted, and dependably hardy. Yet, during severe winters, flower buds of the Chinese wisteria are sometimes damaged, especially in the most northerly parts of the country.

Full sun or part shade suits it, but when planted in shady areas, flowers are seldom produced freely. Many growers offer container-grown specimens which have compact root systems; usually these plants have produced a few blooms. Selected colors of either kind are frequently grafted plants; therefore, any growth appearing below the graft union must be cut out together with shoots from the base of grafted plants. Where sand is predominant, add several shovelfuls of humus in preparing the hole; otherwise, average garden soil is sufficient. Feed sparingly with a low nitrogen fertilizer such as 5-10-10 until its bloom habit has been determined. Even then, do not overfeed, unless an abundance of foliage is preferred to flowers.

City of York, an outstanding white climbing rose

Betty Prior still rates high as a floribunda rose

Rugosa roses thrive by the sea in sandy soil, exposed to wind and salt spray

Pruning roses is a spring chore of prime importance

White Chinese wisteria at its height

Climbing hydrangea, although slow to become established, is long-lived and notably hardy

Hybrid clematis runs the gamut of the rainbow in its color range

Bold-leaved summer-flowering cannas are tropical in appearance

Daffodils are more effective when planted in clumps

Hardy hybrid lilies are best planted in the late fall

When grown in pots, tuberous begonias can be given special care

Hybrid mollis azalea stands out against the fence
and a carpet of thyme

Carolina rhododendron, dramatically placed at the edge of a terrace

Hybrid mock-orange or philadelphus becomes a
splash of white in early summer

11

GROUND COVERS

❧❧❧ Essentially ground covers are low-growing plants that increase mostly by underground stems, or are by nature of trailing or wide-spreading habit. As they develop, they form mats or carpets on the surface of the soil. Some are evergreen such as periwinkle, pachysandra, and moss pink. Certain kinds such as English ivy produce roots along their stems, which serve to keep them flat and hold soil, while the junipers and the dwarf cotoneasters spread by trailing stems in a procumbent manner so as to create a slightly wavy, or billowy effect, without forming roots unless induced. The manner in which these plants develop roots and the depth to which the roots penetrate the soil determine their value as soil binders. The term *ground cover* as used in its broadest sense also embraces a goodly number of dwarf perennials, both native and exotic (including some true alpine plants), miniature or sub-shrubs, ferns, and wildflowers. To this list may be added a selected group of evergreen and deciduous shrubs which by the nature of their growth lend themselves to ground-cover use. In addition, certain tall-growing perennials such as daylilies and plantain-lilies, because of their heavy root systems and broad-spreading foliage are ideally suited to cover large areas where grass is not practical.

Although grass is the most desirable of all ground covers, there are many situations—on slopes and banks, in shady areas—where grass does not grow easily or well, and where it cannot be cared for satisfactorily. Then, too, even on flat surfaces, the time required and the cost involved to maintain a high-grade lawn may not be feasible. Often, the need for continual fertilizing, spraying for insects and pests, and cutting adds up—in terms of man hours and dollars—to a sizable total. Furthermore, in shady areas where homeowners frequently struggle to keep grass growing, more time and energy may be spent than the plot is worth. The solution for such sites is ground covers.

Exposed ground needs to be planted, if only to keep it from becoming infested with weeds. On slopes, erosion may become a serious problem. Actually, ground covers fulfill a variety of needs on home grounds and help materially to reduce maintenance.

The following are typical situations in which they can be used to advantage.

Concealing Exposed Tree Roots. This problem often plagues gardeners, especially if large trees are a part of or adjoin a lawn area. In many instances, grass may be neither easy to cut nor easy to maintain, and exposed roots are a hazard. Cover plants solve both problems.

Carpeting Shady Areas under Specimen Trees and Shrubs. Where grass is not practical, matting plants or taller kinds are needed for soil cover, as well as to provide a pleasing setting for specimen plants.

Clothing Rocky, Uneven Land. Where rough, natural effects are desired, but cover is needed, outcroppings of rock may be greatly enhanced if planted with a variety of ground cover and rock plants.

Covering Banks and Slopes. Erosion is the chief problem in both sun and shade. Most slopes and banks are not suited to grass from the point of easy maintenance. Steep grades require deep-rooted, low-growing plants to hold the soil. Also, suitable ground covers help to tie slopes in with the over-all planting scheme.

Underplanting Tree and Shrub Borders to Keep Down Weeds. Soil under high-branching kinds can be a nuisance to keep attractive, unless some suitable cover is provided. Ferns of various kinds, carpets of wildflowers, and evergreen cover plants are often suitable.

Reducing Weeds among Perennials. This practice has proved to be most satisfactory where large-scale perennials—peonies, hardy asters, chrysanthemums, poppies, iris, daylilies, and the like—are grown in large groups of a single kind. Evergreen candytuft, Silver Mound artemisia, snow-in-summer, barrenwort, and similar plants are desirable.

Binding Sandy Soils. Plants that tolerate salt spray—bearberry, rugosa roses, shore juniper, beach wormwood, and many others—are invaluable for holding sandy soil in seaside plantings and inland.

Solving Problems in Wet Soils. Some creeping plants are by nature adapted to boggy conditions in which they thrive on hummocks. Others prefer moist, heavy soil. Ferns, forget-me-nots, primroses, violets, foam-flower, dwarf willow, and others fill the need.

Settings for Lilies and Other Bulbous Plants. Lilies grow best when they have shade over their roots. The contrasting foliage of ground-cover plants provides a setting and acts as a foil for lilies and other kinds of flowering bulbs, notably the spring-flowering kinds.

General Landscape Value. Unless beds and borders are mulched with peat moss, composted bark, or some other suitable material, or a dust mulch is maintained, weeds appear which require cultivation to eradicate. A good-looking mat of green is preferable to a weedy tangle.

Ground covers in their diverse forms lend a finished appearance to shrub and perennial plantings, thereby eliminating sharp edges between beds and grass areas. Large surfaces of bare ground are not particularly pleasing, since the soil tends to cake and crust.

These versatile creepers have value in the over-all landscape picture by helping the various units of a planting on the home grounds flow into one another. The transition between a lawn and the trees and shrubs that enclose it can be enhanced by the use of suitable carpet. Small shrub groupings can also be softened with ground covers. Plants of varying sizes and shapes within a unit can be linked or tied together with one or more kinds. This is particularly true in foundation plantings.

Year-Round Eye Appeal. Evergreen ground covers are especially valuable for their year-round color and interest. They become eye-catchers in plantings viewed from windows, driveways, and roads adjoining one's property. They are equally important in approach plantings, corner groupings, strips along walks, and other areas adjacent to the house—be it the front door, the service entrance, or the rear driveway. Blankets or sheets of cover plants are the simple and easy solution to tasteful landscaping. They seem to belong in these locations.

The selected group of ground covers in this chapter is but a sampling of the many useful kinds available.

Artemisia, Silver Mound—4-12″—Zone 3

Artemisia schmidtiana

A sturdy perennial, it grows in full sun and poor soil, making handsome mounds of silvery, finely cut foliage, a foot or more in diameter, which are eye-catching all season long. Often used singly in small rock gardens or as an edging for wide borders, it shows off equally to good advantage in broad masses combined with juniper and cotoneaster as a ground cover in rocky areas or on slopes.

Root division is the easiest way to increase stock. Artemisias spread rapidly and are easy to divide at anytime during the growing season. If Silver Mound gets shoddy with too much rain, causing the clump to spread open, cut it back and watch it quickly send up new growth.

Bleeding Heart, Fringed   See Chapter 3.

Bloodroot   See Chapter 3.

Blue Phlox   See Moss Pink.

Bugle-Weed—4-12″—Zone 4   *Ajuga species*

A perennial ground cover for quick cover, it is easy to handle and increases rapidly. It is widely used in shade as a substitute for grass, both on flat areas and on slopes. For carpeting under shrubs and trees, in strip plantings, among rocks, on terraces, or between stone crevices, it is one of the easiest of all ground covers to grow. The blue, pink, white, and variegated forms grouped together make a colorful display. However, it does not stand any great amount of foot traffic. Except in naturally dry soils, this plant flourishes with little care, and may become weedy in a small garden. It is ideal for shade or partial shade, or in sunny locations where there is more than average soil moisture.

The smallest piece with roots will take hold. It can be set out at any time during the growing season, since it requires only ordinary soil and routine care in transplanting. Perennial covers for shade are not too numerous; bugle-weed is one of the most useful and least expensive, because of its rapid method of increase. It has a shallow rooting system and shows the effects of prolonged dry spells in thin soils, but responds quickly to watering.

Candytuft, Hardy   See Chapter 3.

Cinquefoil   See Chapter 6.

Coral Bells   See Chapter 3.

Cotoneaster   See Chapter 6.

Creeping Phlox   See Moss Pink.

Crested Iris   See Chapter 3.

Daylily   See Chapter 3.

English Ivy   See Chapter 10.

Ferns

From the time the fiddleheads unfurl in spring until the mature fronds (foliage) turn gold and brown in late autumn, ferns provide a source of continuing interest and fascination. Once given the right location, they flourish with little care. They are of inestimable value for creating finished effects in the garden in a single season and make good dividers between formal and informal plantings. Used in groups or singly, they supply needed filler material under shrubs or trees. The tall growers may take the place of low shrubs, since their height and habit of growth is certain, once they are established.

City gardeners have learned to use ferns in dark, shady places, largely because they have seen them in old gardens where well-established colonies have proved their ability to persist for half a century or more, despite neglect.

Ferns increase by creeping or running rootstocks, or by enlarging their crowns, as with common types of perennials. The spores (seeds) which appear in brownish sacks either on the reverse of the fronds or on separate stems are another means of perpetuation. They are usually transplanted in spring or fall, but many kinds can be moved at almost any time during the growing season, if handled with care. Many ferns have wide-spreading and fairly deep roots, which means that they must be dug with a sharp spade. In planting, set the crowns no deeper than they originally were growing. Get them off to a good start by digging large holes to accommodate the roots without crowding. Woods soil, leaf mold, or peat moss added to the soil pays dividends. Matting types can be lifted like sod and divided or replanted without breaking the roots. Water as with any newly set plants until they are established. Plants may be obtained from dealers or collected in the wild.

Forget-Me-Not   See Chapter 3.

Fringed Bleeding Heart   See Chapter 3.

Hall's Honeysuckle—18-24"—Zone 5

Lonicera japonica Halliana

One of the most widely used vines for covering banks and slopes in many parts of the country, Hall's honeysuckle can also be the meanest of pests to eradicate. It has clean foliage, delightfully fragrant flowers, and will grow anywhere in any kind of soil. On the other hand, uncontrolled, it makes a tangled mat of growth and twines itself around shrubs and trees. In many areas it is disliked, because birds drop seeds of poison ivy which fall among the stems, take root, and thrive in its dense growth. When neglected, it can become a breeding place for various kinds of weed trees and, because it is so resistant to elements and is often allowed to grow without pruning or restraining, it has rightfully earned the name of pest. Unless very carefully restrained, Hall's honeysuckle is not suited to the small home grounds.

Houseleek—1-3"—Zone 4   *Sempervivum tectorum*

This curious and commonly grown perennial, with rosettes of fleshy leaves, gathers its young around it in a cushion or mat; hence the common name, hen-and-chickens. It fills the seams of rocks with ease and is sometimes used along rocky paths and outcroppings, but always in the sun. When planted in shade, it loses its vigor, becoming soft and loose in growth. On dry slopes as a ground cover, especially where soil is poor and gritty, it flourishes and crowds out most weeds. If interplanted with sedums, especially such weedy kinds as *Sedum acre,* it is soon crowded. Best left to itself, or planted with other varieties (of which there are quantities), it makes a flat, uneven cover of crisp texture and color, depending on the kinds used. There are numerous species and varieties, some with webby filaments giving a cobweb effect and others rich with reddish leaves. Flowers are borne in clusters on stout stalks.

Houseleeks can be planted at almost any time during the growing season. Drainage is much more vital to their survival than soil; avoid wet feet for them at any season.

Iris, Crested   See Chapter 3.

Juniper—1-2'—Zones 2-5   *Juniperus species*

For steep slopes in full sun where grass is difficult to maintain, few plants are more adaptable and desirable than low-growing junipers. Horizontal in habit, evergreen, and soft in texture, these prostrate shrubs are attractive throughout the year. As the branches spread they root, making a wavy carpet. Creeping junipers are often the answer to problems created by the construction of split-level houses, particularly in areas of rolling terrain. Also, when used in masses to link several changes of level on home grounds, they are more effective than grass, because of their height, color, texture, and mode of growth.

Regardless of how poor the soil is or appears to be, junipers will prosper with proper soil preparation. Assuming that the slope has been raked and graded, dig holes wide and deep enough to accommodate the roots; partially fill the hole with equal parts of garden soil and peat moss thoroughly mixed with a handful of acid-soil fertilizer. Water thoroughly and leave a slight depression around each plant to catch water. Additional water will be needed twice a week until the plants are established. Rooted cuttings from flats or potted plants are inexpensive where quantities are needed; balled and burlapped specimens may be used.

Moss Pink—6″—Zone 2   *Phlox subulata*

Blue Phlox—1′—Zone 3   *Phlox divaricata*

Creeping phlox is among the most desirable of native hardy perennials for home gardens. It is vigorous, colorful, permanent, and requires little care. Rating high on the list as one of the most colorful of all ground covers, *Phlox subulata* has many popular names, such as moss pink, ground pink, creeping phlox, and mountain pink. Its evergreen, needle-like foliage makes a desirable mat and the creeping stems develop roots as they spread.

The familiar type, with its magenta flowers, clashes with other colors in the garden, but when used in broad masses with a white variety it can be most pleasing. However, there are so many superior varieties in shades of pink, red, lavender, and purple that there is no point in using the common magenta form.

Blue phlox and wild sweet William are common names for *P. divaricata*, one of the fairest blue flowers native to eastern North America. In its native haunts, it is found in thin, moist woodlands, but grows well in average garden soil in sun or part shade. When in blossom, at tulip time, it makes a vivid display in several shades of blue and lavender. Although not a dense grower, in the sense that we evaluate ground covers, blue phlox is a filler for use in drifts among ferns, wildflowers, and spring-flowering shrubs and perennials.

Low-growing phloxes are of easy culture and free from serious pests. All can be increased by division in early spring, early fall, or at any time during the growing season, if they are given the necessary watering after transplanting.

Pachysandra—6″—Zone 4   *Pachysandra terminalis*

The common name Japanese spurge is probably used less than the scientific name pachysandra. One of the four most widely used ground covers in America, its spoon-shaped leaves, arranged in whorls on trailing stems, make a rippling effect when used in broad carpets. Creamy white spikes of bloom top the foliage in May, and old plants produce whitish fruits in autumn, but these are not common. Easy to grow and propagate, it makes a dense mass for shady areas and grows most satisfactorily even where there is considerable sun. However, it is no plant for hot, dry situations. It burns badly during open winters when planted in exposed areas where wind and sun are its enemies. A variegated form known as Silveredge lends a pleasant contrast to plantings and endures sun with ease.

Pachysandra makes a superbly rich green carpet. It fits under such trees as maples and other shallow-rooted kinds which tend to rob the soil of nourishment, normally making cover of any kind a problem. Interplanted among rhododendrons and azaleas, it gives a pleasing and finished effect. It also combines well with low-spreading junipers, yews, pieris, leucothoë, skimmia, and others. Along the edges of steps and on banks and slopes, it serves all the purposes of a good ground cover.

Few ground covers are as easy to propagate or root more rapidly. Cuttings may be taken after the new growth has formed in early June and rooted in a mixture of sand and peat. Some gardeners simply set out rows of cuttings in garden soil and shade them until roots appear. Once a good healthy set of roots has developed, the plants are given a permanent home, about 8 to 10 inches apart for intermediate effect. Close planting followed by mulching is worthwhile with rooted cuttings and to eliminate considerable weeding.

Periwinkle—6"—Zone 3   *Vinca minor*

Periwinkle and myrtle are common names for one of the most widely grown ground covers. A glossy-leaved evergreen trailer with lively blue flowers that bloom in early spring with the daffodils. There are also white-flowering varieties which are most pleasing. *V. minor atropurpurea* has purple flowers. A double-flowered kind and one with yellow markings on the leaves are sometimes planted. The best of them all is Bowles variety, with larger and deeper blue flowers and more restrained habit of growth than the common periwinkle. Plants tend to increase in size by expansion of the crown rather than by the rooting of trailing stems, which is typical of the species. A recent introduction, Miss Jekyll's White is smaller in scale than any of the others. Not only smaller, in leaf, but more restrained in growth, it is exceptionally free-flowering and well suited as a carpet plant for spring-flowering blubs.

Ordinary soil, well prepared, gives good results in sun or shade. Easy to propagate from division of the clumps or rooted trailers, it can be trans-planted at any time of year. When dividing matted clumps, cut back the runners hard to make the rooted portions easy to handle. Mulch immediately to reduce weeding. Otherwise, a newly planted area has a messy appearance. Heavy pruning induces new growth from the rooted portions, which makes for denser cover. Annual feeding of newly planted colonies induces more vigorous growth, as does continued fertilizing of established plantings.

Phlox, Blue   See Chapter 3.

Phlox, Creeping   See Moss Pink.

Pinks   See Chapter 3.

Plantain-Lilies—1-3—Zones 3-5   *Hosta species*

Plantain-lilies make excellent ground covers under shrubs and trees and in areas where other plants fail to make a presentable appearance. Funkia is the scientific name formerly used for this genus. There are large and small-leaved kinds, some with white margins, others with variegated markings; also blue-green and yellow-green types, as well as some with lustrous, dark green foliage. For textured foliage effects, for accent, or for striking contrasts with smaller-leaved plants, these perennials have great value. Flowers are mostly blue, lavender, or purple, and one kind bears a showy white, fragrant cluster. Blooms appear from July to September and make an attractive display while they last, but their foliage is their prime asset.

Plantain-lilies grow in average garden soil in sun or shade. If planted in rich loam, they grow to enormous size, especially in shade, for which they are well adapted. One feeding a year in ordinary soil produces good results. Plants are easily divided in spring or fall, or at any time during the growing season. They are completely hardy and seldom affected by pests or diseases.

Primrose   See Chapter 3.

St.-Johnswort   See Chapter 6.

Stonecrop—3-12"—Zone 2   *Sedum species*

Mention stonecrops or sedums to most gardeners and they shout "weeds" or "pests," for some of them are precisely that. Yet, where soil cover is needed in sun or light shade and large areas are involved, sedums are often the answer. On stony locations, on slopes or banks, or among ledges where soil is sparse, the sturdy stonecrops have a place. Because of their shallow roots, they are easy to eradicate when they attempt to run away with any given area. Low-growing, free-flowering, and requiring little care, they are often of great use, especially at summer places where low maintenance is essential.

Sedum acre, sometimes called mossy stonecrop, actually grows by the acre in a short time. One of the lowest-growing of all, 2 to 3 inches, its flowers make a carpet of gold above miniature evergreen foliage. There are many kinds of sedum which are well adapted to ground-cover use. Those that develop large rosettes like *Sedum sieboldi* are less rampant than the common species.

Ordinary dry soil, even on the poor side, suits all the stonecrops. The smallest bit with a root will grow, and they can stand drought and neglect with ease.

Thyme, Mother-of-Thyme—2-4″—Zone 2   *Thymus Serpyllum*

Thyme is a plant never forgotten once it has been stepped upon. This carpet plant has many forms, both species and varieties, but most useful of all for a flat cover are forms of *T. Serpyllum*, known as mother-of-thyme. These are white, lavender, crimson, and reddish-purple flowered varieties, one with white margins and another with yellow coloring in its leaves. Lemon thyme has yellow-green foliage, and Woolly thyme is just what its name says, grayish in texture.

A green rug for slight slopes, a covering among rocks, dry walks, and ledges, a crevice plant for walls and terraces and for uneven ground surfaces, thyme is at its best in the sun. Several kinds, or as many as you can collect, will make a bank that you will enjoy working about.

A hot, dry, rocky soil on the poor side where the sun shines all day is the best place for thyme. Since the smallest portion with a root will grow, there is no need to start it from seed unless the aim is to grow some species not easily available. Thyme likes lime, but grows in acid soil.

Veronica   See Speedwell.

Violets—3-18″—Zone 2   *Viola species*

Violets are vigorous and persistent and, however charming and appealing we consider them, they can become the weediest of weeds in the small garden if not restrained. But grow them we will, so they need to be used to best advantage—as ground cover in shady places. Almost every gardener wants a few violets, but some kinds are more desirable than others.

Two kinds of flowers are produced—those we see blooming on the plants and those that we don't see—the greenish, cleistogamus (inconspicuous, usually concealed) flowers under the foliage, near the base of the plants. The concealed flowers, which are only rudimentary in their structure, do not open and are self-pollinated. When ripe, the pods pop open, scattering seed in all directions to a distance of several yards or more; hence, the reason that violets are so weedy.

With few exceptions, violets are shade-loving plants and grow easily in well-drained garden soil. Some kinds, especially the cultivated varieties, need moist, rich loam to produce good bloom. Increase by division can be done in spring or fall or at any time during the growing season.

Wintercreeper   See Chapter 10.

12

HEDGES

❦❦❦ For many properties hedges are more desirable than fences. They both serve the same purposes—to define a boundary, to furnish desired privacy, to provide a background, windbreak, or setting for a garden, and sometimes to keep out the neighbor's dogs and overly enthusiastic children.

Hedges, like fences, require maintenance but, if properly trimmed from the beginning, the job can be comparatively easy. All too often, homeowners get off to a wrong start. They fail to handle young plants properly by cutting them back hard at the time of planting in order to induce dense growth at the base. If a hedge is kept wider at the bottom than at the top, there is little danger that the lower branches will die out, since they obtain the light that they need. However, when a hedge is pruned wider at the top than at the base, it soon becomes leggy and unsightly. Little can be done to correct this condition, unless the hedge is cut back hard or nearly to the ground and given a fresh start. Such treatment is successful with privet, hedge roses, barberry, and many other flowering shrubs, but few evergreens—with the exception of Japanese yew—can endure this harsh treatment. Even so, yew cannot be cut back as drastically as others.

In addition to the formal types of hedges, which require periodical shearing, there are the informal types, often referred to as hedgerows or borders. These may be composed of several kinds of flowering shrubs or evergreens interplanted, which are allowed to grow in a natural state.

Indispensable Privet

Privet is the most widely used of all shrubs for hedges, because of its attractive appearance, rapid growth, and low cost. Ibota privet (*Ligustrum obtusifolium*) and the variety Regel's privet are best suited to the colder sections of the United States. Most popular of all is California privet (*L. ovalifolium*), hardy from Zone 4 southward and partially evergreen. However, where winters are severe, it is often killed to the ground. South from lower

New Jersey, the handsome Wax privet (*L. japonicum*) is widely valued for its leathery evergreen foliage and black fruits.

Japanese Barberry

Japanese barberry has the advantage of thorny stems, showy red fruits, and colorful autumn foliage. Hedges 2 to 6 feet tall and often as wide are commonplace, and it makes an excellent barrier, but its thorny stems make it somewhat difficult to prune. A vastly superior form is the Mentor barberry, distinguished by stiff upright growth, the rich green foliage of which lasts well into winter. It is exceptionally drought resistant. For these reasons, it is worth the price: about twice that of Japanese barberry. Furthermore, it retains its foliage to the base of the plant and, requires little or no shearing.

Rose Hedges

Several kinds of roses make desirable hedges, among them the rugosa rose, known for its ironclad hardiness, its clean foliage, its delightful bloom, and its showy fruits. It belongs at the top of the list for seaside gardens because of its tolerance of salt spray and wind. Varieties with single and double flowers in white, pink, red, and yellow are available. Plants range from 3 to 6 feet in height, spreading even wider if allowed.

Floribunda roses used for hedge purposes are the closest approach to an everblooming fence. The color range is extensive, and by selecting the taller growing kinds such as Betty Prior, a highly ornamental hedge—3 to 4 feet tall—can be developed. Set plants 2 feet apart and prune back to 10 inches at planting time to induce dense growth at the base. Floribunda roses require much less pruning than the hybrid teas. See Chapter 8.

Flowering Shrubs

For informal effects, lilacs are often planted. Well-grown (which means occasional feeding and pruning to keep suckers under control), they create a billowy effect that is pleasing to the eye, and they seem to belong with colonial and federal architecture. Bridal wreath (*Spriea vanhouttei*) also makes a highly decorative and handsome hedge because of its billowy racemes of white flowers, graceful habit of growth, and generally clean appearance. Forsythia, or golden bell, particularly the upright-growing form, is also desirable. The new hybrids of flowering quince have considerable value for their glossy foliage, brilliant flowers, and appealing twiggy growth. Winged euonymus (*E. alatus compactus*) is a clean grower with winged, twiggy growth and rich red foliage in autumn.

Yews and Other Evergreens

Of all the evergreens used for hedges, Japanese yew heads the list. There are both upright and spreading forms which can be used to advantage, depending on the type of hedge sought. For a tall, upright screen, Hick's yew is the answer, or for one of broader habit, Hatfield yew serves the purpose admirably. Upright Japanese yew (*T. cuspidata capitata*) makes an impressive, tall hedge. Various forms of spreading yew are well suited to low hedges. An evergreen hedge of this sort represents a considerable investment, but perhaps no more than that of a well-built fence.

The effect desired, the space available, and the property owner's long-range viewpoint are factors to weigh in making this kind of investment. However, many growers offer small plants in quantity at moderate prices. These can be lined out and grown on for one or two seasons (depending on the size obtained) before planting as a hedge. This is an excellent way to obtain a yew hedge at moderate cost (saving as much as 50 per cent), when time and space permit. Lining out (planting in rows) is recommended to develop sturdy top and root growth as well as sufficient size; unless marked or protected, young plants are often trampled or damaged by mowers. The various forms of Japanese yew produce their most vigorous growth in full sun, but grow satisfactorily even in fairly heavy shade if carefully pruned and fed.

Other evergreens which make desirable hedges are: arborvitae, hemlock—both the Carolina and the Canadian types—

Pfitzer's juniper, white and Scotch pine, and several forms of red cedar and spruce.

Boxwood

For low hedges, tall ones, too, boxwood (*Buxus sempervirens*) has been a tradition in gardens for centuries. Despite its beauty, it is often winterkilled or badly burned in the Northeast, and several pests which attack it are most annoying. In Maryland, Delaware, Virginia, and the Carolinas, box is the shrub that gives the gardens of the region their atmosphere of repose and rare enchantment. Maintenance involved is often more a case of what not to do, since many of the plants are extremely old and require only moderate care. A useful and practical substitute is littleleaf or Japanese boxwood (*B. microphylla*) which endures extreme winter temperatures, even those of Canada. The foliage is light green, sometimes on the yellow-green side in winter, but its summer appearance is excellent. Its ironclad hardiness and vigor are its chief assets.

Dwarf Hedges

Dwarf hedges have special merit for many properties where space is limited and a low, slow-growing barrier is needed along walls, to outline a formal planting, or to enclose a terrace or patio.

Boxleaf Holly

A glossy evergreen form of Japanese holly valued for its box-like foliage, compact growth, and the ease with which it can be kept to a desired size (1½ to 3 feet) by clipping. Hardy from Zone 4 south, it flourishes in sun or shade and needs a well-drained acid soil. Many selected forms of low-growing habit are available.

Cranberry Cotoneaster

Cranberry cotoneaster lends itself to use as a dwarf hedge. Foliage is evergreen or partially so in cold climates, and the showy fruits in autumn are of special merit. Well suited to hot, dry locations, it can be maintained at 2 feet or less, developing a pleasing, irregular effect of great charm.

Dwarf Red Barberry

Dwarf Red Barberry is a tailor-made plant for dwarf hedges. The variety Crimson Pygmy with its bronzy-red foliage, spiny stems, and compact growth has many uses in sunny locations. It averages a foot high and spreads half again as wide.

Floribunda Roses

Floribunda roses are often used for this purpose, particularly the dwarf varieties which are bred especially for hedge use. Also, any of the low-growing kinds are possibilities for colorful and free-blooming low fences about 2 feet tall.

Korean Boxwood   *Buxus japonica koreana*

Korean Boxwood is an ironclad form of this beloved hedge plant. Useful for sun or shade, its slow, compact growth makes it easy to maintain so there is no need to clip it tightly. It can be kept at a foot in height by constant pruning and shearing or allowed to grow to 2½ feet.

Wintercreeper   *Euonymus radicans*

Wintercreeper, discussed in detail under Vines, Chapter 10, is sometimes used for a low evergreen hedge in sun or shade.

Yew

Yew, particularly the selected forms (*Taxus cuspidata densa* and *T. canadensis stricta*), make effective evergreen hedges of low stature (under 2 feet) for sun or shade.

13

GARDENING
IN THE SHADE

❧❧❧ Most plants require sun for at least half a day to produce sturdy growth as well as satisfactory bloom. However, there
are a surprising number that are either true denizens of shade or
adaptable to it, some tolerating considerably less direct and
reflected light than others. Shade created by buildings, walls, and
fences presents a problem of less than normal sunlight and
daylight, and little can be done to change the situation. Because
it is elusive, shade cannot be measured with any degree of
precision. Consequently, trees, shrubs, perennials, bulbs, and
annuals to be planted under these conditions must be selected
with more than average care, since not all kinds bloom or grow
well in limited light.

On the other hand, when trees create a dense canopy excluding
sun and daylight, the possibility of growing a greater variety of
plant material may be increased, since light conditions can be
altered by pruning and thinning the tops of trees to allow filtered
sunlight to enter. Often, the removal of a few branches makes the
difference. (See Pruning, Chapter 20, Creating High Shade.)
Even trees such as maples, which have extremely heavy root
systems and develop dense top growth, robbing the soil of
considerable moisture and plant food, are amenable to this
treatment.

Actually, on properties where there are a considerable number
of trees, opportunities for creating a green garden offer a challenge. The play of light and shadow on woody growth, perennials, and bulbs, as well as lawns creates a new kind of eye
appeal. Furniture and garden ornaments, thoughtfully placed,
enhance such a setting and become objects of more than casual
use and interest. In the absence of bright masses of lower color,
they often provide needed contrasts when painted suitably.

Gardening in the shade, with all its seeming limitations, frequently opens the way to a new awareness of leaf pattern, its
texture, its form, and the subtle variations of green. There is
more to green than meets the eye at first glance. When foliage
masses of varying textures are grouped, the diverse tones of
green are readily apparent. The inherent richness of rhododen-

drons, laurel, and Japanese andromeda are contrasted with the black-green of yews and the lighter tones of hemlock. Clumps of broad-leaved plantain-lilies, yellow-green or glaucous, variegated or white-edged, provide needed contrasts. The delicate texture of ferns as exemplified in finely cut fronds is another aspect of interest in a green garden. Ground covers fill a multitude of needs for carpeting effects, their flowers and foliage contributing to the over-all picture. Blue-green, yellow-green, olive, and bottle green, together with overtones of bronze, gold, silver, red, and purple—according to the season—achieve a kind of distinction that the brighter hues of flowers do not possess.

In spring, before the leaves appear, color is provided by drifts of bloodroot, foam-flower, trillium, blue phlox, and other native wildings. Flowering bulbs such as scillas, crocuses, species tulips, daffodils, glory-of-the-snow, and many others are easily established, since they seldom need to be disturbed once planted. Hardy perennials—bleeding heart, foxgloves, false spirea, sweet rocket, peach-bells, snakeroot, and bee balm—make for continuity of bloom.

For summer and autumn there are innumerable varieties of daylilies, plantain-lilies, hardy ageratum, and other hardy plants. The colorful annuals, patient Lucy in shades of red, salmon, pink, and white and flowering tobacco with fragrant white, pinkish, purple, or chartreuse flowers contribute their share of color. Begonias in variety (particularly the tuberous kinds), coleuses, and fuchsias, all tender plants, make shady gardens a source of sheer delight from late spring to frost, filling the color needs for summer admirably.

Success in the shady garden is based largely on careful plant selection, placement, sufficient moisture, staking, pinching, and feeding. Encroaching roots of shrubs and trees are ever greedy for moisture and plant food and offer continual competition, so that frequent watering and feeding with complete fertilizers, dry or in liquid form, are vital. Overshadowing branches of trees and shrubs need constant heading back during the growing season to provide all the light possible.

In preparing beds and borders, root pruning of trees and shrubs is often necessary. Long-handled pruners and small saws are useful in making the job easy. A sharp spade is another useful tool. Little or no harm results from cutting back the invading roots of most trees and flowering shrubs. Naturally, no attempt should be made to tamper with or even dig close to rhododendrons, laurel, and other broad-leaved evergreens. Root pruning may be required every two years. The alternate approach is to sink plants in six-inch pots up to the rim and mulch heavily. This practice has proved especially satisfactory with tender plants, such as tuberous-rooted begonias, fuchsias, and others.

Gardening in the shade usually involves more effort than growing plants in full sun, but it has its compensations. The presence of shade itself, especially in the hot days of summer, is one of them.

Evergreens for Shade

The most satisfactory needle-type evergreens for planting in shade are the Canadian and the Carolina hemlock and all types of Japanese yew. For description and culture, see Chapter 9. Arborvitae and false cypress tolerate light shade. Firs, junipers, pines, and spruces need full sun or direct sunlight for considerably more than half of the day to prosper. Otherwise, they become thin and ragged in appearance.

Broad-leaved evergreens are much more adaptable in this respect. The following list includes the leading kinds that may be used effectively. Growth is usually looser and less compact than when grown in full sun, depending on the amount of light available and the competition from roots of adjoining trees and shrubs. More than average attention to pruning and feeding is required to keep growth trim and tidy. In like manner, flowering is not as profuse, but blooms last longer than when grown in full sun. This is true particularly of azaleas and rhododendrons. Windburn of foliage and buds during severe winters is not likely to be as severe under shady conditions. Consult the index for descriptions and culture of the following kinds:

American Holly	Inkberry	Pachysandra
Andromeda	Japanese Holly	Periwinkle
Azaleas	Leucothoë	Skimmia
Boxwood	Mountain-Laurel	Rhododendron
English Ivy	Oregon Holly-Grape	Wintercreeper

Flowering Shrubs and Trees for Shade

Flowering shrubs and trees—not including broad-leaved ever-greens—which grow satisfactorily in the shade are not numerous, but there is sufficient variety in the following list to find kinds suited to most gardens. When combined with the various broad-leaved kinds, the textured effects of both are greatly enhanced. Flowering is not as abundant as when these woody plants are grown in full sun.

Azalea	Flowering Dogwood	Summer Sweet
Barberry	Honeysuckle	Viburnums
Blueberry	Hydrangea	*except:*
Bush Cinquefoil	Privet	V. *Burkwoodii*
Cotoneaster	Redbud	V. *Carelsii*
Enkianthus	Sour-Wood	V. *Carlcephalum*
Firethorn	St.-Johnswort	Winged Euonymus

Perennials for Shady Sites

A sizable number of hardy perennials flourish in light shade. Others can endure a considerable amount of subdued light. Discussed in detail in Chapter 3, these are carefully coded as to the degree of shade.

Ground Covers

The following list of ground-cover plants includes those well suited to shady sites. Of particular significance is the representative list of ferns, which are desirable adjuncts to any shady garden. Substitutes for grass include bugle-weed, English ivy, pachysandra, and periwinkle. All are described in Chapter 11.

Barrenwort	Ferns	Lily-of-the-Valley
Bloodroot	Foam-Flower	Pachysandra
Blue phlox	Fringed Bleeding	Periwinkle
Bugle-weed	Heart	Plantain-Lilies
Coral Bells	Goutweed	Speedwell
English Ivy	Hall's Honeysuckle	Violets

Annuals for the Shade

Many annuals produce fairly good bloom where there is sun for half or slightly less than half of the day. A few perform well even in heavy shade. Annuals grown in shade tend to become rangy and loose in habit as they reach for light. As a result, tall kinds often need staking. All require pinching back several times to induce branching and sturdy growth. On the whole, annuals used to provide color in shady gardens require more care than those grown in full sun, but they are worth the effort involved for the effect created. The following list includes tender, woody plants such as the fuchsia which are treated as annuals, since they cannot be set out until the soil is warm. In turn, like true annuals, they are cut down by the first hard frost in the fall.

Balsam—8-24″   *Impatiens Balsamina*

A sturdy, self-branching, tropical annual resembling a stocky tree with blooms like tiny camellias borne in the leaf axils. Colors are white, pink, salmon, red, and purple. There are dwarf forms, those a foot high, and 2-foot varieties of easy culture; seed is sown in the open at tulip time. Set plants a foot apart in good garden soil.

Begonia—12-15″   *Begonia semperflorens*

These are the bedding begonias in pink, white, and red, mostly single flowers but sometimes double, averaging a foot or less in height, sold by florists in small pots or flats. They are ideal for edgings, for planting in drifts, or for window boxes and various kinds of containers. Professional growers raise them from seed or propagate by cuttings—the easier and faster method—but most beginners get their start with these free-blooming plants by first buying a few. Cuttings rooted in late summer make window gardens bright in winter. Their appeal lies not only in their showy flowers and free-blooming habit, but in their glossy foliage which may be a rich, light green or bronzy red, according to variety. Although their requirements are easily met, they must not be allowed to dry out. Allow a foot of space between plants each way, and give them humusy soil. Periodic feeding pays dividends. (Tuberous begonias are discussed in Chapter 5.)

Blue Salvia—2-3′   *Salvia farinacea*

Blue or white spikes on attractive plants which branch freely and produce bloom until hard frost. Seed may be sown in the open ground or seedlings obtained from a local grower.

Browallia—15″

A superb, steel-blue, flowering annual with shallow-tubed, petunia-like blossoms borne on wiry stems. Constant pinching produces trim growth. It makes an ideal plant for hanging baskets, pots and boxes; browallia may also be used as a border or in drifts with other annuals and perennials. There is a good white form also. Many growers offer plants. Seed needs an early start.

Coleus—2'   *Coleus Blumei*

A tender plant valued chiefly for its richly textured and brightly colored foliage, coleus belongs in shady gardens. Yet, it grows equally well in full sun. The spikes of tiny flowers have little merit and are best pinched off before they develop. It is easily raised from seed and even more easily increased by cuttings. Growers offer small plants in pots or flats at moderate cost, and this is a convenient way to get a start with coleus. If the tops of young plants are removed—2 to 3 inches—and rooted, double the quantity will be available for a summer and fall supply of colorful foliage. Plants grow to 2 feet or more in a single season, often developing into shapely specimens resembling small shrubs. Pinching does the trick, along with frequent watering in dry spells and a booster feeding or two during the season. Space plants at least 1½ feet apart.

Feverfew—8"-2'   *Matricaria species*

A commonplace, old-fashioned garden flower, feverfew is actually a biennial which flowers the first year from seed. Its habit of self-sowing makes it weedy—even a pest, if not controlled. The creamy white or soft yellow, button-like flower heads, in sizable clusters, are long lasting, showy, and bloom well even in considerable shade. Once planted, there are always seedlings on hand which can be used to fill in bare spots. Plants average 1½ to 2 feet in height and are spaced a foot apart. There are several forms that are less than a foot tall.

Flowering Tobacco—1-2½'   *Nicotiana affinis*

Flowering tobacco is a free-branching annual, valued not only for its showy flowers but its fragrance as well. Colors include white, lavender, mauve, crimson, and chartreuse (the variety Lime Green). It self-sows readily, but one cannot be sure of color in this way. When white is desired, it must be planted annually. Blooms of the typical forms of nicotiana close in the bright sun and open on cloudy days and during the evening hours, but the newer varieties remain open all day. Plants range from 1 to 2½ feet, according to the hybrid strain, and bloom freely from midsummer until cut down by severe frost. An excellent filler plant, flowering tobacco has many uses. Space plants a foot apart.

Forget-Me-Not   *Myosotis*

Forget-me-nots, although biennials, are often treated as annuals and make their display of pink, white, or blue flowers in spring when the weather is cool. They self-sow readily, sometimes to the point of becoming naturalized.

Fuchsia—1-3′   *Fuchsia species*

Fuchsias are tender, woody plants, actually shrubs, which are commonly treated as annuals in cold climates. They make a notable display in shady situations when planted in the ground or handled in containers. Somewhat exacting in their requirements, they need humusy soil, ample water, and frequent feeding. However, they are worth the effort, for, if well grown, theirs is a display of superb bloom from late spring until hard frost. Hundreds of varieties are cultivated, and most florists and garden centers offer small, rooted cuttings or small plants which may be set out when tomatoes are planted. Two or three pinchings induce side branches which produce abundant bloom. Both upright and pendulous forms are popular. The latter are well suited to window boxes and hanging baskets in the shade. Space plants at least 1½ feet apart. Mulching helps to conserve moisture, which is essential for top-quality growth. Dry conditions for extended periods prove harmful to both bloom and growth, and the effects are soon noticed. Do not plant them unless you are willing to care for them.

Madagascar Periwinkle—10-18″   *Vinca rosea*

Not well known but deserving to be, Madagascar periwinkle is a truly handsome annual of bushy habit with rich, dark-green, glossy foliage. Flower colors are rose, pink with a deeper eye, and white. The tall form grows to 18 inches, while the dwarf type is less than a foot in height. Seed is slow to germinate and needs a very early start to obtain fair-sized plants for summer bloom. However, more growers are now offering seedlings in small flats or in pots. Space plants a foot apart. This sturdy annual flourishes in light soils and withstands drought. Its trailing relatives are *Vinca minor,* one of the best of ground cover, and *Vinca major,* a favorite trailer with variegated foliage for window boxes.

Patient Lucy—6-24″   *Impatiens Sultanii*

A soft-stemmed, tender annual, Patient Lucy is valued for its glossy, light green foliage topped by clusters of brilliant red, orange, pink, or white flowers. Long a favorite house plant, it flowers well even in deep shade and is particularly effective in window boxes and other types of containers, as well as in beds and borders. Few annuals make brighter splashes of color throughout the summer than this old-time favorite, but it is nipped by the first frost. Pinching out keeps it compact. New strains, that range from 6 to 12 inches in height, are self-branching, making low mounds, are notable for their free-flowering habit. The tall kinds grow 1½ to 2 feet tall and spread nearly as wide. Allow at least 15 inches between plants of both tall and dwarf kinds. It is raised from seed, which needs an early start indoors, or cuttings may be rooted in water or sand. Patient Lucy flourishes in moist soil; long periods of dry weather are hard on it. Many growers offer plants in small pots or boxes of a dozen.

Lobelia—4-6"   *Lobelia Erinus*

A sun-loving annual, lobelia blooms well—even though more sparsely—in part shade, but growth is neither as neat nor as compact as in full sun. Easily grown from seed, this edging plant, averaging 4 to 6 inches in height, is prized for its bright blue flowers. Space plants 6 inches apart and plan to cut them back in midsummer to induce new growth from the base for late season bloom. Do not let lobelia dry out.

Wishbone Flower—12"   *Torenia Fournieri*

A charming tropical annual, the wishbone flower contributes attractive foliage and curious tubular, purple or white flowers to the summer garden. Within each deep-purple, velvety-textured bloom that is lined with yellow, the stamens shaped like a wishbone are easily seen; hence, the common name. Plants such as this one are grown for delight and amusement, as well as for their landscape effect. Seed must be started early indoors. Space plants a foot apart.

Other annuals for shade include the following kinds:

Baby Blue-Eyes	Mignonette	Satin-Flower
Clarkia	Monkey-Flower	Snapdragon
Cleome	Pansies	Sweet Alyssum
Cosmos	Petunias	Toadflax

14

AN EASY
APPROACH TO
LANDSCAPING

❦❦❦ "It's not a home until it's planted," is more than an over-worked slogan coined by the American Association of Nurserymen to sell plants. Suitable trees, flowering shrubs, evergreens, and ground covers thoughtfully placed are the materials that tie a house in with its surroundings.

When new houses are erected in subdivisions, frequently an attempt is made to provide some planting. The contractor puts in a row of shrubs across the front of the house and, occasionally, a tree, but rarely are they suitable. Quick-growing evergreens are planted, and invariably they are placed too close to the house to develop properly. Or, big-scale flowering shrubs are used which soon outgrow their setting. However, with proper planning and a careful selection of material, the home grounds can be planted appropriately and pleasingly from the beginning.

For convenience and practical use, most home grounds are best considered in the following manner:

(1) The public area; (2) The service area; (3) The private—or living—area.

Thus, the home grounds become a series of outdoor rooms. Hedges, fences, or walls serve as the dividers. Trees, shrubs, and flower beds become the furnishings, together with those accessories which provide ornament and comfort in enjoying the outdoor living room. The lawn and whatever ground covers are chosen become the carpet.

The Public Area, or the approach, includes the land between the house and the sidewalk, the approach walk, and usually part of the driveway. The manner in which it is handled reflects not only the taste of the owner, but also the impression which he wishes to achieve about his residence. For eye appeal as well as for easy maintenance, the planting must be simple, uncluttered, pleasing in composition and scale, and so arranged as to fit the house and make it blend with the surrounding landscape. In many instances today, houses are located fairly close to the sidewalk, so that it is essential to create a feeling of greater space than actually exists.

To impart a feeling of welcome, the walk should be wide enough (4 to 5 feet) so that two people may walk abreast comfortably. When an approach walk is narrower than the width of the front door or only slightly wider, the effect is not only uninviting but, usually, it is out of scale with the area as a whole. Surfacing with such materials as brick, flagstone, concrete, or asphalt is much more practical than steppingstones set in sod. Broad, hard surfaces are also much easier and more comfortable to walk on and to maintain in all kinds of weather. Whether the approach walk is to be straight or curved depends primarily on the placement of the front entrance and its relationship to the setting. The driveway should be wide enough to accommodate a car without damaging sod on either side. Cleanly defined edges of the planted area, the walk, and the driveway give a neat and trim effect, which may well serve as the keynote in developing the area.

In contrast to the days when houses were placed on high foundations and usually treated with a skirt or fringe of shrubbery around one or all sides, contemporary buildings usually hug the ground and need much simpler treatment. Planting is used to accentuate the entrance and soften the corners. Ground covers, which are slightly higher than the grass, serve as connecting links. Or, planting may be decidedly sparse, serving to point up the lines or architectural features of the house. An espaliered shrub or a vine may be used to provide tracery on a chimney. A strategically placed small tree or specimen evergreen may be a dominant feature. The present-day approach to planting is based on thoughtful selection to achieve distinction, which can be accomplished easily with a little "know-how" and imagination.

The Service Area includes the laundry yard, a permanent place for trash and garbage containers, and such space as may be needed for a compost pile, a vegetable or a cutting garden, cold frames, and the like. Its size will be determined by the needs of the family and may include an enclosed play area for small children. Screening may be done with a hedge, a fence, or trellis work. If space is strictly limited, portable clothes reels may be used, and the area so arranged that no enclosure is needed.

The Private or Living Area of the home grounds is frequently revamped to meet the needs of a growing family. Often, especially on small lots, the transition from play area to outdoor living room is gradual. In any event, the first aim is for privacy. A fence, a hedge, a row of shrubs, or a combination of small trees and shrubs may be used for enclosure to provide a setting for flower beds and borders and such planting as suits the taste of the owner. The creation of a lawn, uncluttered by beds and specimen shrubs, gives any outdoor living room, regardless of size, a feeling of spaciousness. Shade trees need careful placement.

A setting for garden furniture is usually desired. Accessories such as pools, birdbaths, sundials, statuary, and other types of garden ornament require thought before placing. Any feature used as a focalpoint requires a suitable background and a reason for its being there. (These are discussed in detail later in this chapter.)

The first step in landscaping your home grounds is to make a plan on paper. It need not be elaborate as to presentation, simply diagrammatic, but your plan should be plotted with sufficient accuracy as far as measurements and other important details are concerned to be useful and practical. It is essential to know the part that each segment of the home ground is to play in the overall scheme of things.

Procedure for Making a Simple Plan

Use a sheet of graph paper. On it, plot the areas occupied by the house and other structures, existing trees and all permanent features on the grounds. The scale for plotting should be convenient, easy to use, and determined by the size of paper being used. Graph paper 17″ x 22″ is easily available. For the small property, "1 inch equals 5 feet" may be a convenient scale, or you can use an inch to represent 10 feet.

With the use of a pencil, an eraser, ruler, a "T" square, a triangle, a French curve, and a compass, you can plot all of the necessary areas.

A piece of tracing paper the same size as the graph paper can be laid over it and secured by masking tape. Rough sketches made on the tracing paper will enable you to visualize the desired effect before the actual outlines of your planting areas are made on the graph paper. Then proceed to arrange your plant groups and number them to correspond with the names on your plant list.

Since order is Heaven's first law, planning and placement need to follow this principle. There is more to landscape design than simply deciding where to place plant materials and garden accessories. With their transient color, even flower beds and borders are less significant than the permanent aspect of trees and the texture and enduring quality of evergreens and flowering shrubs.

The Need for Composition

The task is to visualize the over-all picture and the parts which the various elements play in it. Developing well-landscaped home grounds involves knowledge of composition and under-standing its importance. Composition is the putting together of the elements of the design so that the result is pleasing—it hangs together. For example, harmony is seldom created by using too many different kinds of shrubs and trees. Nor, is it achieved by using too much plant material. Composition involves selection and placement—the right plant for the right place.

The Importance of Scale

The trees that exist on a property or are planted set the scale for the entire planting scheme. The term *scale* as used here refers to the visual relationship of each part of the grounds to the other units and to the design as a whole. In essence, scale means the right size. For example, on a small property, the aim is to create the feeling, or the illusion, of greater space than actually exists. Therefore, the size of the tree or trees chosen is not the only factor. The type and texture of the foliage, the bark, the flower-ing and fruiting habit, as well as the branching characteristics and the over-all habit of growth are all important. Of course, the size of your house is a prime factor in selecting suitable trees. A large tree makes an average-sized house look smaller than it actually is. It dwarfs the structure. Small trees and small-scale planting, used in conjunction with a small house, create the illusion of greater size than exists. Trees of medium height have little distinctive effect on the aspect of the small house, except to underscore its true size.

The Significance of Proportion

Proportion is the relationship of the width to the length of a given area. We look to classic architecture or to well-designed formal gardens for easy-to-recognize examples of good proportion. Proportion, like scale, is an essential characteristic of good design. We come to understand it by instinct, by keen observation, by comparing known, good examples with those that lack satisfying harmony. Since we are dealing with living, growing material, proportion cannot be applied to landscape design with the same precision that is possible in architecture. When trees and shrubs are harmonious in size, good proportion is the result.

Color, Form, Texture

Flower color, at best, is of fleeting beauty. Rather, it is the enduring value of green, in all its variations, that needs consideration in planning home grounds for year-round interest.

Form brings into sharp focus the typical shapes that trees, shrubs, and massed groups of plants assume as they develop their mature forms. They may be round-headed, columnar, or broadly or narrowly pyramidal. It is the wise selection and use of these forms that creates a pleasing landscape effect. Thus, plant selection is based not so much on favorite varieties as it is on the choice of desirable forms that can be combined or related to achieve harmony in the over-all design.

Texture refers to the degree of fineness or coarseness of foliage, its arrangement on the branches, and the amount of light it reflects or absorbs. Combining masses of varied textured foliage often points up and gives distinction to even the simplest planting.

Maintenance

Easy maintenance is essential. Over-all planting from the beginning needs to be based on this important factor. Elaborate plantings and formal areas demand considerable care.

Shady areas and slopes where grass cannot be grown and cared for easily may require ground covers.

Poor maintenance creates a bad impression. Better to have a simple grounds layout that can be kept trim and neat than an elaborate development that is poorly maintained or cared for casually.

Important Maintenance Practices.

1. Feeding is essential to healthy growth.
2. Weeding is a part of maintenance that often makes all the difference.
3. Pruning is essential to creation of good form.
4. Mulching is a means of conserving moisture.
5. Spraying is often essential for pest control.
6. Over-all care needs to be kept at a minimum.

"It's Fittin' to Be Settin' There"

Some 20 years ago a family from the Midwest chose a small Cape Cod town for their permanent residence. They built a trim Cape Cod house and planted a dooryard garden, filling it with lilacs, roses, boxwood bushes, and a few other old favorites, enclosing it with a white picket fence. The garden was a joy not only to its owner but to all who passed by. One day the local postmaster asked an old native what he thought of the house. His reply was, "It's fittin' to be settin' there." In practically every community in America, there are properties so tastefully planted as to be similarly described, but they did not just happen. Often, by taking a good hard look at a well-landscaped house, the true meaning of proportion, scale, harmony, form, balance, unity, and all the other technical terms used in landscape design come to be realities as we strive to plan and plant with a little "know-how."

The common mistakes made by most beginners in planting the areas around a new house include the following:

1. Shrubs and trees are usually planted too close to buildings. As a result, they fail to develop properly on all sides. Plants need air, light, and adequate space for development; otherwise, they become one-sided, producing considerable dead growth. Evergreens suffer considerably in this respect.

2. Equally common is the error of placing fast-growing evergreens in foundation planting or flanking the front entrance to a house. Arborvitaes, spruces, firs, upright yews, and hemlocks are usually offered as well-branched, tightly sheared specimens, 2 to 3 feet tall; however, they soon outgrow the space allotted to them. Low-growing evergreens—both the needle and the broad-leaf types and dwarf flowering shrubs which, with an annual pruning, remain in scale with the site—are preferable. To be sure, low-growing evergreens are usually more costly but well worth the price, since they remain in scale with a minimum of care.

3. Most present-day houses are built without gutters. When shrubs are planted in the drip line, they soon come to grief from too much water or are damaged by ice during the winter. Plant shrubs beyond the drip line. A layer of crushed stone, pebbles, or smooth stones, extending from the wall of the house to a point several inches beyond the drip line, helps absorb the excess water. Various types of ground cover may be planted in the stone mulch to soften it and, eventually, conceal it. This arrangement allows for adequate light and air circulation for the shrubs, which are planted in front of the stone mulch. The effect created is not only much more pleasing but more permanent.

4. Many plantings look bare and unfinished for several years, because the use of filler plants or ground covers is neglected. Low-growing carpeting plants are invaluable to tie in the various elements of a planting.

5. All too often, contractors bury all kinds of rubbish around the foundation of the house, including rubble from masonry work, which contains a considerable amount of lime. This debris is often harmful to plants, particularly those that require acid soil. If azaleas, rhododendrons, laurel, pieris, and other acid-loving plants are to be used in such locations, every vestige of lime must be removed.

6. Adequate soil preparation is often neglected when planting around newly built houses. For satisfactory results, most soils in developments require improvement *before* planting. If it is not possible to remove soil to a depth of 15 inches from the area around the foundation, at least prepare the hole for each shrub to be planted thoroughly by digging it at least twice as wide and deep as required by the roots. This practice is important whether planting a balled and burlapped specimen or a bare-root shrub. Use compost, well-rotted manure, peat moss, or chopped sod to provide the needed organic matter. The old rule of digging a $25 hole for a $5 shrub is sound.

7. Failure to apply fertilizer when planting in new ground is commonplace. Feeding plants and providing for the constantly expanding roots a year hence is important. Soil under shrubs and trees should be thoroughly prepared with fertilizer before planting, but commercial fertilizer should not come in contact with roots when the plants are set in place. This task, which takes but a few minutes, pays big dividends.

8. Watering newly set plants spasmodically is another fault of beginners.

Ample and thorough watering two to three times a week until the plants become established, followed by attention during dry periods, is of prime importance. Failure to follow this routine may result in losses, or plants, at best, get a poor start.

9. Drainage is sometimes overlooked; this factor is especially important in heavy, clay soils. If a sub-layer of hardpan or clay exists in your area, be sure to provide for ample drainage under the plants by using coarse gravel so that water will not stand around the roots. Poor drainage can be as deadly as extended periods of drought to new shrubs.

10. Setting plants too deep may seriously affect the vigor of trees and shrubs. Woody plants may languish for several years, because the root ball was buried rather than planted. Rhododendrons, azaleas, and other shrubs producing a sizable but shallow root system need to be set at the same level at which they were growing in the nursery. Usually, there can be no mistaking the soil level, if the burlap is rolled back before filling in the soil around the roots. To correct a too-deep planting, replant at the proper level. When this condition exists with fair-sized trees, which cannot be lifted easily, excavate the soil to the top of the root ball, opening a circle 18 to 24 inches in diameter and replace the soil with coarse, screened or washed gravel to provide needed aeration.

11. Mounding up loose soil around trees and shrubs, sometimes to a height of 6 to 8 inches or more, is unwise. This practice causes surface roots to develop at the expense of essential underground root development.

12. Changes in grading in which large amounts of earth are moved may seriously affect the vigor of an established tree, especially if the grade is raised appreciably. In this situation, provide a well around the trunk.

13. Failing to stake newly planted trees may prove disastrous. Young trees often produce vegetative growth more rapidly than they develop root growth. This condition is apparent when young trees are transplanted. To encourage a more vigorous root system, prune the top growth. Also, to assure needed protection against wind, a young tree needs to be adequately staked with a solid wooden or metal support that is kept in place for 2 or 3 years. Make several ties along the trunk, allowing enough play for movement without injury to the bark.

14. Improper guying of trees and shrubs where wire is too tight or too loose sometimes occurs. Girdling woody stems is bound to kill them.

15. Failure to remove suckers that emerge from the understock of grafted trees and shrubs frequently results in the loss of a grafted hybrid as the wild or less desirable understock takes over. This is common with roses. The condition is easily detected by simply comparing the foliage of the usually vigorous sucker growth with that of the grafted hybrid.

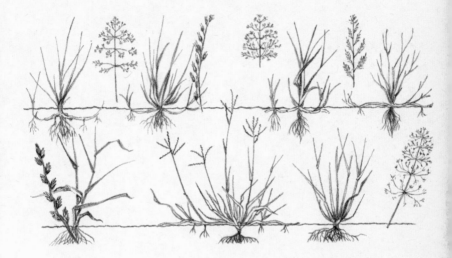

BUILDING A LAWN

❧❧❧ More new lawns are built in spring than in the fall. Yet, autumn is the ideal time to plant grass. At this season of the year, temperature and moisture conditions are better suited to the growth of grasses. Soils are warm and in good, workable condition. In spring, late thawing frequently presents problems of adequate drying out for planting seed. Unless new grass areas are well established before hot weather, they are soon overgrown with annual weeds. Then, too, seasonal rain is a normal expectancy in the fall. Shorter days and cool nights aid in conserving moisture. Annual weed seeds, especially the several types of crab grass, are dormant at this time. The rush of spring planting is over and the hot, humid weather of summer has passed. The earlier in the fall the new lawn is established, the longer period of ideal growing weather it will have to become established before winter.

Depending on the size of the area, preparation of the seedbed usually involves a rotary tiller to loosen the surface of the soil to a depth of 6 inches. Improving soil texture—be it sandy or clayey (see Soils, Chapter 1)—based on the time available, cost, and other practical considerations is all to the good. However, where large areas are involved, seldom is it possible to add the amount of organic matter desirable. Every available bit should be dug in. If compost is not available, thoroughly moistened peat moss, spread at least an inch deep and turned under, is a valuable adjunct, particularly during dry weather.

Raking to break up lumps of soil, remove stones and other debris, and to obtain a flat surface is best done by hand. When lawns are built by professionals who use mechanical equipment, raking takes less time. Nonetheless, a certain amount of handwork is necessary to obtain a flat surface of crumbly soil texture for seeding. Actually, there is no point in obtaining a finely screened surface, since the cost in time and labor of screening soil is out of proportion to the results achieved. Actually, a slightly rough, crumbly surface is more desirable, since it enables the seed to become well anchored between the particles. When autumn rains are heavy, wash is more likely to occur in finely screened soil, forming deep ridges. Then, too, excess moisture often causes caking as soil of fine texture dries, creating poor conditions for seed germination.

While preparation is in progress, the soil may require lime, but it is a waste of time and effort to apply it, unless needed. Under normal conditions, soil of average quality can be expected to produce a good crop of grass. The ideal condition for grasses is found in soils that are neutral or nearly so. Thus, a slight degree of acidity or alkalinity has little effect on growth. However, where soils are known to be highly acid, lime is essential. A soil test is the simplest method of determining the amount of lime needed. The recommended amount may vary from 50 to 100 pounds per 1,000 square feet. Based on experience, local practice can be obtained by a call to the local county agent or to an experienced gardener. This comment is offered to guide those who are confused by various recommendations regarding lime. For details on the functions and uses of lime, see Chapter 1.

Fertile soil is of prime importance in growing a good crop of grass. Scatter a complete fertilizer over the area, mixing it thoroughly in the top 3 or 4 inches of the seedbed. Since the amount will vary according to the formula used, apply as directed on the bag. For even distribution, use a spreader.

Seeding is best done in the same way, for even and quick coverage. Since the quality of a lawn depends primarily on the type of seed used, and the cost of the seed is the least part of the expense in making a lawn, only top quality seed should be used. There are many formulations of grass seed on the market, ranging from cheap to fairly expensive mixtures. There is also a vast difference in quality. Inexpensive mixtures are made chiefly of the coarse seeds of annual grasses, principally rye. These germinate quickly, grow rapidly, and die at the end of the season, leaving the lawn surface with bare areas where weeds quickly find a home. Actually, when counted pound for pound, there are only an eighth as many seeds to a pound of rye as compared to an equal amount of blue grass. This fact alone indicates that the most "costly" mixtures are actually cheaper than inexpensive seed and cover a much greater area.

Top grades of lawn seed are mixtures of several kinds of perennial grasses. Percentages of the kinds selected for a given mixture are determined largely by the area in which they are used. By law, formulas must be clearly printed on containers. The amount needed for a new lawn is 2 to 3 pounds of top quality seed per 1,000 square feet. There are mixtures for sun and shade, and this fact should be borne in mind when shady areas are being planted.

On a pebbly surface, raking in the seed may not be essential, but a light raking is general practice. If the soil is light and dry, raking is a necessity. Watering with a fine spray from a hose or sprinkler helps to settle the seed. Depending on weather, wind, rain, and temperature, watering every 3 or 4 days may be required. Moisture hastens germination.

In exposed areas and on sloping surfaces, some cover may be desirable. It can be a mulch of weed-free straw, marsh hay, grass clippings, or finely screened peat moss, scattered lightly. Cheese-cloth, lightweight burlap, or any lightweight cloth, stretched in strips over the area make excellent protective cover, but these must be removed immediately when germination occurs. In windy areas on high exposures or near the sea, this type of cover usually eliminates watering, or reduces the amount normally required.

The critical time for all seedlings is the period from germination until they are 2 to 3 inches high, and grass is no exception. Therefore, watering is vital if the weather is abnormally dry or windy. It should be remembered that wind dries bare soil rapidly. Usually germination occurs within 8 to 14 days after seeding, depending on the weather.

Grass can be mowed when it is 2 to 3 inches tall. Set the mower at 1½ to 2 inches high, enough to trim the tips of the blades, but not so low as to shear it tight. If lawn building is begun early enough in the fall, a second or a third mowing may be needed, and this is all to the good. At this time, a light feeding of a complete fertilizer (half or less of the amount originally used) followed by watering, benefits a new lawn greatly.

Weed Control

New lawns are seldom free of weeds. Even in established sod where growth is vigorous, certain kinds of weeds become invasive and often grow unnoticed until they are well rooted. The problem of weed control in lawns could be reduced to a minimum, if all the neighbors in a given community took the necessary control measures at the right time, but such communal action is rare. For example, if the residents of a given area waged war on dandelions and eliminated the possibility of reseeding, by removing the blossoms, they could soon be eradicated with the use of selective weed killers.

Weed control of turf is possible with comparative ease, but it is a continuing practice, one that has to be carried out periodically during the growing season. In early spring, control of many broad-leaved weeds is accomplished when the lawn is treated with a "weed and feed" mixture of fertilizer and weed killer. (Some preparations contain pesticides as well.) Crab grass is controlled with the use of pre-emergence or post-emergence chemicals. These are effective in combating the most annoying of all midsummer weeds in lawns, but they must be applied at the right time. Directions need to be followed carefully in using all weed killers, for they can cause serious damage to flower beds if handled carelessly.

Lawn Pests and Diseases

Since it requires time, energy, and money to make and maintain an attractive lawn, a careful check should be made periodically to note any unusual condition in its appearance. Lawn pests and diseases are not common to all lawns but can be serious when and where they do occur, if not controlled. Most kinds of damage are conspicuous, because of the discoloration caused in the grass.

Chinch bugs, which occur in hot weather in sunny locations, cause brown patches that look as though the grass had dried out. Damage is done by tiny, white-winged insects, which suck the juices from the blades. They are controlled with Chlordane.

Earthworms can be a nuisance if too many are present in a lawn. Their presence is noted by little piles of soil which appear on the surface after rains. Both the large, native, brown kind and the smaller, tropical earthworm are sometimes a problem. Treat the soil with Chlordane, using three times the amount applied to control beetle grubs and water thoroughly.

Earwigs, which do considerable damage throughout the garden in early summer, lay their eggs in grass. See Chapter 19.

Japanese Beetle. Grubs are usually found a few inches under the soil. Skunks, moles, and birds make holes in turf to get at these grubs. Large, dry patches of brown grass result from such damage and from grubs eating the roots. Since the roots are usually severed from the soil, it is possible to roll back the damaged areas and find the evidence.

When examined closely, the Japanese beetle is a most attractive insect. Its metallic-green coloring and coppery wings are actually striking. Adults, which are active throughout the summer months, devour more than 200 different kinds of fruits, flowers, and vegetables. Each female Japanese beetle lives 30 to 45 days and produces 40 to 60 eggs, which are usually deposited in lawns. Grubs hatch in less than two weeks and devour grass roots until cold weather comes. Then, they work their way into the soil to a depth of 8 or 10 inches, where they hibernate over winter. As spring approaches, these pests work their way upward to feed again on grass roots before they emerge. The grayish-white grubs, which have brownish heads, are approximately an inch long. The brown spots in a lawn, which develop into large patches of brown or dead grass, can be pulled or rolled back, revealing the grubs.

Control of Japanese beetles, which fly rapidly from late June on except in extreme heat, can be most exasperating. For instance, spraying during long periods of hot weather is only moderately effective. For control, there are a number of easy-to-use preparations on the market. Methoxychlor, Chlordane, lindane, DDT, and other insecticides are ingredients of these mixtures. To control the grubs in lawns, Chlordane dust (5 per cent), applied at the rate of 5 pounds per 1,000 square feet and watered in thoroughly, is easy to use. Because the grubs are found in great quantities in sod, treating lawns as early spring is practical.

Sod webworms devour patches of grass, causing small whitish squares in the turf, giving lawns an unkept appearance. These pests are the size of small grubs but with a hairy coat and nest in silk-lined burrows beneath of the sod. Use Chlordane.

Termites, so injurious to all types of wooden structures, sometimes nest in lawns. They look like flying ants and are white, but not all have wings. The workers which do the damage are wingless, plump in appearance, and white. Use Chlordane.

Lawn Diseases. In long stretches, humid summer weather may cause diseases that disfigure and damage grass. Thin growth or discolored patches are indicators of trouble. Brown patch, leaf spot, damping off, mildew, molds, and algae—as well as fairy ring and toadstools—are evidences of diseased turf. They are best controlled with specially prepared fungicides for lawns.

16

FEEDING PLANTS

❧❧❧ Plants, like people, need food. Proper feeding with adequate amounts of a complete fertilizer that is applied periodically brings results in top-quality flowers, fruits, vegetables, as well as permanent growth on trees and shrubs. When to feed, how much to use, and what to apply are the questions.

Gone are the days when stable manure was available in plentiful supply. Now we must depend on compost, organic, and commercial fertilizers, in proper balance, to provide the essential elements which our plants need. In most home gardens, commercial fertilizers prove to be the chief source of plant food. A "complete" fertilizer includes nitrogen, phosphorus, potash, and minor amounts of "trace" elements. By law, formulas must be printed on bags and packages to indicate the proportions of the various elements used. For example, the formula 5-10-5 means that it contains 5 per cent nitrogen, 10 per cent phosphorus, and 5 per cent potassium. The rest is inert material used as a filler. Minor elements included are magnesium, iron, copper, boron, aluminum, zinc, manganese, molybdenum, and other so-called trace elements, for the general well-being of plant growth. Trace elements essential for the health and vigor of plants are needed in minute amounts to ward off or resist disease.

Nitrogen, the number one factor in controlling growth, is essential to the production of foliage for flowers, vegetables, fruits, and grass. A surplus of nitrogen in the soil produces lush growth and few flowers. It is highly soluble in water and disappears rapidly during heavy rain.

Phosphorous stimulates root growth, hastens the maturity of plants, and the production of flowers, fruits, and seeds.

Potassium is the element that provides plants with the vigor they need to tolerate changing weather conditions and build up resistance against diseases. Since it is needed for the manufacture of starch and sugar, it aids the plant in developing firm stems.

The beginning gardener who feeds his plants with a complete fertilizer is likely to have little difficulty. Complete fertilizers are packaged for general garden use, and these should be applied at the rates specified on the container. (The amount is usually 3 to 5

217

pounds per 100 square feet.) Recommendations for the amount to use on a given area are based on sound judgment. Follow them carefully. Manufacturers package a wide variety of formulations in containers of varying weight. It is sound economy to buy 50-pound bags of the kinds commonly used, since packages of smaller amounts usually cost more.

Why Fertilizers Burn Plants

The statement is frequently made that commercial fertilizers may "burn" plants if they come in contact with foliage and roots in dry form. The term *burn* refers to injury in the form of dehydration, which occurs when the chemical salts absorb water from the green tissues of stems and leaves or the roots. Stems and leaves lose their green color and show a brownish color, paper-like in texture. Therefore, the recommendation is made to water the soil thoroughly after applying commercial fertilizer so that the salts contained in it are in the solution. Then, the fertilizer becomes effective as plant food, and plant roots can absorb it. Furthermore, instructions that state to mix fertilizers thoroughly with soil before planting are based on this premise. Organic fertilizers, derived from sewage, can cause "burning."

In feeding plants, bear in mind that most perennials need at least two applications of commercial plant food annually. The first should be applied early in the spring and the second about eight weeks later. A formula like 5-10-5 or 4-12-4 is well suited to most perennials. Chrysanthemums, hardy asters, and other kinds that bloom in autumn need at least three feedings.

In the interest of economy, supplementary fertilizer applied to annuals and vegetables can be scattered around the plants and watered in. (It is assumed that fertilizer was mixed with the soil at the time it was prepared for plantings.)

Flowering shrubs—including roses—and most kinds of trees can be fed in the same manner as perennials. Roses fed in late summer (after August 1) are encouraged to produce new growth, which may not harden before winter; this practice often results in winterkill.

Adding Superphosphate

In some soils, phosphorus may be lacking or unavailable to plant roots. Flowering or fruiting can be hastened by adding it to the soil in the form of superphosphate, a quick-acting fertilizer. It needs to be dug in so that it is as close as possible to the root area of the plant being fed. Use it at the rate of 3 to 5 pounds per 100 square feet.

Organic Fertilizers

The nature of manure and other organic fertilizers—as contrasted with the commercial or inorganic types—is sometimes puzzling to beginners. Organic plant foods are raw materials which become accessible to the roots of plants only with bacterial action. These include rotted manure, mushroom compost, dried manure, bone meal, cottonseed meal, dried blood, treated sewage sludge (milorganite), and others. The bacteria which break down these organic substances are low forms of plant life that become active in the soil as it warms up in the late spring. In light, sandy soils, they begin their work much sooner than in heavy, clay soils. Therefore, early applications of plant food used to stimulate growth require the use of commercial or inorganic plant foods. Where organic materials are used exclusively, they often need to be supplemented periodically with balanced commercial fertilizers, which contain all the essential nutrients required by plants.

Chemical Fertilizers

Chemical fertilizers are salts mixed with inert ingredients, which are readily absorbed by plant roots once they are in solution. In fact, they can only benefit plant growth when they are soluble, thus the need for thorough watering after applying them. When they are added to compost piles, they are absorbed by the bacteria in the pile and are returned to the decomposing matter when the bacteria themselves die. Thus, commercial fertilizer scattered in a compost pile aids in the breakdown of vegetable matter and is returned to the garden when the compost is added.

Acid-Soil Fertilizers

Ordinary types of commercial fertilizer are not suited for use around acid-loving, ericaceous plants such as rhododendrons, azaleas, pieris, blueberries, and others since the salts are inclined to produce toxic residues in the soil. Use the specially prepared acid-soil fertilizers which are generally available. These contain organic nitrogen, preferred by acid-soil plants. Cottonseed meal is also good; it is high in nitrogen with a small percentage of phosphorus and potash. When feeding broad-leaved evergreens, plant foods are best applied early in the growing season, so that new growth stimulated by feeding will have ample time to harden before cold weather sets in.

Peat Moss—Not a Fertilizer

Because peat moss is in wide use in home gardens everywhere, some beginners believe that it is a form of fertilizer. To be sure, some types may contain plant food in small amounts, but it should be considered primarily as a soil conditioner.

Foliar Feeding

Concentrated plant foods, which are readily soluble in water, have made foliar feeding a popular method of feeding certain types of plants in recent years. The liquid plant food is absorbed by the leaves and stems through tiny openings (stomata) not visible to the naked eye. These concentrates, applied with a watering can or sprayer, have merit for stimulating growth, and there is actually little waste, since the liquid which falls on the ground is absorbed by the roots. Where an immediate effect is desired, foliar feeding, although somewhat costly, produces good results. Applications are made at 10-day intervals.

17

INCREASING

YOUR PLANTS

✿✿✿ Half the fun of gardening is often derived from propagating plants to increase favorite kinds. All of the methods described in this chapter can be carried out on a small scale in the garden without special equipment. However, if a quantity of various kinds of plants are needed, more cold frames are essential for the control of light and moisture as well as winter protection for those plants propagated late in the season.

With perennials, propagation is essential, since some kinds require renewal by division every 3 to 5 years, depending on the kind and size of the plant. Some perennials tend to die out in the center as they mature, while others produce such dense masses of roots that they literally impoverish the soil in their search for nutrients. In addition to the fibrous-rooted kinds (typical of most perennials), bulbs, corms, tubers, and rhizomes also need division. Stock of scarce and expensive kinds may be multiplied in several ways.

Perennials, shrubs, trees, vines, and ground covers are increased by cuttings, division, layering, suckers, runners, grafting, and budding. Once the know-how is mastered, the procedures are easy, and the results most rewarding.

Cuttings—Increasing plants by cuttings is an easy and quick method with many kinds of annuals, perennials, and woody plants. A cutting is a segment of a plant, usually a stem or a leaf—sometimes part of a root. When removed from a parent plant and given the required medium, it produces roots. These may appear at the end of the cut stem or at nodes (points from which leaves emerge) along the stem. Amateur gardeners often refer to them as "slips." Some kinds need only water for root formation, but with most cuttings, sand, peat moss, vermiculite or shredded sphagnum moss, or mixtures of these materials are used.

Green or Softwood Cuttings. The most familiar kinds used by home gardeners are taken from tender plants such as begonias, coleus, and geraniums. Cuttings are preferred to seed for perpetuating distinct varieties, since these do not come true to seed. The growth used is referred to as half-ripened wood.

Annuals which may be propagated in this manner include: ageratum, double petunias, snapdragon, and others. Actually, the practice is not much used with annuals, except where it is desired to perpetuate a particular plant for its color and quality of bloom. Such plants are useful for late flowering in the garden or for use in window gardens.

Perennials include: alyssum, candytuft, chrysanthemums, hardy asters, phlox, and many others. Among perennials, chrysanthemums are most commonly increased in this way to obtain clean stock, since insects and diseases are often harbored in the crowns of the plants and are transmitted by division of the roots. (See Chapter 19.)

Ground Covers. Cuttings are the best method of increasing ivy, myrtle, pachysandra, wintercreeper, and other woody types in quantity.

Flowering Shrubs and Trees, Vines. Many kinds root easily and quickly, but some do not respond to this method, or the percentage of rooting is so small as not to be worthwhile. With shrubs such as roses, for example, which root easily, it is not advisable to propagate hybrid teas, floribundas, grandifloras, and large-flowering climbers from cuttings, because the root system which develops is not sufficiently vigorous to assure permanent winter hardiness in the Northeast.

This is, however, an excellent way of obtaining needed shrubs for hedges and mixed borders, particularly when budgets are limited and quantities are needed. Kinds listed under layering are best suited to that form of increase, since they either do not root readily or require a fairly long period to form roots. The following flowering shrubs are best suited for beginners.

Blue Spirea	Honeysuckle	Rose-of-Sharon
Butterfly-Bush	Hydrangea	St.-Johnswort
Deutzia	Kerria	Spirea
Forsythia	Mock-Orange	Viburnum
Glossy Abelia	Privet	Weigela

Leaf Cutting. A leaf cutting may be an entire leaf or part of a leaf with or without a portion of a stem attached. The method is used chiefly with house plants. African violets, snake plant (sansevieria), peperomia, and Rex begonias are typical examples. Although house plants are not treated in this book, the method is included here since many gardeners find it advantageous to increase their house plants in the summer months. Sometimes these are rooted in water, as with the African violet, or the leaves may be inserted in a rooting medium.

Leaf Bud. One or several buds with a portion of the stem attached are severed from a plant and handled in the same manner as a leaf cutting. Coral bells and sedum are typical examples, but most home gardeners will be able to divide these plants by obtaining divisions with roots already formed. This method is also more generally used with house plants.

Root Cutting. Some plants form new buds for reproduction from their roots. A root cutting is a segment of a root, often fleshy, inserted in a suitable medium to produce a plant. Oriental poppies, phlox, plantain-lilies, gaillardia, and other perennials are typical examples of this method.

Roots are dug in early spring (with the exception of poppies, see Chapter 3). Remove the soil by washing and cut the roots into sections 2 to 3 inches long. A mixture of equal parts sand, peat moss, and soil makes a good rooting medium. Insert with tops (widest portions) upright a half inch below the surface. When buds develop and appear above the surface, they can be transplanted (like seedlings) to rows in a nursery bed.

Rooting Media. A mixture of equal parts sand, peat moss, and soil is ideal for many kinds of cuttings. Leaf and leafbud cuttings are best rooted in a mixture of sand and vermiculite, or shredded sphagnum moss to avoid decay of fleshy parts. The mixture may be placed in pots, flats, or in the open ground. Allow for a depth of at least 3 inches.

Plant Hormones. These are chemical preparations used to induce rapid and heavy rooting. Plant hormones have proved to be invaluable for commercial purposes and home gardeners as well. They not only hasten root formation on easy-to-root kinds, but induce development on certain types of plants that are normally slow in forming roots. Yet, they are of no value on stems which are known to be non-receptive to increase by this method. The moistened stems of the cuttings are dipped in the rooting powder a half to an inch deep before inserting them in the rooting medium.

Mist Sprays. This is essentially a commercial process by which a fine mist is applied to cuttings to hasten rooting. The constant presence of moisture keeps the stems and leaves turgid, preventing wilting, and root formation is hastened.

Factors for Success with Cuttings

Softwood cuttings, the commonest kind used, are best taken when in prime condition.

Perennials. The test is growth that snaps or breaks easily when bent and is firm in substance. Select top growth about 4 inches long.

Flowering Shrubs. Softwood cuttings are made in June, selecting top growth or side shoots 4 to 6 inches long. Make all cuts with a sharp knife or shears and strip lower leaves clean, so that only a few remain at the top. If these are large, cut back a third of the foliage.

Insert stems in the medium which has been previously packed with the pressure of a brick. After inserting, firm the mixture by pressing around each cutting with the thumb and forefingers of each hand. Water and shade. The rooting mixture must be kept moist. Shading with a cloth frame prevents wilting.

Roots form within 10 to 20 days, according to the type of shrub. A wooden plant label or trowel can be used to lift one to check on root development.

Remove any leaves that drop or decay together with any cuttings that show signs of decay. Otherwise, decaying vegetation aids fungus growth, which is harmful to cuttings.

Trees. Willow is the easiest of all trees to root from cuttings at any season. These may be placed in water. Flowering dogwood, crab-apple, maples, birches, lindens, and other kinds of shade and flowering trees not usually attempted by beginners, may be rooted using this method.

Evergreens. With few exceptions, broad-leaved and needle evergreens are slow to root and require bottom heat. Most beginners will find layering an easier and surer method. Boxwood and Japanese holly are the exceptions; the former is most satisfactory and produces roots rapidly when cuttings are made of new growth in June.

Root Division. This is the quickest way to increase most perennials and those woody plants, shrubs, and vines, which produce several stems or increase naturally by means of underground stems. Dividing is usually done in spring or fall, but most plants can be divided at any time during the growing year, if given the needed care—primarily adequate watering after planting.

Perennials to be divided are dug with all their roots intact. For clumps of any size, shake the soil off the roots or wash it off with the hose. If top growth is present, cut it back half way. Depending on the type of root structure, sections may be pulled or cut apart with a sharp trowel or knife. However, if roots are heavily meshed, a sharp knife is essential to avoid splitting them and growth buds as well. Cut out all dead or decayed growth and stems, as well as damaged parts, and shorten long, stringy roots. Reset divisions in well-prepared soil as soon as possible after dividing and water thoroughly.

When perennials are divided in the fall, it is advisable to complete the job as early in the season as possible, so that the roots become established before winter. Otherwise, they tend to heave in periods of alternate thawing and freezing. For late planting, a protective mulch of marsh hay, straw, or evergreen boughs (put on after the ground has frozen) is essential.

Flowering shrubs and vines which produce an abundance of stem growth can be dug and divided in early spring or fall. Dig shrubs carefully and use a sharp spade or pruning saw to make divisions. Frequently, it is unnecessary to remove all the soil from the roots to accomplish this task. Shrubs such as bayberry, coralberry, flowering quince, inkberry, leucothoë, lilacs, shrub roses, summer sweet, and others can be increased in this way. These divisions, particularly those from the outer circle of growth, are often referred to as suckers or stolons.

Layering is a sure way to propagate plants. The process involves increase by inducing branches, brought in contact with the soil, to form roots while they are still attached to the mother plant. This is a natural method with many plants of prostrate habit, such as English ivy, and those which develop side shoots near the base. Results are more readily obtained when the soil is in good workable condition and contains sufficient organic matter and moisture to aid in development of a healthy root system.

Mound layering is effective for shrubs such as heather and cinquefoil, which produce many stems from the ground level. A mixture of moist sand and peat moss is heaped up around the crown of the plant to a height of 3 or 4 inches. Roots form along the covered portion of the stems. These may be cut and planted when roots have developed a half to three-quarters of an inch in length.

Air Layering. This is an ancient Chinese method of propagating new plants from "leggy" specimens (long stems) with good top growth (such as house plants) and certain woody plants, which are difficult by other methods. Select the stem or stems to be layered. Make a diagonal slit or cut in the stem extending a third of the way through. Insert (upward) a tiny bit of wood to keep the wound open, then dust the opening with a rooting powder. Cover the cut area with a ball of moist sphagnum moss, 2 to 3 inches thick and slightly longer. Wrap it with polyethelene, holding it in place with string. When roots penetrate the moss, they can be seen through the polyethelene, indicating that the rooted portion may be removed for planting. Water thoroughly after planting and keep shaded for a few days until it is well established. Rhododendrons, azaleas, and most kinds of trees, shrubs, and vines can be increased in this way.

Grafting. The union of two plants, usually woody, by joining the cut surface of a stem with another to which roots are attached is known as grafting. The plant which results from this union has a top or scion of a selected variety and an understock of sturdy rooting habit, which may be similar in kind or a related plant. For example: a named variety of lilac or rhododendron may be grafted on a common species of the same plant. Lilacs are sometimes grafted on privet.

There are many variations of the process including bark, bridge, cleft, or ship grafting.

Grafting requires considerable skill and care to produce a

satisfactory union, but the principles involved are simple. Few beginners are likely to attempt this method of propagation. However, a knowledge of the procedure helps in the care and maintenance of grafted plants in the home garden.

This process assures a sturdy rootstock for greater hardiness than the variety itself may possess, due to difficulty or slowness of increase by other methods. It is also a method by which plants of formal upright or pendulous form may be developed quickly. With fruits, it is a means of dwarfing or controlling growth, as well as the usual procedure by which fruit trees are produced commercially.

Evergreens and various types of ornamental trees, flowering shrubs, and some vines are increased in this way. Evidence of the graft union is noticeable on the stem near the soil level or, in the case of pendulous growth, where the weeping stems originate on the trunk. Part of the maintenance includes a close watch for growth which may develop from the understock.

Bud Grafting. Rose varieties are increased by bud grafting. The understock may be any one of several species (or wild) roses, raised from seed to produce sturdy tops and vigorous roots. The tops are cut back, and a bud of a named variety is inserted in the bark of the selected understock and tied in place. When the bud unites with the cambium layer under the bark of the rootstock, it puts forth growth, developing into one of several stems. All other top growth is cut back and, after two years, it becomes a salable plant.

Suckers. Woody plants which spread by underground stems send up stems which produce leaves and eventually flower. Commonly referred to as suckers, these are usually dug out or cut back to induce older wood to flower. The lilac, the coralberry, inkberry, and summer sweet, are typical examples. When named varieties of lilacs are grown on their own roots (rather than on grafted stock), they may be increased by digging out the suckers and replanting them in new locations. The other shrubs mentioned may be increased in the same manner. A sharp spade is used to sever the suckers, obtaining as much root as possible. Use a sharp spade to sever them from the clumps and dig deeply enough to obtain a good root system.

Stolon. Stems which tend to grow downward from a plant and take root when they make contact with the soil are known as stolons.

Examples: Forsythia—especially the weeping forms—jasmine, and other woody vines with arching or pendulum branches have this habit of reproduction.

Runner. A stem of woody plants or a perennial which lies on the ground and produces roots.

Examples: English ivy, many kinds of woody vines.

When cuttings are made, they are best taken from plants growing in soil that is moist rather than dry. If necessary, water the parent plants thoroughly and allow them to dry off before making cuttings.

Temperature. For rooting cuttings in the garden, late spring or early summer are ideal times.

Moisture. The rooting medium must not be allowed to dry out. Keep it moist, but not waterlogged. In hot weather, tops may need to be sprinkled daily to prevent wilting. A shaded location or shade provided by a simple frame covered with burlap or cloth is essential.

Ten-year-old rock-spray cotoneaster used as specimen plant

The double form of the double-file viburnum is horizontal in habit

Approach planting comprised of mountain laurel, holly, cotoneaster, and pachysandra

Hinoki cypress contrasts with low hollies and rose daphne

Dwarf mugo pine, an ideal evergreen for rock gardens

Dwarf Alberta spruce is compact and very slow growing

Pink flowering dogwood, edged with a border of pachysandra

Japanese or Kousa dogwood flowers in June

White flowering Sargent crab-apple has a spreading habit

Saucer or soulangeana magnolia blooms when very small

Doorway of a charming house is framed with wisteria and pieris

Borders of petunias add sparkle to a modest house

Needle and broad-leaved evergreens offer variety in texture and form

An apple tree shades the terrace of a small city garden

Small house is pleasingly framed by trees and low shrubs

Wood chips mulch controls weeds and retains moisture

18

USING MULCHES

TO ADVANTAGE

❧❧❧ The beginning gardener often indulges his enthusiasm for a season or two before discovering the value and importance of mulches. However, it requires only a year of dry weather and water shortages to convince him of their merit. Mulching means *furnishing a protective cover*—preferably with some type of organic material—*for the soil around and between plants in beds and borders,* including flower, vegetable, and fruit plantings. It is a practice gardeners have adapted from Nature's way of forming a protective carpet on bare ground. Naturally formed mulches are composed of leaves, needles from evergreens, fruits, seed pods, bits of wood, twigs, bark, and various kinds of decaying plant life. Ground cover plants discussed in Chapter 11 serve a similar purpose.

Among the materials commonly used by gardeners are peat moss, buckwheat hulls, sawdust, rotted manure, wood chips, chopped bark, oak leaves, pine needles, and others discussed in this chapter. Some have greater merit than others, and few gardeners would have the opportunity or the need to utilize all of them. A few are man-made such as aluminum foil, black plastic film, and tarpaper, but these are of small importance to most home gardeners.

Mulches keep the soil temperature even at all seasons, conserve soil moisture, allow moisture to enter the soil easily and efficiently, eliminating run off. They reduce the growth of weeds and make it easier to pull out those that appear. These materials eliminate the necessity for cultivation by preventing the formation of soil crust. Chopped bark, wood chips, well-aged sawdust, buckwheat hulls, peat moss, and others are neat in appearance and contribute to the eye appeal of a planting. Erosion control is another prime-value asset of mulches on sloping ground. They are essential to keep strawberries clean. Also, mulching newly set plants and those already established is an easy and effective way to provide organic matter, thus improving soil texture. To be effective over an extended period of time, a mulch must be maintained continually. By constantly adding organic debris to the existing mulch layer, the vital topsoil in a garden is benefited by the nutrients which leach into it as the organic material breaks down.

What to use for a mulch depends primarily on the type of area to be covered, what is available, the cost involved, and the desired result. When large areas need to be covered, the item of cost must be kept in mind, as well as the amount of preparation required to use the mulch. For example, a goodly number of mulching materials remove existing nitrogen from the soil as they break down. However, once deterioration is complete, the nitrogen cycle is reversed, and this essential plant food is released to the soil, becoming available to the roots of plants as they need it.

To compensate for the loss of nitrogen in soils where such mulches as sawdust, wood chips, chopped bark, grass clippings, straw, hay, corncobs, and various kinds of hulls are used, apply a complete fertilizer such as 10-6-4 to the soil before the mulch is put on, using 2 to 3 pounds per 100 square feet. Some gardeners mix nitrate of soda or ammonium sulfate with these materials before they are spread. To each cubic yard of mulch applied, add 1½ pounds of ammonium nitrate or ammonium sulfate or 3 pounds of nitrate of soda. If organic materials are preferred, use 5 pounds of dried blood or hoof and horn meal.

Feeding plants before any type of mulch is applied, especially in large areas, is another point to consider. If fertilizer is applied before the mulch is put on, time and labor are saved. Actually, the best time to mulch new plantings is immediately after they are planted. However, if plants are partially or well established and mulches are needed to control weeds and conserve moisture, these are best put on in early spring when the plants are beginning their growth and before weed seeds have germinated.

How much mulch to use must also be considered. If not put on thick enough, a mulch will not accomplish its intended purposes. Tests have proved that mulches applied 2 to 3 inches deep actually insulate the soil, a point of vital importance where summers are exceptionally hot and dry and, particularly, in seaside gardens where wind is a constant factor. In addition, it should be remembered that many plants have comparatively shallow root systems. With some plants, roots do not penetrate more than 6 to 12 inches below the soil and others extend only 1 to 2 inches deep. When adequately mulched, these plants thrive. To be effective, loose materials such as straw, hay, and the like need to be 2 to 3 inches deep; others that pack down easily are applied to a depth of 1½ inches.

In selecting a mulch the problem of fire hazard needs consideration. Straw, hay, peat moss, wood chips, and many other desirable mulches burn readily when dry—a point to remember when working with them.

The following list is sizable, since practically all the materials in use are included. Some are of regional importance because of their availability in quantity at low cost. High transportation costs make it uneconomical to use certain mulches in areas where the supply is scarce, but most home gardeners soon learn to locate sources of the most desirable kinds at moderate cost.

Before applying any type of mulch, the area to be covered needs a thorough weeding and leveling of the soil, followed by a thorough soaking. Then scatter a light sprinkling of fertilizer over the surface of the soil. After the mulch has been spread, it may need raking or leveling for even coverage. Keep mulch away from the stems of woody plants at ground level to eliminate decay caused by wet mulch and rodent damage in winter. Apply mulch as soon as the area can be readied in spring or at any time during the growing season, and replenish it as materials become available.

Alfalfa Hay. See Hay.

Bark: Chopped or Shredded. Derived from sawmills, the bark of hemlock, pine, spruce, and other trees, with a little birch mixed in, is shredded and composted for several years before it is sold. It makes an excellent mulch and, where available at moderate cost, it may be used to advantage throughout the garden. Unlike redwood bark, this material breaks down rapidly and needs partial replenishing every two years. It is an excellent and efficient source of organic material for building soil.

Black Plastic Film. As with aluminum foil and tarpaper, black plastic film is used commercially and, while most effective, not always easy to handle or attractive in home gardens.

Buckwheat Hulls (Mul-tex is the trade name) rates high as an ideal mulch, particularly for roses. The one objection to this material—if large quantities are needed—is its cost, but, the dark brown color and its light weight make buckwheat hulls a joy to handle. It absorbs little or no moisture from the ground, allows rain and water from sprinklers to penetrate easily. Rich in organic content, it decomposes slowly. Buckwheat hulls have no apparent effect on nitrogen depreciation in the soil. Gardeners who have used this mulch for years simply add more each year, keeping the thickness to 1½ inches with amazingly good results. Not suited to exposed areas because it is sufficiently light in weight to blow away easily, this mulch is also not practical on sloping ground.

Burlap has value for temporary effects, as in seeding lawns on flat or sloping surfaces.

Cocoa Shells have been used extensively in the gardens at Hershey, Pennsylvania, and elsewhere in areas close to chocolate factories. The hulls of the cocoa bean make a coarse-looking but effective dark brown mulch which turns black as the hulls age. Because they tend to cake and form a mold when used alone, sawdust is added for greater effectiveness. (One-third sawdust to two-thirds cocoa shells). The hulls add nitrogen to the soil as well as humus, and the chocolate odor usually disappears a week or so after spreading. They are slimy when wet and absorb considerable heat, so keep them away from tree trunks and the bases of shrubs.

Compost from a homemade pile is useful, but few gardeners have enough to spare for covering areas of any great size. Likewise, composted manure is desirable but usually scarce.

Corncobs, Ground, serve in areas where they are plentiful such as the Midwest. As with sawdust, nitrogen must be added to the soil before the mulch is applied. Also the soil needs a thorough soaking before the dry mulch is put on. A cover 2 to 3 inches thick is applied, avoiding close contact with the stems of plants. Fertilizing and watering of mulched areas are accomplished easily.

Cottonseed Hulls. Like peanut shells, ground corncobs, cocoa shells, and other regional materials, the hulls of cotton seed make a useful, inexpensive cover.

Cranberry Vines, sometimes offered commercially as Cran-mulch, are used for winter mulch on Cape Cod and in areas to which they can be shipped at reasonable cost. The material, handled in bales, is easy to spread, making a most attractive and effective form of winter cover for perennials and shrubs.

Crushed Stone, pebbles, stone chips, and washed gravel give a certain finish and pattern, as well as contrast to plantings. These materials are well suited to tailored gardens where flat areas need mulch. When subtle color effects are desired, colored gravel may be obtained. If light colored or white chips or pebbles are used, the harsh effects can be softened by the planting of ivy or some other trailing plant, which breaks the surface and makes a pleasing kind of tracery. These materials provide a means for achieving unusual patterned effects, but require sturdy dividers between mulched areas and sod; otherwise loose stones may cause serious damage to lawn mowers.

Dust Mulch is the result of loosening the soil with a scuffle hoe or cultivator to form a layer of dust which discourages shallow rooted weeds and keeps the soil beneath from drying out.

Evergreen Boughs are used as a winter mulch to keep soil temperature even, thus preventing the heaving of shallow rooted plants. This type of cover provides shade for evergreens, the foliage of which is often damaged by winter sun.

Grass Clippings are sometimes used; however, they are not particularly pleasing in appearance and break down so rapidly that considerable quantities are needed to make an adequate soil cover. During moist, humid weather they give off an unpleasant odor as they decay as well as pulling needed nitrogen out of the soil—a point to be remembered. Once decomposed, however, they add vitally important organic material to the soil. A layer 2 inches deep that has been mixed with peat moss or some other mulch material is essential if grass clippings are to be effective.

Gravel, Screened. Use like pebbles (See Crushed Stone).

Hay. Various kinds, including clover and alfalfa, afford good cover for soil but break down rapidly, adding nitrogen to the soil. Apply nitrogen fertilizer to the soil before spreading. Hay is best suited for fruit trees, grapes, strawberries, and vegetable and shrub plantings (where appearance is not a prime factor).

Hay, Marsh. See Salt Marsh Hay.

Hops, Spent, make a good fireproof soil cover, sometimes available for the hauling, but they have an objectionable odor. This may not be offensive if the material is used away from the house or sitting-out area.

Lawn Clippings. See Grass Clippings.

Leaf Mold in various stages of decomposition is a good and useful mulch. In its coarser forms, it can be used on slopes, especially if mixed with the surface layer of soil. Spread it at least 1½ inches deep. Unfortunately, it is seldom in plentiful supply, since most gardeners use it to improve soil.

Manure. Well-rotted stable manure and spent mushroom compost are ideal for level ground or easy slopes. These materials have the advantage of supplying plant food as well, but they are not easily obtainable everywhere.

Mushroom Compost. See Manure.

Oak and Beech Leaves are a natural mulch for acid-soil plants. They break down slowly, have strong eye appeal, and are ideal for naturalistic settings. Use them 2 to 3 inches deep around rhododendrons, azaleas, and other ericaceous plants.

Peanut Hulls. Like ground corncobs, peanut hulls are used in regions where they are plentiful. They break down adding humus to the soil, but are coarse in appearance. Covering with a layer of pine needles greatly enhances their appearance.

Peat Moss is easy to handle and obtain; cover should be at least an inch deep. The coarse, brown peat sold in bales (usually imported), derived from sphagnum moss, makes a satisfactory cover. However, it tends to cake when the top surface dries. This condition may be overcome by mixing soil, pine needles, or chopped bark with it. Peat from local bogs is often more desirable, since it is finer in texture and often can be obtained at moderate cost if purchased in quantity. Actually, the finer grades of peat are easier to spread than the sphagnum type (which is fibrous in texture), and they are also easier to soak. Peat absorbs ten times its weight in water, and this point should be borne in mind when applying it. Never spread bone-dry peat on soil as a much or incorporate it with fairly dry soil, since dry peat tends to pull the moisture from the soil with which it comes in contact.

Pebbles. See Crushed Stone.

Pine Needles, when obtainable, are the best of mulches for acid-soil plants, particularly the various types of broad-leaved and needle evergreens. This kind of cover is always good to look at and allows moisture to penetrate easily. If the mulch can be applied thickly enough, it can be used on fairly steep slopes. Two inches of cover are desirable.

Plastic Film. See Black Plastic Film.

Redwood Bark and composted bark are readily available. This material is not blown away by wind, allows water to penetrate easily, breaks down slowly, and is dark in color. Nitrogen is sometimes included in packaging; otherwise, it must be added as previously mentioned. (Coconut and yucca fiber are also considered useful mulches on the West Coast.)

Salt Marsh Hay is primarily a winter mulch, spread after the ground has frozen to protect perennials, rock plants, and roses. It may be used to good advantage for strawberries, vegetables, or among shrubs. As it rots, it provides organic matter for the soil. Although fine-textured as contrasted with straw, it is not pleasing in tailored plantings of perennials and annuals. For winter protection, it is ideal and easy to handle. In spring it can be raked and used for the purposes suggested as a summer mulch.

Sawdust makes a practical mulch and is being more widely used by home gardeners throughout the country. Usually it is obtainable for the hauling from any local sawmill. The coarse grade is preferable, because it does not pack together and crust as quickly. The use of nitrogen, as discussed in the beginning of this chapter, is essential. Fresh sawdust is apt to be unsightly when first applied because of its light coloring. However, it can be piled and allowed to weather before using, or it can be mixed with soil. Sawdust does not blow around easily and does not absorb moisture from the soil like dry peat. It allows the rain to penetrate, and it is gradually added to the soil as it deteriorates. If applied at least 1½ inches deep, it controls weeds satisfactorily and functions as a useful mulch.

Seaweed, kelp, and eel grass are sometimes applied, as gathered, for winter mulch in seaside gardens. These materials are untidy for summer use in plantings close to dwellings, but make excellent materials for coarse compost.

Shavings from the carpenter's bench or sawmill used alone are light in weight and of little value, unless mixed with wood chips.

Spent Hops. See Hops, Spent.

Stone Chips are particularly appropriate and practical in rock gardens, especially when they are exposed to wind. Peat moss is actually harmful to most alpines, a fact which some gardeners learn too late. Actually, many of the choicest alpine plants grown in American rock gardens are afforded the best kind of prolonged life in summer and winter with the use of a stone-chip mulch.

Straw, provided that it is free of seed, and salt marsh hay are adaptable and practical for large surfaces and sloping areas where erosion is a factor. However, these materials are fire hazards. As with sawdust, add fertilizer to the soil before the hay or straw is used.

Tarpaper. See Black Plastic Film.

Tobacco Stems, available in areas where tobacco is raised, serve for perennials and shrubs. Their nicotine content is a repellent to many kinds of insects. Avoid using tobacco stems in conjunction with tulips, lilies, and tomatoes, since the stems may transmit mosaic disease.

Walnut Shells, particularly those of the black walnut, are sometimes used where available. They break down slowly and make an attractive appearance.

Wood Chips make an excellent mulch for permanent use, because they are slow to deteriorate. The particles vary in size, allowing water to penetrate the soil easily. Although light in color when applied, this material weathers in appearance as it ages, and its rough texture is pleasing to the eye. Apply it at least an inch deep. When new, it can be darkened by scattering a thin cover of peat, pine needles, or soil over it. Wood chips, sometimes

composted, are available from garden centers and nurseries. Arborists and
municipal tree departments are excellent sources, since practically all of
them use chipping machines to reduce the bulk of cut branches. Leaves and
twigs make the mixture coarse at first, but it soon breaks down. Truckloads
are often available at small cost.

19

CONTROLLING
PESTS AND DISEASES

❦❦❦ Pests and diseases that attack garden plants are more prevalent some seasons than others. They need not plague the beginner, if control measures are taken as soon as they are discovered. These pests have always been with us, and the chances are that they are here to stay. Undoubtedly, Adam and Eve knew the tribulations of bugs and blights. One noted entomologist delights in recalling a passage from Joel 1:4: "That which the palmerworm hath left hath the locust eaten; and that which the locust hath left hath the cankerworm eaten; and that which the cankerworm hath left hath the caterpillar eaten."

Quotations from the Bible offer little consolation when Japanese beetles descend in great numbers on your favorite plants. Control of garden pests has been made comparatively simple in recent years with the appearance of all-purpose sprays and dusts. These are available in many forms, including aerosol types which are easy to apply. For over-all spraying, attachments made for the garden hose (hose-end sprayers) assure the gardener of adequate coverage with little effort, providing water pressure is adequate.

Instructions are carefully printed on insecticide containers, and materials should be used precisely as directed. Since many spray materials are highly toxic, they must be kept out of reach of children.

Birds and Friendly Insects

Not all the insects that we see in the garden are harmful, but would that there were more friendly ones to help in checking those that ravage our plants.

Birds. Berry-bearing shrubs, bird feeders, and bird baths help to attract birds to a garden, and every effort should be made to encourage their presence since they eat quantities of insects in various stages of development.

Fireflies. On summer nights fireflies, appear in many gardens. Like the ladybug and the praying mantis, this insect is one of the gardener's best friends. It eats tiny pests of various kinds, as well as snails, slugs, and cutworms, in addition to making its presence welcome by a streak of light in the dusk.

243

Ladybugs. Rejoice when you see ladybugs, for they live on the various kinds of aphids or plant lice, mealy bugs, and tiny-scale insects that appear on the stems and leaves of practically all kinds of plants. Several California firms advertise them for sale.

Praying mantis. It resembles a giant grasshopper, is light green in color, and often blends with the surrounding foliage. It poses motionless among plants and waits patiently for its victims. While waiting for his prey, it secures itself firmly and holds arm-like tentacles upward as if in prayer, hence the common name. Actually, the praying mantis should be known as the *preying* mantis, for it preys on a wide variety of injurious insects, ranging from aphids to various kinds of beetles and flies.

Eliminate Breeding Places for Pests

Maintaining order and neatness on the home grounds by clearing away debris frequently helps to eliminate breeding places for various kinds of pests. Areas where trash containers are kept—particularly if adjacent to compost piles—or where peat moss, soil, sand, pots, stones, bricks, or lumber may be stored are likely breeding places for earwigs, slugs, and other pests. Burn or dispose carefully of all disease- and insect-ridden vegetation gathered from plantings, woody stems removed in pruning, as well as discarded plants.

Some Common Pests and Diseases

The pests discussed here are the kinds most likely to be encountered in the average garden. No attempt is made in this brief chapter to describe all of the common plant pests and diseases. Rather the presentation is aimed at describing typical kinds and how to control them.

Insects are divided into two broad groups; those that chew leaves, stems, flowers, and roots, and those that suck juices from growth. Chewing insects—which include beetles, cutworms, caterpillars, grasshoppers, grubs, slugs, and others—are controlled by stomach poisons. Sucking kinds—aphids, lacebugs, leafhoppers, mites, scale insects, and others—are controlled only with contact insecticides. Stomach poisons have no effect on this group.

Diseases that affect garden flowers include anthracnose, black-spot, botrytis blight, crown rot, damping off, fireblight, leafspot, mildew, rust, and wilt. Some occur during prolonged seasons of damp weather when temperatures are high; others during prolonged dry spells. Poor air circulation in enclosed areas is also a factor. Various fungicides are used to check these diseases with good results. However, garden sanitation is also sound practice. It is often safer and easier to dig up and burn one or more badly diseased plants than to run the risk of spreading the disease to nearby healthy specimens. Winds scatter disease spores quickly —a point to remember.

Ants on Peonies and Roses. Although their appearance is often disturbing, ants do little damage, since they are seeking the sweet secretions given off by the buds or by aphids often found on the buds.

Aphids. These tiny, sucking insects attack the new growth of practically all types of plants from the tallest tree to the smallest annual. Some seasons they are more annoying than others. When they appear in great numbers, they considerably weaken new growth by sucking the sap, often disfiguring foliage, fruit, and flowers. Furthermore, aphids spread diseases. Control with contact sprays.

Bagworms. Early spring is the time to look for bagworms on such evergreens as junipers, cedars, arborvitae, larch, hemlock, spruce, and pines. Brownish in color, they look like tiny, elongated bags. Since they harbor eggs of ravaging caterpillars, they should be cut off and burned in late spring.

Birch-Leaf-Miner. See Leaf-Miner.

Borers in Trees and Shrubs. Evidence of borers in dogwood, lilacs, birch, as well as many kinds of evergreens, shade trees, and flowering shrubs is usually detected by tiny piles of sawdust at the base of the plant, or particles adhering to the bark. Use a flexible wire and work it into the hole as far as you can push it, then plug holes with borer paste or coarse soap so that additional eggs cannot be laid by flying insects.

Brown Canker. See Chapter 8.

Capterpillar Nests. These appear as cobwebby masses in the crotches of apples, cherries, and crab-apples and should be destroyed before they hatch. In suburban areas, examine wild cherries, which are favorite nesting trees for the webbed caterpillar—a most annoying and destructive pest, if not checked. Nests in high branches can be torched out with a long pole.

Cinch Bugs. See Chapter 15.

Cutworms are an annual plague in many home gardens, and spraying does not always do the job. The soil can be treated with Chlordane before young plants are set out, or poison bait may be used where the infestation is serious. Since poison bait can be harmful to children and animals, its use is not always advisable.

Cyclamen Mite. Delphiniums are particularly subject to infection from the cyclamen mite, which causes the leaves to curl and become distorted, and the lower stems to turn black. Spray with a miticide such as aramite, making sure to hit the undersides of the leaves and the crowns of the plants, where these tiny black pests congregate. If choice delphiniums are being grown and only a few are infected, dig up and burn the infected plants and spray the remaining ones.

Earthworms. See Chapter 1.

Earwigs. The European earwig, which looks like a water bug on springs with long, pincer-like appendages at its tail, moves rapidly indoors or out. In addition to being repulsive in appearance, it is an omnivorous eater of plants. Furthermore, this pest is easily transported indoors on flowers, clothing, or on any article momentarily left on the ground. Once inside, earwigs may be found around the kitchen sink, in the bathroom, or even in beds and overstuffed furniture.

One of its most annoying characteristics is the tendency to hide during the sunny hours of the day, becoming active in the early morning and evening hours. It feeds on most flowering plants, many kinds of vegetables, and also attacks fruits.

Earwigs can be controlled with poison bait scattered in beds and borders, using an ounce of Paris green to each pound of moistened crumbs. Several insecticides can be used for control. Among these are DDT and Chlordane, both available either in powder or liquid form. Use according to instructions on the container. Any control measure is best applied before the earwigs are fully developed, usually from early to mid-June. Spray around the foundations of buildings, under shrubs, near compost piles, or wherever there is decayed vegetable matter for these insects to eat.

Elm-Bark Beetles. To check the ravages of these pests, which spread the deadly Dutch elm disease, spray thoroughly with DDT in early spring before the buds begin to swell. Early spraying checks the beetles before they penetrate the bark. For trees more than 10 to 12 feet tall, this is a job for a tree surgeon and is well worth the cost. Urging your neighbors who have elms to do likewise is good community effort for checking the ravages of this serious disease.

Fireblight. A disease that attacks cotoneasters, hawthorns, pears, crab-apples, and other members of the rose family, it is easily recognized by darkened stems with a burned look, dieback, and defoliation of the infected parts. Cut and burn diseased parts immediately and sterilize the pruning shears after using to avoid spreading.

Holly-Leaf-Miner. See Leaf-Miner.

Iris Borers become active in early summer. If iris foliage looks sickly or flower stems topple, examine the stems or roots (rhizomes) at once for these pests. Use a sharp knife to remove the offender and cut out all soft growth. Dust wounds with sulfur.

Japanese Beetle. See Chapter 15.

Lacebugs attack rhododendrons, azaleas, and other broad-leaved evergreens during late spring. These are tiny insects approximately an eighth of an inch long and are so-called because of lace-like wings. Evidence of lacebug damage is indicated by a mottled, grayish appearance on the upper sides of the leaves. Usually they are most troublesome to plants in full sun. Spray with malathion, hitting both sides of the leaves. For heavy infestations, several sprayings may be necessary.

Lawn Pests and Diseases. See Chapter 15.

Leaf-Hopper. See Chapter 8.

Leaf-Miner. Birch and holly are two of a number of woody plants the leaves of which are punctured by the sawfly. Disfiguring is conspicuous. Spray with malathion in May, when these insects are emerging and laying eggs. With birches, second and third broods occur 8 and 10 weeks after the first. Spraying is repeated.

Mildew. See Chapter 8.

Red Spider. A tiny mite known as red spider attacks all kinds of evergreens—particularly spruce and junipers, causing the needles to turn brown—and such broad-leaved types as azaleas, rhododendrons, and others, giving the under surface of the foliage a rusty appearance. Red spider is found also on the undersides of the leaves of annuals, perennials, and flowering shrubs; it causes rose foliage to turn yellow and drop. Few gardeners have ever seen a red spider, because it takes 50 of them, stretched end to end, to cover an inch of a ruler. When infection is suspected, test by placing a piece of white paper under the foliage and rub your hands on the under surface. The tiny mites look like specks of red dust.

Where infestations on evergreens are light, the cobwebby nests made by these pests can be washed away easily by a strong hose spray, a practice to be followed every few days. However, to control these pests where infestation is serious, use a miticide. Follow application instructions carefully, and be sure to hit the undersides of the foliage where these pests tend to nest.

Rose Chafer and *Rose Midge.* See Chapter 8.

Scale. The commonest and most annoying scale insect is the euonymus scale, which commonly attacks wintercreeper (euonymus), pachysandra, and other broad-leaved evergreens. This encrusting insect collects along the stems and on the undersides of leaves. Apply a dormant oil spray in early spring, coating the infected areas thoroughly; where infection is heavy, spray later with malathion when the tiny pests begin to crawl. If only small areas are infected, branches or stems can be cut out and burned. Without control, this pest causes serious damage. Various kinds of scale which attack other shrubs such as lilacs are similarly controlled.

Slugs nest under boards and debris around compost piles and other parts of the garden where it is damp. Remove litter where they nest, and spread lime around plants where slugs are numerous. They cannot crawl over it without injury.

Sod Webworm. See Chapter 15.

Tent Caterpillar. See Caterpillar.

Termites. See Chapter 15.

Thrips. See Gladiolus, Chapter 5 and Roses, Chapter 8.

Wasps. See Chapter 15.

20

PRUNING

❦❦❦ The primary purpose of pruning woody plants is to keep them in vigorous growth, improve their appearance, and control the space they require or the area available. This practice not only increases flowering and fruiting habits, but prolongs the life of trees, shrubs, and vines. The removal of dead, diseased, and damaged growth is also part of the why of pruning. The term *pruning* as used here refers to the cutting of growth for the purposes mentioned. In contrast, the terms *trim, shear,* and *clip* describe the types of cutting commonly performed to give shrubs and hedges a neat outward appearance. Yet, pruning shears can be a dangerous weapon in the hands of those who use them thoughtlessly. Actually, the basic principles involved are simple and, once understood, easy to practice. Such descriptive phrases as "whiffle-cuts" and "shear horrors" describe only too well much of the present-day pruning done by untrained landscape service and maintenance crews and amateur gardeners as well.

For decades, hedges, flowering shrubs, and evergreens have been butchered and barbered into grotesque shapes, patterned somewhat after the topiary of Old World gardens, but often lacking completely the imagination, skill, and placement which made the art of topiary a kind of living sculpture. Certain types of houses call for formal planting, and in such locations clipped shrubbery—particularly evergreen—has a distinct place. Formally trimmed hedges also are highly ornamental and add greatly to the beauty of a tailored landscape planting. However, shrubs sheared formally, either as specimens or hedges, should be handled with the idea of encouraging new growth all the way to the ground. All too often, the tendency is to trim them wider at the top than at the base, causing the lower branches to die out. The effect is a leggy, unsightly mass of foliage, often top heavy.

In an attempt to control the growth of big-scale evergreens, they are frequently sheared and barbered until only the outer tier of growth is green, while all the branches within the framework are brown and bare. Severe drought, a heavy infestation of insects, or the damage created by low temperatures during an unusually severe winter are causes of dead growth, which fre-

252 ❦ GARDENING FOR BEGINNERS

quently appear in large patches on mature evergreens that have
been tightly sheared. The result is an unsightly effect, and often
these shrubs are fit only for the rubbish pile.

Retaining Natural Form

On the other hand, the pruning shears in the hands of the
thoughtful gardener can be used skillfully to thin dense growth,
emphasize the significant lines and shape of a tree or shrub and,
generally speaking, retain its natural aspect, whether pyramidal,
global, or columnar. The distinct forms of Japanese holly (*Ilex
crenata*), when allowed to grow naturally, typically develop
mound shapes. Certain arborvitaes have a definite globular habit
of growth, while others are columnar in form. Many of the
evergreen azaleas are compact in habit, mound-like, and low
spreading by nature. Such shrubs as these require only light
pruning annually. It is done by shortening new growth to retain
the typical form, but allowing the entire surface to remain fluffy
and irregular. To trim shrubs of this sort by close shearing them
is to detract greatly from their natural beauty.

Pruning Tools

Use sharp shears or a saw to make clean cuts, and be sure that
the blade of the shears you use is adequate for the size branch
you attempt to cut. Long-handled pruners are used for big-scale
shrubs and trees which produce heavy wood. Several "handy-to-
use" types of pruning saws are sold in hardware stores and
garden centers. These are comparatively inexpensive and most
practical for cutting big branches, since they have interchange-
able blades in several sizes. For removing tree limbs out of
normal reach, there are pole pruners and pole saws. Keep tools
clean, well oiled, and sharp, and have a convenient place for
storing them.

Using Tree Paint

When sizable branches (more than three-quarters of an inch
in diameter) are removed from trees or shrubs, wounds should

be treated with tree paint which can be applied by using one of the new aerosol type sprays. These are most efficient and easy to use, since none of the paint is wasted and spraying covers the surface evenly. If moisture is present on exposed surfaces after cuts have been made, allow it to drain away before applying tree paint.

Forsythia—Right and Wrong

Forsythia is often a victim of unfortunate treatment. It has a natural fountain-like, vase-shaped form. Some types are stiffer and more upright than others, and a few are notably pendulous. With either type, there is distinct grace and beauty in the appearance of a well-grown specimen of forsythia that has been pruned to preserve its natural habit. Most kinds reach a height of 8 or 9 feet when mature, often spreading even wider than their height. Frequently, the space required may be greater than is desired. However, by shortening the individual stems and branches to the desired size, the entire shrub can be kept within bounds. Branches need to be cut back at varying lengths, while preserving the typical character of the growth. In the process, some of the old growth should be removed entirely from the base. The time to prune forsythia is after flowering.

What happens when a forsythia is trimmed in geometric fashion? In summer it looks like a green ball, pyramid, or block, whereas in winter it has the appearance of a bunch of ugly sticks. The same is true of spirea, flowering quince, mock-orange, and any number of the other flowering shrubs, trimmed or sheared (not pruned) in this manner.

Basic Rules for Shrubs

A basic rule in pruning most flowering shrubs is to remove the oldest stems at the ground level to encourage new growth from the base. The ideal time to prune is immediately after flowering. However, there are times when pruning must be done during the dormant season, and some flower buds are bound to be cut away. Sometimes new growth or lateral branches are awkward in habit, or they detract from the symmetry of the plants. These need to be removed, together with all dead, diseased, and weak growth; branches that rub against one another; and gnarled wood. Then the growth of the remaining branches is shortened individually, all the while bearing in mind the natural habit and form of the shrub being pruned.

Actually, few plants grow in perfect symmetry without some manipulation by the gardener, but within the structure of any well-grown shrub or tree, there exists a basic symmetry of form that can be followed after a little study.

Since most beginners are a bit wary about pruning shrubs as drastically as is often essential, the following procedure may prove helpful. First, remove less of each branch than is desired; pull out or "tuck under" the branch to be removed before actually cutting. Then, stand back and observe the effect before you cut. In most cases, it is best to make two cuts rather than one drastic move; thereby, not eliminating an important, irreplaceable branch.

Pruning Shade and Flowering Trees

Flowering and shade trees often need pruning to improve form, as well as to remove lower branches and those damaged by insects and weather. If stems are unusually large, several sectional cuts may be required. Remember that the final cut should be made flush with the main trunk, taking care not to skin the bark as the limb is severed. Any damage that occurs to the bark surface should be trimmed clean and painted. Where large trees are involved, the job is more wisely and safely handled by a skilled arborist, who is experienced at climbing and is usually attended by a competent helper.

Handling Lilacs

Lilacs are often disappointing in the bloom they produce, even after they have reached a fair size. Many times, this condition is the result of allowing too many suckers to develop at the base. When these suckers develop in quantity, the large flowering stems do not produce the bloom which should be normally expected of them. Therefore, keep lilacs clean at the base, if free-blooming plants are desired. With neglect, old growth may become borer-ridden, and this should be entirely removed. Then, too, lilacs are often allowed to grow taller than is desirable. Reducing height involves drastic cutting which is best done immediately after flowering.

Rejuvenating Old Shrubs

Through neglect, shrubs often become decrepit and over-grown. The question often arises "Shall they be removed or replaced?" In many instances, they can be revived by judicious pruning. First remove the least desirable growth. Considerable thinning may be required, and the immediate result may be a mere skeleton, but this is often the treatment needed for renewal. When the operation is done in early spring, new growth quickly transforms the appearance of such a bare shrub. Feeding and watering after pruning will stimulate growth. Practically all flowering shrubs that lose their leaves in winter respond to this treatment. Examples include:

Beauty-Bush	Honeysuckle	Rose-of-Sharon
Deutzia	Kerria	Shrub Roses
Firethorn	Lilacs	Viburnums
Flowering Quince	Mock-Orange	Weigela
Forsythia	Privet	Winged Euonymus

Pruning and Topping

Evergreens—particularly yews and rhododendrons—are often victims of bad pruning. But it is an easy matter to study their natural habit of growth and cut here and there to check rampant growth, at the same time preserving the natural appearance of the plant.

In controlling the height of evergreens, small flowering trees, and big-scale shrubs, "topping" is often necessary to retain good scale in a planting. One or more leader branches may need to be cut. Then several side-growing branches will develop. These, in turn, need to be "headed back," as the expression goes. This type of pruning, done frequently, controls growth effectively.

Replacing "Leaders" in Trees

Sometimes "leaders" (the tips of main stems) are damaged by borers, storms, or heavy snow. The damaged part should be cut back to healthy growth, and the wound treated with tree paint if it is more than three-quarters of an inch in diameter. This precaution prevents insect attack at the cut surface. Usually a vigorous side branch can be induced to form a new leader by staking it to grow upright. If leaders are split so that the bark is not seriously injured all the way around the stem, they can often be taped and made secure with the aid of a splint. In many cases they will continue to grow normally after the wound heals.

Creating "High Shade"

Shade is a handicap to bloom in many gardens where trees are allowed to develop dense growth, preventing light from entering sizable areas. Crab-apples, elms, lindens, locusts, maples, oaks, tree-of-heaven, and others are offenders in this respect. Branches of these kinds can be cut back to the trunk without disturbing the appearance of the trees. The process may have to be repeated every few years. Thinning heavy growth and lifting or removing low limbs produces what is known as "high shade," an ideal condition for growing azaleas, rhododendrons and a host of perennials, as well as annuals. This job requires at least two people, one or more to do the cutting and one to direct it. By increasing light, flowering plants in the undergrowth will produce more bloom; flowers produced in shade last longer than those in full sun.

21

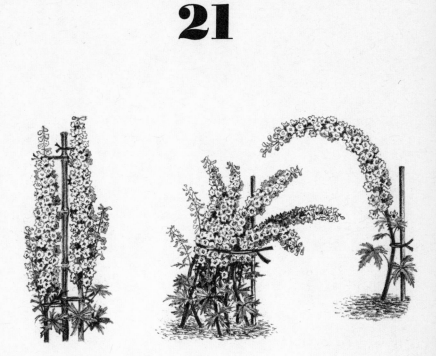

GENERAL CARE
AND MAINTENANCE

❦❦❦ All garden plants have definite soil, moisture, drainage, and light requirements. If these are met, there is reasonable assurance that a plant will grow without special attention. Curiously enough, some gardeners tend to pamper plants. They are impatient, expecting them to take root and produce an abundance of bloom and foliage almost overnight. But this is not the way of Nature. Certain plants require a fair amount of time to become established. Flowering dogwood may be sparse of bloom for one or several years after it has been set out. Frequently, peonies may take two, full-growing seasons to produce a crop of full-size flowers. (Some gardeners remove all buds the first year after planting to benefit root development.) In contrast, roses, especially hybrid teas and floribundas, make a creditable showing the same year they are planted.

Although newly set plants may be stimulated by heavy application of fertilizer and frequent watering, this is not sound practice. Sturdy root development is as prime a requisite for over-all vigor as foliage and stems. When a tree or shrub is transplanted, a portion of the established root system is heavily pruned in the process. Consequently, time is required for the development of new roots. This process may be slower than the vegetative growth above ground. The same is true of deep-rooted perennials such as peonies.

Sometimes, newly set plants develop abundant foliage with few or no flowers for several years. Usually, this condition is traceable to an excess of available nitrogen in the soil, which stimulates leaf growth, or it may indicate a lack of available phosphorus, essential to the production of flowers. This occurrence is frequently corrected by applying superphosphate. (Flowering dogwood, lilacs, crab-apples, wisteria [see Chapter 1], and other trees and shrubs are typical.) For 4 to 6 foot specimens, scatter 3 handfuls of superphosphate around the base of the plant and water it in thoroughly. For each additional foot of growth, add a handful. Superphosphate is most effective when applied immediately following the normal bloom-time of a woody plant, since flower buds for the succeeding year are then being developed. Normally, flowering shrubs and trees need at least one complete growing season or even two to become well established.

The essential phases of maintenance discussed in this chapter relate to the basic care required for most plants in the home garden. They are treated in topical form for easy reference. Each and every gardener soon develops his own procedures and short cuts to achieve easy and efficient maintenance, but only by experience in one's own garden are these practices learned and put into effect. The beginner has no need to fear the complexities involved, since the procedures outlined become second nature with practice.

Control of Insects and Diseases, which may affect some plants, vary with weather conditions and other essential factors. The chores involved are discussed in Chapter 19.

Late Transplanting. Annuals and perennials transplanted on warm days tend to wilt quickly. Water thoroughly and provide temporary shade. When large quantities are being transplanted, it is often difficult to find enough strawberry and peach baskets to cover plants, but shade can easily be provided by cutting twigs from flowering shrubs. These are struck in around the plants to provide temporary shade for a few days. When the leaves on the twigs have shriveled, they can be pulled up; by that time plants will be well established.

Prolong the Life of Pansies, English daisies, and forget-me-nots by snipping off dead blossoms regularly. Feeding with liquid manure encourages new growth and improves the size of the blossoms as warm weather approaches. When pansies have been blooming for 6 to 8 weeks, they need to be cut back to encourage new growth from the base. "Kill two birds with one stone" by cutting pansies for indoor decoration with longer stems that include some foliage, thereby keeping the plants compact.

Booster Feeding for Annuals and Perennials. In midsummer most annuals and late-blooming perennials, such as phlox, chrysanthemums, hardy asters, and others, respond readily to an application of a complete fertilizer. Scatter it lightly around plants and water it in. Some gardeners prefer foliar feeding. See Chapter 16.

Summer Pruning. After bloom has faded, flowering shrubs usually need pruning, which improves and keeps them within bounds. See Chapter 20.

Cut Back Overgrown Annuals. Certain annuals are benefited by being cut back in midsummer after having produced heavy bloom. Growth may become rank in wet seasons due to excess moisture. This type of pruning induces new growth and assures improved bloom for late summer and autumn. After cutting back ragged stems and loose growth, apply a booster feeding of a complete fertilizer. Scatter it around the plants and water it in. Among the annuals which respond to this care are:

Annual Phlox	Mignonette	Snapdragon
Calliopsis	Petunias	Sweet Alyssum
Cornflower	Pinks	Wishbone-Flower

Watering. Unless a thorough soaking job is done, there is little point in watering. A mere sprinkling with the hose simply brings roots toward the surface of the soil in search of moisture. Mulches (see Chapter 18) reduce the amount of watering required, even in seasons of prolonged drought. Soil soakers and sprinklers allowed to remain in a given area for a long enough period to soak the soil thoroughly are the easiest and most effective means of watering. To determine the depth of moisture penetration after watering, dig down into the soil and see firsthand. A thorough watering at regular intervals is preferable to casual, daily sprinkling.

Weeding. Getting weeds out by their roots, instead of breaking them off at ground level, is the most efficient way to eliminate unwanted plants. (A weed is a plant out of place and may refer to seedlings of annuals, perennials, trees, or shrubs that self-sow or germinate readily.) Seedling maples, elms, tree-of-heaven, Japanese barberry, honeysuckle, and the like can be a nuisance to remove, if left for one or more seasons. Seeds of many kinds of trees and shrubs germinate in hedgerows and even among the stems of shrubs, where conditions are ideal. They bear watching.

Small trowels or three-pronged forks are practical when removing most shallow-rooted weeds which are more easily removed when the soil is moist. In dry weather, it is advisable to soak an area thoroughly before weeding in order to get out all the roots. Deep-rooted kinds such as dandelions can be removed by using weed killer in the crowns or lifting them with a long-bladed weeder.

Mulching (see Chapter 18) greatly reduces the problem of weeding in beds and borders. Most of the weeds that may appear have their roots in the mulch and, thus, are easily pulled out. Weeds allowed to form seed on any part of the property make next year's task all the harder.

Pinching. This is the gardener's way of pruning annuals and perennials to make them compact by producing side branches and new growth along the stem near the base and, in turn, to obtain maximum flowering.

Annuals. Left to itself even in full sun, an annual usually produces a single stem, topped by a sizable, single bloom, a cluster, or a spike of flowers. Unless pinched back at the proper stage, it produces seed after flowering. By nature, others are self-branching, and this tendency shows itself as the plants develop, when shoots begin to break along the stem near the base.

First pinching is done when plants are 2 to 3 inches tall. Snapdragons are a prime example of this requirement. A second and even a third pinching naturally delays flowering, but the result is a multistemmed plant bearing an abundance of blossoms. Pinching is even more important when annuals are grown in any degree of shade, since they reach for the strongest source of light and quickly become leggy.

Perennials. Hardy chrysanthemums, Michaelmas daisies, veronica, summer-flowering phlox, thermopsis, and several others need their first pinching when 3 to 4 inches tall. With chrysanthemums and Michaelmas daisies, two or three pinchings before August 1 will assure compact, many-branched plants.

Staking perennials requires time but is worth the effort. It is always disturbing to see a well-grown clump of delphiniums blown about by the wind. While stems may appear sturdy, flower spikes are heavy, and skillfully concealed stakes can greatly add to the appearance of a well-grown plant. After the plants have finished blooming, the stakes can be used in other parts of the garden. Whether raffia, soft twine, or twistems are used, allow for some movement of the plant. Otherwise, the stems may break off in a heavy rain or wind storm. Plants tied tightly have a bunched effect that is unnatural and unappealing. There are many kinds of bamboo, wooden, and metal stakes on the market, which, if put in an old golf bag or some other container, are quickly accessible. Perennials with slender stems can be held up with brush.

Sprayers. Spraying can be tedious and annoying, if equipment is not kept clean. All sprayers should be thoroughly washed out and completely rinsed each time the spray tank is emptied. Remove the nozzles and clean them also. Furthermore, some chemicals tend to react unfavorably on metal containers, and this is another good reason for keeping them clean. When weed killers are used, be sure to keep a separate sprayer for applying these liquid chemicals. Separate sprayers are desirable when considerable amounts of weed killers are used. Since it is often difficult to clean sprayers with complete thoroughness, you may kill desirable plants when applying insecticides or fungicides if a weed-killer sprayer container is used.

22

FALL CHORES AND
WINTER PROTECTION

✿✿✿ Fall maintenance is important, even in the smallest garden. There are leaves to be raked and placed on the compost pile, weeds to be pulled, and dozens of other chores. From late August until mid-October is the ideal time to restore or renew lawns. It is the season for planting bulbs, flowering shrubs, vines, and evergreens, as well as ornamental and shade trees. Perennials can be divided at this season.

Annuals. As plants fade and are blackened by frost, they should be pulled up and placed on the compost pile or destroyed. Those showing evidence of mildew, rust, or other diseases need to be burned.

Biennials. For winter protection, see Chapter 3.

Perennials. Foliage of most kinds can be cut to the ground and disposed of as suggested with annuals. Iris is cut back fan-shape, 4 to 6 inches above the soil. Those with evergreen foliage, such as creeping phlox, candytuft, English lavender, and others, are best left undisturbed. Chrysanthemums need special protection. See Chapter 3. For the handling of perennial seedlings and plants raised from cuttings, see Chapters 3 and 17.

Roses. See Chapter 8.

Watering at periodic intervals for flowering trees, shrubs, and all types of evergreens is essential, particularly if drought has been serious during the summer. In fact, soaking at intervals during the fall is vital to the survival of newly planted shrubs and trees of all kinds. Otherwise, winter damage can be serious during prolonged freezing spells that are followed by periods of alternate thawing and freezing, especially when snow cover is light.

Mulching of newly planted trees, shrubs, and evergreens is best done at planting time, but mulches can also be applied in autumn for winter protection to conserve moisture and keep the soil temperatures even. The soil around well-mulched plants freezes more slowly and less deeply than bare ground. This fact is of prime importance in the culture of all types of evergreens; unlike those woody plants which drop their leaves, evergreens are never completely dormant. Thus, they require available moisture to combat the drying effects of wind and sun. For mulching materials, see Chapter 18.

Winter Protection

Many curious misconceptions exist regarding winter protection for plants. The object of a protective mulch is to keep the soil frozen and to maintain an even temperature, not to keep the roots warm. The function of protective cover and shading around and above stems and foliage is to provide insulation against wind and sun. Exposure is concerned as much with windy sites as it is with those parts of the home grounds where winter sun is reflected from a building or shines directly on evergreens. Wind causes excessive transpiration, resulting in the drying out of stems and leaves. The play of sunlight has a similar effect on foliage, and, being unable to draw water from the frozen soil, it tends to dry and burn. Winter damage is usually most severe when temperatures remain abnormally low for extended periods and snow cover is sparse or non-existing.

Protecting Tender Plants. Many gardeners—both beginners and experienced amateurs—grow plants known to be of questionable hardiness and are often successful in keeping them over a period of years by providing adequate protection. Young hollies, the mophead hydrangeas, boxwood, crepe myrtle, and others may require special winter care. Heavy watering, mulching with straw and leaves, and wrapping with burlap are necessary. Some gardeners use building paper or chicken wire to form a protective barrier. Wooden frames and plastic covering are also used.

Using Plastic Sprays. A transparent plastic spray (applied for wilt-proofing when transplanting) is being more widely used on all types of evergreens, especially the broad-leaved kinds for winter protection. It is most effective in reducing transpiration when applied in late November or early December on days when the temperature is approximately 50° F. Recent experience has proved that a second application in midwinter, prior to March, is worthwhile on windy, exposed sites.

Snow on Evergreens. Snow and ice can often do considerable damage to evergreens, both the broad-leaved and the needle types. Excessive weight may cause branches to snap and break, with the result that a plant becomes misshapen and unattractive in appearance. Get out as soon as possible after each snow storm and gently knock the snow from the branches with a broom or stick. It only takes one experience with this kind of damage to convince most homeowners that evergreens in exposed places are worth protecting. They can be wrapped in burlap, or snow guards can be set up which need not be eyesores. Then, too, trees used indoors at Christmas can be put to use to protect evergreens from both the snow and the damaging effects of winter sun.

January Thaw is usually an annual event throughout the colder regions of the country. Several days of above average temperature cause the ground to thaw with the result that plants are sometimes awakened from their dormant period. Dandelions may flower in the lawn, a few johnny-jump-ups may blossom in your rock garden or border, and spring flowering bulbs may venture forth with a leaf or two. This is the time to be wary of what is usually bound to follow—a sudden drop in temperature, which causes both plants and humans to shiver.

Double Duty for Chrismas Greens. Having had their heyday, Christmas trees and greens are usually dismantled shortly after the New Year, but they should not be piled on the rubbish heap. Make the most of every cut evergreen branch for winter cover. Perennial and rock plants with shallow roots often heave during mild spells in winter. By covering them with evergreen boughs, the ground will remain frozen and winter sun and wind will not affect them.

Holiday trees make ideal shade for broad-leaved evergreens in exposed areas, especially newly planted specimens. Rhododendrons, pieris, the various kinds of holly, evergreen azaleas, and other broad-leaved evergreens will benefit greatly from this type of protection.

Living Christmas Trees, large or small, should not be kept indoors for more than a week, or they will shed their needles at an excessive rate. Move them outdoors as soon as possible. If convenient, set them in the ground immediately. Otherwise, place them in a sheltered location and do not let the roots dry out. After planting, mulch the roots heavily with peat moss and soak the ground thoroughly.

23

COMMON

MISTAKES

OF BEGINNERS

❦❦❦ In the pursuit of any hobby, beginners often learn the fundamentals faster by the mistakes they make, and this is especially true of gardening. Efficient techniques are the real shortcuts in reducing maintenance labor. The following list is offered in the hope that when checked at the end of the growing season, it will point up the importance of some of the basic precepts of good gardening.

1. Most beginners plan and plant larger areas than they can maintain adequately, with the result that weeds often smother their precious treasures.

2. Watering is apt to be either neglected or done casually, and a vacation in midsummer may result in dried-up flower beds. See *Watering*, Chapter 22.

3. Overcrowding plants by not allowing adequate space between them creates a jumbled effect. This is a mistake common to many gardeners, both experienced and beginner.

4. Treating weeds casually by failing to dig out deep-rooted kinds results in their return, often twice as vigorous. This is particularly true of dandelions and the various forms of witch grass. Allowing weeds to produce seed means twice as much work the following year.

5. Planting broad-leaved evergreens such as rhododendrons, evergreen azaleas, Japanese andromeda, and other kinds in exposed situations where the wind whips the foliage means a short life, unless they are moved.

6. Neglecting to stake tall plants such as delphinium before the flower spikes develop fully often brings destruction of blooms by wind and heavy rain.

7. Failure to remove dead flowers from annuals and to cut back rank growth hastens seed development, shortening the flowering period.

8. Carelessness in spreading commercial fertilizer is a common error. When it falls on stems and foliage and is not washed off immediately, serious burning of the foliage occurs. See Chapter 16. Failure to water it in, especially on lawns, causes burning.

9. Overlooking seedling trees that appear spontaneously in shrub plantings, hedges, or close to buildings, and failure to pull them out when small, results in considerable effort to dig out roots later.

10. Hesitancy to do an adequate job of pruning on flowering shrubs after bloom has passed is based on the erroneous notion of harming the shrub. See Chapter 20.

11. Planting shrubs too close to the walls of a building or a fence is one of the commonest errors of many homeowners. No allowance is made for growth or air circulation, and it only requires two seasons of vigorous growth before a shapely evergreen becomes lopsided.

12. Cutting lawns too close in midsummer gives crab grass an ideal start. Cut high and set the mower 1½ to 2 inches above the soil level.

13. Setting shallow-rooted plants such as rhododendrons too deep results in poor growth. With few exceptions, most plants are best planted at the same level that you find them in the nursery.

14. Using the wrong kinds of plants in the shade produces sparse flowering and soft, rangy growth. See Chapter 13.

15. Applying too much fertilizer to annuals, especially formulas high in nitrogen, usually produces superb foliage and few flowers. Marigolds and cosmos are typical examples.

16. Neglect of pest control, both insects and diseases, takes its toll on favorite plants. See Chapter 19.

17. Planting peonies too deep and covering iris rhizomes with too much soil cause sparse bloom.

18. Beginners should be wary about accepting surplus, rapidly multiplying plants from neighbors. The decidedly weedy perennials are undesirable for the small place. See Chapter 3.

19. New trees are often set out without considering their size at maturity or their expected rate of growth. Adequate staking or guying is often also overlooked.

20. Apply mulches thickly enough to accomplish their purposes. See Chapter 18.

Every beginner can profit by keeping a list of his own mistakes and those of his neighbors and be the wiser and the richer in experience for so doing.

POSTSCRIPT: LOOKING AHEAD TO ANOTHER GARDEN YEAR

❧❧❧ Most beginners plant flowers, particularly annuals, in rows or in symmetrical groups. This is the logical way to start, but learning to plant them in drifts or irregular masses is the first step toward more picturesque effects.

Using sizable groups of a few kinds of annuals, suited to sun or shade, can be more rewarding than attempting to grow 57 varieties in a small garden. Try one or two new kinds each year, or more, if space allows. This is an excellent way of broadening one's knowledge of flowering plants—particularly annuals—which provide the major display of color in summer and fall.

A notebook kept handy to record ideas observed in other people's gardens is always helpful. Notes covering outstanding varieties of plants, ways in which to combine them, their preference for sun or shade, and their landscape value give point to such a record.

The importance of clean lines, carefully edged beds, neatly maintained plantings, and restful color schemes add up to more than mere theory or book talk after one or two full years of gardening.

On most home grounds, soil building is a continuing project, and there are always areas which can be improved by adding organic matter, such as peat moss or compost. This can be done in fall or spring. Long-range plans for a garden should include a place for a compost pile, as well as a program for soil improvement. There is more to good gardening than feeding plants. The quality of the soil is the determining factor for good plant culture.

The majority of new gardens are started with little or no planning. Usually the desire to grow plants for cutting and for their beauty is the basis for the venture. But, after a few years, without some kind of over-all plan, the effect is usually something of a hodgepodge. Thus, the importance of order enters the picture, and the answer is a plan. What started as a few flower beds or borders soon develops into a project of landscaping the home grounds.

Indoors, the tasteful selection and arrangement of the furnishings makes for pleasant living. The same is true of the home grounds, where trees, shrubs, vines, and flower beds may be considered as the furnishings. Arranged effectively, the home garden becomes a series of outdoor living rooms. This is a logical approach in looking ahead to another garden year, even though it may require several years to accomplish the desired results.

The longer we garden, the more we realize how little we know of the mysteries of Nature. As one great gardener wrote several decades ago, "If I knew more, I should enjoy less." The exhilaration and the excitement that a gardener experiences when he plants a seed is the most rewarding part of the great adventure.

INDEX

Hardiness is indicated on the basis of the "Zone Map of Plant Hardiness," revised in 1960 by the United States Department of Agriculture. In some instances the plants discussed in *Gardening for Beginners* have proved to be hardy in selected areas north of the zone indicated. It is practically impossible, however, to designate precise limits for some kinds of uncertain hardiness, because of environmental factors.